the BIG PICTURE *of* BUSINESS

"Hank Moore is a thought leader. Cognizant of the past, he weaves the accomplishments of others into dynamic strategies. I've worked with him and admire his writings."

—**George P. Mitchell**, Chairman of Mitchell Energy & Development. Developer of The Woodlands and downtown renovation in Galveston.

"Whether I'm at the office, at home, or on the road, I always have a stack of books I'm looking forward to reading. We all need people who will give us feedback. That's how we improve. Success has really been based on partnerships from the very beginning."

—**Bill Gates**

"Hank Moore truly embodies the concept of the Renaissance Man, from his worldly connections and involvement to his almost eerie sense of business acumen, in forecasting trends and patterns of commerce. To those of us who deal in the often delicate balance of customer and company, it is blessing to have, in Hank Moore, a resource we can depend on for fair, statesmanlike and balanced observation. I count him as a valued business friend."

—**Dan Parsons**, President, Better Business Bureau

"Every book that Hank Moore writes is a keeper. That's because of his thought leadership and ability to target what is paramount. Houston Legends is not only required reading, it is blessed reading for those of us who are Houstonians and those around the world who wish they were. Hank Moore brings out the grits and guts of these pioneers like nobody else could. You will be recommending this book to your friends."

—**Anthony Pizzitola** MBA, CFM, CBCP, MBCI,
Quality Assurance Manager—Jones Lang LaSalle.

"You can have brilliant ideas, but if you can't get them across, your ideas won't get you anywhere. Management is nothing more than motivating other people. The speed of the boss is the speed of the team. Get all the education you can, but do something and make it happen."

—**Lee Iacocca,** past-Chairman, Chrysler Corporation.

"Hank Moore knows more people than a person who just got elected as President of the United States, and more importantly he knows how to bring out their traits. I don't know how he does it."

—**George W. Strake Jr.,** Chairman-President, Strake Energy, Inc.

"Hank Moore works miracles in changing stuck mindsets. He empowers knowledge from without by enthusing executives to reach within."

—**Dino Nicandros,** past-Chairman of the Board, Conoco.

"Mr. Moore is one of the true authority figures for business and organization life. He is the only one with an Ethics Statement, which CEOs understand and appreciate."

—**Ben Love,** Vice Chairman, Chase Bank.

"Hank Moore's Business Tree™ is the most original business model of the last 50 years."
—**Peter Drucker**, business visionary.

"Always ahead of the trends, Hank Moore's insights are deep, applicable beyond the obvious."

—**Lady Bird Johnson**, former First Lady of the United States.

"Hank Moore provides fresh approaches to heavily complex issues. His step-by-step study of the business layers makes sense. It shows how much success one could miss by trying to take shortcuts. There cannot be a price put on that kind of expertise."
—**Roy Disney**.

"How can one person with so much insight into cultural history and nostalgia be such a visionary of business and organizations? Hank Moore is one of the few who understands the connection."

—**Dick Clark**, TV icon.

"Hank Moore is a million dollar idea person. He is one of the few business experts whose work directly impacts a company's book value."
Peter Bijur, Chairman of the Board, Texaco.

"30 minutes with Hank Moore is like 30 months with almost any other brilliant business guru. He's exceptional, unlike any other, and with a testimonial list to prove it. As a speaker, he's utterly content rich, no fluff, no 'feely-touchy' nonsense, right to the point and unashamed to tell the truth. There is nobody better. Every CEO needs him."

—**Michael Hick**, Director, Global Business Initiatives.

"I could not have wished for a better boss and mentor in my first professional job than Hank Moore. He leads by example, and taught me valuable lessons not only about business, but also professionalism and ethics that have stood me well throughout my career. Indeed, when I was in a position to mentor others, I've often repeated "Hank Moore stories" to my staff, and they've all heard of my first boss. Over time, I grew to understand more and more that Hank Moore treats others with respect, and thereby commands respect. I was privileged to be trained by this creative and brilliant thinker who gets more accomplished in a day than most do in a week."

—**Heather Covault**, Media Relations Manager, Writer, Web Editor at Kolo, Koloist.com.

"Hank Moore brings alive the tales of these important individuals in a rich and detailed way that affords us all the opportunity to appreciate their contributions to our world and way of life. Well researched and experienced, Legends reflects Hank's personal relationships with those legends shaping the past, present, and future. Legends is a must read."

—**Nathan Ives**, Strategy Driven.com.

"Hank Moore has a wealth of knowledge. Not only is he fascinating to talk with, he's a fabulous writer as well. I'm so glad that he put all of his extensive knowledge of pop culture and business history down in a book for generations to come. Now we can all have access to the amazing stories behind many of the histories, corporations and who's who. Thanks Hank for sharing these wonderful stories. You Rock."

—**Kathryn Wheat Wiggins,** author, *Networking: Naked and Unafraid.*

"Important Ideas Efficiently Presented. Hank Moore is a real king of business strategy in a time when there are all too many pretenders to that throne—and he knows how to write. The Business Tree is not for those who like their information presented slowly and interlaced with fluff. Moore's ideas are clearly and concisely presented. The book is all meat; and therefore needs to be read and pondered, then read again. Hank's books contain an enormous amount of useful information that will help any executive to function more effectively. Highly recommended."

—**Daniel Krohn**, attorney at law

"Hank Moore writes this book from a fascinating and unusual point-of-view. He is both an advisor to top-level managements of business and non-profit organizations, and an avid student of popular culture, especially of pop music. Combining these two perspectives, he offers valuable and entertaining insights about motivating excellence in organizational behavior. Hank's book is full of warmth and good humor, as well as keen insight. It is also stuffed with facts—my favorites are: a description of a sizeable list of young inventors and entrepreneurs (many under ten years of age, all under twenty), and a list of cities describing the origins of their names. This book is an enjoyable and thought-provoking read."

—**Thomas J. Perrone**

"Hank Moore is one of the legends of business, as well as pop culture. He connects the genres for ultimate wisdom. This is an adventurous book, his 10th. The next one, "Pop Music Legends," will go out of the stratosphere. This book series is a major undertaking. Hank Moore has crafted it masterfully."

—**Nancy Lauterbach**, *5.0 out of 5 stars* Must Read

"Hank Moore is a prolific writer with an amazing knowledge of his subject. Everyone will love this book."

—**Douglas B. Gehrman**

the BIG PICTURE *of*

BUSINESS

—————— BOOK 2 ——————

COMPREHENSIVE REFERENCE
for BUSINESS SUCCESS
Doing Business in a Distracted World

HANK MOORE

NEW YORK

LONDON • NASHVILLE • MELBOURNE • VANCOUVER

the BIG PICTURE *of* BUSINESS BOOK 2
COMPREHENSIVE REFERENCE *for* BUSINESS SUCCESS
Doing Business in a Distracted World

Published in New York, New York, by Morgan James Publishing. Morgan James is a trademark of Morgan James, LLC. www.MorganJamesPublishing.com

ISBN 978-1-64279-351-2 paperback
ISBN 978-1-64279-352-9 eBook
ISBN 978-1-64279-353-6 hardcover
Library of Congress Control Number: 2018913251

Cover Design by:
Rachel Lopez
www.r2cdesign.com

Interior Design by:
Bonnie Bushman
The Whole Caboodle Graphic Design

In an effort to support local communities, raise awareness and funds, Morgan James Publishing donates a percentage of all book sales for the life of each book to Habitat for Humanity Peninsula and Greater Williamsburg.

Get involved today! Visit
www.MorganJamesBuilds.com

Dedicated to Joan Moore.

TABLE OF CONTENTS

ACKNOWLEDGEMENTS

Remembrances to some of the business legends whom I knew and worked with: Malcolm C. Baldridge, George R. Brown, George & Barbara Bush, Winston Churchill, Dick Clark, John & Nellie Connally, Stephen Covey, Philip B. Crosby, Michael Dell, W. Edwards Deming, Roy Disney, Peter Drucker, Michael Eisner, Bill & Melinda Gates, Max Gotchman, Dr. Norman Hackerman, Gerald Hines, Ima Hogg, Lee Iacocca, Lady Bird Johnson, Lyndon B. Johnson, Ben Love, Clare Boothe Luce, J. Willard Marriott, Glenn McCarthy, Marshall McLuhan, Harris & Carroll Masterson, George & Cynthia Mitchell, Bill Moyers, Dino Nicandros, Earl Nightingale, Cactus Pryor, Anthony Robbins, Eleanor Roosevelt, Colonel Harland Sanders, Vidal Sassoon, Peter Senge, Allan Shivers, Roger Staubach, Jack Valenti, Dottie Walters, Jack Welch, Gus & Lyndall Wortham.

Also, acknowledgements to Imad Abdullah, Sharon Connally Ammann, Tom Arbuckle, H.E. Madame Sabine Balve, Jim Bardwell, Robert Battle, Jennifer Bayer, Ann Dunphy Becker, Betty Bezemer, Judy Blake, Tom Britton, Robert Brooks, Dr. Lee P. Brown, Margie Nash Buentello, Sarah Buffington, Neil Bush, Crissy Butts, Tony Castiglie, Glenn Chisman, Sandra Collins, George Connelly, Mike Contello, Rob Cook, John Cruise, Hector & Arleigh De Leon, Jenna & Michael Devers, R.J. Diamond, Kallen Diggs, Sue Ditsch, Deborah Duncan, Tom &

Anna Dutta, Alan Erwin, Dr. Ron Evans, Margarita Farmer, Mike Flory, Felix Fraga, Dr. Yomi Garnett, Martin Gaston, Douglas & Christine Gehrman, Nick George, Andrea Gold, Diane Payton Gomez, Glen Gondo, Sonia Guimbellot, John Harris, Brett Hatfield, Phillip Hatfield, Bubba & Glenna Hawkins, Royce Heslep, Michael Hick, Mary Higginbotham, Bruce Hillegeist, Ann Hodge, Derrill Holly, Richard Huebner, Susan & Robert Hutsko, Hiett Ives, Chris Kelso, Dana Kervin, Soulat Khan, Jon King, Kirby Lammers, Nancy Lauterbach, Torre Lee, Wea Lee, Steve & Barbara Levine, Mike Linares, Craig & Vicki Loper, Stuart & Laura Lyda, Jackie Lyles, Carol & Michael Marcantel, Hon. Tammy Collins Markee RCC, Aymeric Martinola, Wayne Mausbach, Cynthia Mazzaferro, Don McCoy, Bertrand McHenry, Kathleen McKeague, Bruce Merrin, Eugene Mikle, Mark Montgomery, Julie Moore, Larry Moore, Phil Morabito, Bill Nash, Howard Partridge, Dan Parsons, Monte & Linda Pendleton, Carla Costa Pereira, Leila Perrin, Tom Perrone, Joe & Courtney Peterka, Sue Pistone, Anthony Pizzitola, Travis Posey, Dino Price, Michelle Puckett, Karen Griffard Putz, Doug Quinn, Sally Mathis Ramsay, Roy & Gail Randolph, Connie Rankin, David Regenbaum, Ronney Reynolds, Jimmy & Lindsey Rogers, Tamra Battle Rogers, Donna & Dennis Rooney, Mike Rosen, Rob Rowland, Tony Rubleski, Monica Ryan, Jordan Rzad, Tina Sanchez, Rita Santamaria, Rick Schissler, Jack Shabot, Lisa Trapani Shumate, John Solis, Previn Sonthalia, Bill Spitz, Maggie Steber, Rod Steinbrook, Kalen Steinhauser, Gail Stolzenburg, George Strake, Bill & Cindy Taylor, Deborah Taylor, Jon & Paige Taylor, Jane Moore Taylor, Charlie & Laura Thorp, Rich Tiller, James & Carolyn Todd, Linda Toyota, Candy Twyman, Mary & Paul Vandenberg, David Wadler, Cameron Waldner, Jack Warkenthien, Louie Werderich, Kathryn C. Wheat, Chris Wiggins, Sara Wilhelm, Robert Willeby, Chanel Williams, Melissa Williams, Ronald Earl Wilsher, Kyle Wilson, Beth Wolff, Dr. Martha Wong, R.D. Yoder, Tom Ziglar.

Special dedications to the Silver Fox Advisors and the Better Business Bureau.

Chapter 1

THE SIGNIFICANCES OF DOING BUSINESS IN A DISTRACTED WORLD

Dealing with Weapons of Mass Distraction

Many people have lost the ability to focus. Every time that you hear a ring, a buzz or a ding, you jump and focus on those distractions. When people get in your space or prioritize their momentary need to control your time, it takes you away from important matters and priorities. Attention is scarcest commodity.

Distractions are caused by someone doing something. Distractions may be visual, mental or cognitive. Your accepting the distraction depends upon your inability to pay attention or your lack of interest in what you were paying attention to. Some distractions are so momentary or attractive that you have to shift attention. Distractions come from both external and internal sources.

There are seven reasons why people get distracted:

1. That's what they know. People maintain comfortable viewpoints and are victim of circumstances.

2. They are aspiring to be something else.
3. They maintain a niche focus.
4. They are susceptible to prejudices and vested interests.
5. They are influenced based upon societal pressures.
6. False and deceptive messages creep into and often dominate the communication landscape.
7. We experience the harmful downstream side effects of a distracted society.

Too Much Information

The average person is bombarded by 1,200 messages everyday. More active people may encounter up to 3,000 messages per day. Messages come from other people, phone calls, e-mails, texts, billboards, publications, radio, television, the internet, phone apps, junk mail, website views, social media people you know and people who network. It has created a "too much information" environment.

The average attention span is 8 seconds. Most humans cannot stay focused on one thing for more than 20 minutes at a time. This is attributable to transient and selective attention. 11% of children have been diagnosed with Attention Deficit Hyperactivity Disorder. Males are three times more likely to be diagnosed with ADHD than females. 4% of adults now have ADHD.

Distractions to the routine and thought processes can and will:

- Derail productivity.
- Cause people to spend more time on tasks.
- Overload memory capacity.
- Get in the way of multi-tasking.
- Cause people to not clearly ear what others are saying.
- Kill time.
- Ravage thought processes and the development of creative ideas.
- Reduce quality of work.

The Interruption Cycle

Here are some statistics on what distractions do to us:

- Most of us spend 70% of all waking hours in some form of communication: 9% writing, 16% reading, 30 percent speaking, and 45% listening. Studies also confirm that most of us are poor and inefficient listeners.
- Over 6 billion texts are sent out everyday.
- Of the calls received on your phone, 58% are robo-call junk solicitations. 46% of e-mails are vendor solicitations from lists purchased by people trolling for business. 43% in your home mailbox is direct mail advertising.
- 97% of college students use their phones during class time for non-educational purposes, according to a study published in the *Journal of Media Education*. Only 3% said they do not use a device during class for non-class-related activities on a typical day.
- Distracted driving accounts for 25% of all motor vehicle crash fatalities. Driver distraction is reported to be responsible for more than 58% of teen crashes. In 2018, 391,000 injuries were caused in distracted driving related accidents. Distracted driving was cited as a major factor in 3,477 traffic deaths.

Sensory overload occurs when one or more of the body's senses experiences over-stimulation from the environment. There are many environmental elements that affect an individual. Examples of these elements are urbanization, crowding, noise, mass media, technology, and the explosive growth of information.

Here are statistics on what happens when one is interrupted:

- Employees report 9% higher rates of exhaustion and 4% increase in physical ailments, headaches or back pain.
- One minute of interruption is enough to wipe out your short-term memory, effectively halting your work and mental progress.
- 95% of employees experience a drop in general work quality.
- Work interruptions can cost you six hours per day.
- Interruption leads to greater error rates. The longer the interruption, the greater the chance of errors: 2.8 seconds of interruption doubled the rate of errors, and 4.4 seconds of interruption tripled the rate of errors.

This is what omnipresent phones are doing to us:

- Interrupting your activities.
- Interrupting your thoughts.
- Interfering with family time.
- Harassing robo-calls disturbing your relaxation, sleep and concentration.
- Spoiling vacations and holidays.
- Affecting socializing activities.
- Interfering with events that you attend.
- Texting behaviors that thwart personal interaction.

Many distractions are ingrained into the system:

- News segments that always begin with "breaking news" and ominous music.
- Crawls at the bottom of TV screens.
- Insufficiently staffed retail counters, thus inviting interrupters to your turn at the counter.
- Pop-up advertisements on the computer, which send you links and rabbit-holes of visiting websites.
- Apps on phone that encourage you to buy special deals, attend events or pay attention to someone's website.
- Differences in personality type, language and cultural orientation lead to further distractions.

These are societal factors that feed distractions:

- People have shorter attention spans nowadays. Research showed that young people could focus for only three minutes before looking for and accepting distractions.
- Book readership is down.
- Stress causes people to make excuses to enable distractions
- Research indicates that constant interruptions make people dumber.

Subtle distractors change what we are doing more than obvious ones. They depend upon how well we know the distractor. Strangers can be more easily dismissed, such as at networking events. Media distractions can be turned off or muted. Needy friends can be limited. The way that the action system expresses itself is affected by perceptions of those who distract.

Small distractions have big consequences. They factor the kinds of activities that you are doing when distracted, such as driving in heavy traffic, speaking at a crucial meeting, something that might trigger a healthcare crisis and situations that might jeopardize your safety and that of others.

There are people that you meet at events, networking, receptions and business groups. They may fit into these categories:

- Some are judgmental or envious of you.
- Some are control freaks who make points of interrupting people's conversations.
- Some are arrogant about needing what they want from you when they want it.
- Some play the parts of victims and try to draw positive energy from others seen as self-confident.
- Some are liars, not truthful about what they are interrupting you for.
- Some are negative, looking for someone with whom to commiserate.
- Some are gossipers. The lowest form of conversation is to gossip about others. The level higher than that is talking about specific concepts. The highest form of conversation is to talk about deeper topics in positive, motivating terms.

And then there is the concept of purposeful distraction. They seek to embolden groups of people to their viewpoints. These can be very dangerous people. Techniques in its cause include:

- Dis-information. This involves communicating selective facts and omitting others.
- Mis-information. This uses statistics, events and positions to craft a false narrative.

- Confusing the issues. Muddying the waters.
- Misleading people into submission for beliefs and positions.
- Conflating multiple ideas together in order to create an alternate reality narrative.

Gaslighting

The term gaslighting is a psychological manipulation that sows doubts, causing people to question their sanity or norms. Communication techniques include withholding, countering, blocking, diverting, trivializing, and denial. According to "Psychology Today," people who gaslight use such techniques as:

- Telling lies and repeating the practice of lying.
- Denying that they said something.
- Using what is near and dear to you as ammunition.
- Having their actions not matching their words.
- Giving you positive reinforcement to confuse you.
- Knowing that confusion weakens people.
- Projecting their own behaviors onto others.
- Seeking to align people against you.
- Telling you and others that you are crazy.
- Telling you that someone else is a liar.

The term "gaslighting" originated in the 1938 play by Patrick Hamilton, "Gas Light." This play was made into a popular 1944 movie starring Charles Boyer, Ingrid Bergman and Joseph Cotten. Gaslighting in business refers to leaders pushing agendas, expecting compliance. Most conflict is a series of distractions, some unintentional and some deliberate.

High Costs of Interruptions

Disruption costs for distractions and interruptions include:

- Time necessary for the recovery of tasks after interruptions.
- Having to conduct make-good for bad or shoddy work.
- Time to re-orient back to the task at hand.

- Time to re-think the creative ideas that were lost.
- The harm it may have done to your schedule, skewing your workload.
- Make-good for bad or shoddy work. Shuffling time in the recovery mode,
- Stress and frustration caused by frequent distractions.

The contexts of the interruptions matter a lot. First, look at the distractions to see if they are single incidents, recurring problems or part of a continuing effort to get you off your game. Examine the time required to perform tasks, before and after distractions. Look at the number of errors that you make and what is required to get back to where you were when distractions transpired. Also, look at your disposition during the recovery process and your politeness to those who interrupted you.

Any interruption has an effect on work patterns, output and the sustainability of activity. Similarities of interruptions and patterns of such behaviors have effects on your work style. Interruptions cause people to change work rhythms, strategies and mental states. A certain amount of interruptions may be tolerable, but each of us needs to limit, set boundaries and not fall prey to those who continually interrupt.

Learning to pursue life is predicated upon learning how to deal with distractions, both internal and external. Behavioral psychologists call that metacognition. By knowing how the brain functions, we must learn how to focus.

Multi-tasking may affect the quality of each task that you perform. It is difficult to quantify what would have transpired had not so many distractions occurred. Some people are addicted to multi-tasking, feeling that it is a badge of perseverance to accomplish a lot at once.

These recommendations on reducing interruptions are offered:

- Silence your phone.
- Shut the door to your office.
- Set a schedule for texting time.
- Use productivity tools responsibly.
- Think before you interrupt others.
- Disable notifications from social media.
- Reduce the timing and frequency of interruptions.

- De-clutter your mind. Streamline your daily schedule.
- Schedule your checking of e-mails and reading messages.
- Learn and practice time management.
- Write down creative ideas because you may be distracted before you can fully develop them.
- Consider changing the daily habits that make you more susceptible to distractions.

Practice time management. This is the process of planning and exercising control of your time spent on specific activities, in order to increase effectiveness, efficiency and productivity. Understand why you need time management skills and what you will do with them.

The best solution to interruptions is to tune them out. Music may or may not help you to concentrate on tasks at hand. Video games, TV sets with crawls on the bottoms of screens and activity outside of windows and cubicles serve as constant distractions. Look carefully at the space in which you work and how it can be redesigned to exclude visual distractions.

There is an art to learning and achieving under distracted circumstances. Spending extra time does not regain last productivity. Creative ideas lost due to distractions may not return to your mind. Technology brings extra distractions.

Take your time back. Stop feeling you are a hostage of the distractors. Reinforce positive behaviors. Hear the good messages more often.

Chapter 2

THE STATISTICS TREE

Understanding Figures and What They Symbolize, Relating Directly to Your Business Success.

Business bases much of what it does on statistics. Most often, they're financial numbers or sales goals. More importantly are the Big Picture statistics that affect every aspect of business growth and success. The way in which the bigger issues are interpreted has direct bearing on strategy and implementation.

Here are some of the most significant statistics that relate to your ability to do business:

Only 2% of the businesses have a plan of any kind. What many of them think is a plan include some accounting figures or sales goals. That is not a full-scope plan. Of the companies who continue to operate without a plan, 40% of them will be out of business in the next 10 years.

Only 2% of those who call themselves Consultants really are just that. That 2% includes all the doctors, lawyers, accountants and engineers, those of us who actually advise clients on what to do and how to do it best. Most so-called consultants are vendors who peddle what they have to sell, rather than what the client companies really need. The answer is for companies to utilize seasoned advisers, rather than coaches and other vendors.

Research shows that change is 90% positive and beneficial. Why, then, do many organizations fight what is in their best interest? The average person and organization changes 71% per year. The mastery of change is to benefit from it, rather than become a victim of it.

92% of all business mistakes may be attributed to poor management decisions. 85% of the time, a formal program of crisis preparedness will help the organization to avert the crisis.

The average person spends 150 hours each year in looking for misplaced information and files. One learns three times more from failure than from success. Failures are the surest tracks toward future successes.

One-third of the Gross National Product is sent each year toward cleaning up mistakes, rework, make-goods, corrective action and correcting defects. Yet, only 5.1% is spent on education, which is the key to avoiding mistakes on the front end.

50% of the population reads books. 50% do not. Of all high school graduates, 37% will never read another book after formal schooling. Of all college graduates, 16% will never read another book. Thus, a declining overall level of education in our society and serious challenges faced by organizations in training the workforce. Yet, the holdings of the world's libraries are doubling every 14 years.

Today's work force requires three times the amount of training they now get in order to remain competitive in the future. 29% of the work force wants their boss' job. 70% of corporate CEOs think that business is too much focused on the short-term.

The human brain has more than 300 million component parts. The human brain connects to 13 billion nerves in the body. The human body has 600 muscles. The human body has 206 bones. The average person speaks 30,000 words per day. The average person is bombarded with more than 600 messages per day. More enlightened, actively communicating people are bombarded with more than 900 messages per day.

98% of all new business starts are small businesses. 45% of small business owners are children of small business owners. 83% of all domestic companies have fewer than 20 employees. Only 7% of all companies have 100 or more employees.

The current success rate for organizational hires is 14%. If further research is put into looking at the total person and truly fitting the person to the job, then the success rate soars to 75%. That involves testing and more sophisticated hiring practices.

Retaining good employees, involving training, motivation and incentives, is yet another matter. According to research conducted by the Ethics Resource Center:

- Employees of organizations steal 10 times more than do shoplifters.
- Employee theft and shoplifting accounting for 15% of the retail cost of merchandise.
- 35% of employees steal from the company.
- 28% of those who steal think that they deserve what they take.
- 21% of those who steal think that the boss can afford the losses.
- 56% of employees lie to supervisors.
- 41% of employees falsify records and reports.
- 31% of the workforce abuses substances.

On any given day, Americans spend over $33 million buying lottery tickets. On that same day, 99 American families fall below the poverty line. 68% of Americans do not like to take chances. 5% of all Americans go to McDonald's every day.

99% of American women think that contributing to or bettering society is important. 35% of Americans are involved in community service and charity activities. During the last 3,500 years, the world has been at peace only 8 percent of the time.

Data from the Census Bureau shows that 69% of new companies with employees survive at least two years, and that 51% survive at least five years. An independent analysis by the Bureau of Labor Statistics shows that 49% of new businesses survive for five years or more. 34% of new businesses survive ten years or more, and 26% are still in business at least 15 years after being started.

Small businesses really do drive engines of the economy. Many people believe that businesses frequently fail because there are a large number closing every year. In 2009, for example, more than 550,000 businesses were opened, and more than 660,000 closed. This occurred during a recession. However, during an economic expansion, the number of new businesses would outnumber the closures.

Many people may not realize how many small businesses there are in the country. In 2011, the Department of Commerce estimated that there were 27.5 million businesses in the United States. Only 18,000 of those businesses had more than 500 employees, and the rest were considered small businesses.

29% of companies are still in business at the end of year 10. And the biggest drop comes in the first 5 years, when half of startups go belly up. This shows that the odds are against startups staying in business. The internet home based business success rate is only 5%.

These are the seven Primary Factors of Business Failure:

1. Failure to value and optimize true company resources.
2. Poor premises, policies, processes, procedures, precedents and planning.
3. Opportunities not heeded or capitalized.
4. The wrong people, in the wrong jobs. Under-trained employees.
5. The wrong consultants (miscast, untrained, improperly used).
6. Lack of articulated focus and vision. With no plan, no journey will be completed.
7. Lack of movement means falling behind the pack and eventually losing ground.

What Could Have Reduced These High Costs:

1. Effective policies and procedures.
2. Setting and respecting boundaries.
3. Realistic expectations and measurements.
4. Training and development of people.
5. Commitments to quality at all links in the chain.
6. Planning.
7. Organizational vision.

Success is just in front of our faces. Yet, we often fail to see it coming. Too many companies live with their heads in the sand. Many go down into defeat because it was never on their radar to change.

Chapter 3

WHAT BUSINESS PEOPLE REALLY KNOW ... AND CAN BENEFIT FROM KNOWING.

T imes of crisis and economic downturn get people thinking differently about the conduct of business. Organizations say that they need to re-evaluate and get back to basics, that nothing is guaranteed. They realize that the old ways of doing business will no longer work. They seek to better themselves as professionals and to rethink the business models. Changing times require new perspectives.

For some, these are stark new approaches. This is the reality in which the small business and entrepreneurial worlds have always experienced. Welcome to the paradigms that many of us have operated under for some time.

Accepting change as a positive guiding principle, one then seeks to find, analyze and apply fresh approaches toward addressing the old problems. For many, times of crisis mandate that they think boldly and get used to doing business that way henceforth.

This book is an exploration into the creativity, the opportunities and the potential rewards of reflecting differently upon business. Our intention and the experiences of many companies who have followed the model presented here is that organizations must now learn how to paint their own "big pictures" of business, rather than focusing upon certain niches. They benefit from change, while the non-change stagnates become additional casualties.

A gun without instructions on its safe use becomes a deadly weapon. Medication usage without diagnosis and treatment by a properly trained and skilled physician is also dangerous. Making financial investments without conducting research and developing a strategy will lead to economic crisis. Continuing to turn a dead ear to the voices of reason and alternate opinions leads to the condition of hubris, which brings companies and societies down.

The purpose of this book is to offer enlightened insights into running a business. These are the kinds of insights that others before me did not have when they embarked upon careers. This is not the approach that is taught in business schools and really should be. As one who has seen, heard and influenced good companies, my hope is to show the good organizations how to become much greater through a larger-scope focus, backed by the strategies to accomplish high goals.

I offer the voice of encouragement to the two youngest generations in the workforce. The objective is to help readers to avoid falling into the same traps that brought their elders' companies down before their times had come.

This book includes many of the insights that the elder generations never had, never were taught or couldn't see on the paths up the career ladder. I have seen many good companies go down in flames because management would not open up the focus any further or make the necessary changes before it was simply too late.

You could call this book the experiences and observations of a credible second opinion, sometimes a third or fourth one. I'm the one who comes in after businesses made the wrong turns or had the wrong consultants dispensing inappropriate advice. I'm the one who suggests that getting back to basics and rethinking where they've been and where they're going might be prudent.

Narratives are from the perspective of myself as your business mentor. This body of wisdom reflects lessons from excellent mentors, teachers and role models whom I had the pleasure of knowing. It is a book filled with the things that I was never taught in business school but learned in the real world.

Most people who have followed my work say that the ideas and insights are 90% common sense, and the creative ideas reflect the gemstones inside each company's goldmine. People always ask, "Why don't we hear this common sense approach more often. Why do few look wide enough at business opportunities? Why don't ethics and best practices get portrayed as profitable business strategies? Why are the same niche perspectives always heard?"

My response is that business people are more wider-picture oriented than they might perceive or allow themselves to be. However, society is more inclined toward favoring certain niche perspectives.

Business is all too often lumped with finance. Economic advisors propose bailouts, while seasoned business advisors recommend marketplace corrections and corporate culture changes. Bean counters see business as mostly numbers.

Trainers see a learning organization filled with classes of students, thus becoming a vendor commodity in the eyes of buyers. Marketers always look toward the next campaign and view business in terms of slogans and images. Process people see only the steps necessary to produce goods.

Every niche perspective figures into a big picture but does not constitute the whole by itself. It is vital to view the relationship of all necessary components to each other and in support of a discernable whole.

I have learned that good businesses do not set out to go bad. They just don't set out with a delineated plan, backed with cohesive strategies to make the plan workable. Widening the scope and conducting meaningful planning are the only true routes toward surviving, thriving and moving forward…when times are tough, when times are prosperous and during every business cycle in between.

Yes, those who waited until they were in dire trouble to re-think and move in different directions could have attained those strategies much earlier. Exceptional lawyers, accountants and other top business advisors all know that calling them sooner rather than later would have lessened the damages on the clients' ends.

Human beings are not perfect and don't do everything right on the front end. We learn more workable strategies through trial and error. Organizations full of human beings need the impetus to think new creative thoughts, without the judgment of past mistakes. Those who continue to make the same mistakes thus become the case studies from which good companies learn the next round of lessons.

That's the rationale for this book. It is predicated upon thinking more holistically about company operations. It poses a business landscape populated by new thoughts that address seemingly insurmountable problems. There is and always will be a fresh new panorama just ahead and ready to paint. The ways in which we build, nurture and compost the landscape will reap the true and more continuing rewards.

The business climate ahead is tough and is filled with uncertainty, all of which translates into opportunities for those who are alert. Those others who believe that the old ways still work shall fall by the wayside. Innovation and the ability to fill new niches will signal the successful businesses of the future.

Messages from the Marketplace

Take this quick test, as part of your strategic planning for the next two to five years. Ask yourself some questions.

Does your company have a cohesive business plan, with results-oriented positioning and marketing objectives, tested and updated every year?

What is the nature of your business now, as compared to when you entered it? What has changed, and who are the new entrants?

Which marketplace factors are within your grasp? Which are out of your control? Which factors do your competitors control? Which opportunities to overtake the competition are within your company's plan of action?

How well does the marketplace understand your organization and its value to the business bottom line? Are there misperceptions that need changing?

How much has your company given back to the communities in which you do business? Is there an organized plan of reciprocation, with a business development design? Do you know who your stakeholders are and how they might benefit you by working more closely with them?

How well trained are your employees? Do they know, hold and embrace the company vision? With some fine-tuning, how much could you multiply the effectiveness of your empowered workforce?

In an era of downsizing, cutbacks and a reluctance to expand, there are four principles of growing a company:

1. **Sell new customers.** Without adding to the base, the business goes flat.
2. **Cross-sell existing customers.** Most customers are not fully aware of all the product-service lines that you offer. It's your obligation to inform

buyers about all that you have to offer, facilitating their ability to make wise choices. A satisfied clientele is easier to see credibility in your company.

3. **Create and market new products-services.** Having one good mousetrap does not mean that the public will automatically beat a path to your door. One must be alert to the next trends, the newest products and the next logical extension of his-her company in the marketplace.

4. **Creatively partner in order to create additional marketplace opportunities.** By combining disciplines, you can attract new business and pursue new, creative solutions for clients. Business can no longer do business as a bunch of lone rangers.

In order to tackle the challenges of the future, each company must assess its current position. One must presuppose that little or no strategic planning was previously done and then paint a fresh landscape.

Only 2% of the businesses in the world actually have functioning strategic plans. This means that 98% of all the companies in the world have no real strategic plan. They may have sales quotas or financial projections, but a collection of such memos does not constitute authentic strategic plans. Is it any wonder that so many businesses steer off course or never really make their journeys in the first place?

Research and "what if" scenario building are what comprise the foundation for effective strategic planning. Company leaders must weigh all of the circumstances and situations in crafting plans. Then, they should formulate workable strategies. Always, we should measure the process and its results.

This book is about building successful strategies to navigate business in the new order. With turbulence and accelerated changes, the opportunities for survival and long-term success are quite varied.

82% of all the companies that exist are small and emerging businesses. 98% of all new business starts are small and emerging businesses. 70% of all companies die in their first five years. 40% of those whop do not plan will fail soon.

90% of firms are out of business by year 10. The 4-year survival rate in the information sector is 38%. The 4-year survival rate in education and health services sector is 55%. The average start-up in education and health sector is 50% more likely than the average start-up in the information sector to live four years. 40% of all start-up restaurants fail.

45% of small business owners are children of small business owners. 83% of all domestic companies have fewer than 20 employees. Only 7% of all companies have 100 or more employees.

The primary categories of small businesses are: retail, build a new mousetrap, clone other mousetraps, pursue a dream that was started elsewhere, transition company (nurturing to grow and then sell to someone else), investment company and the providing of professional services.

I have talked with many entrepreneurs and founders of companies that rapidly grew from the seeds of ideas they had germinated. Most admitted enjoying the founding phase but lost interest shortly after giving birth. Over and over, they said, "When it stops being fun, I move on."

After the initial honeymoon, you speak with them and hear rumblings such as: "It isn't supposed to be this hard. Whatever happened to the old days? This seems too much like running a business. I'm an idea person, and all this administrative stuff is a waste of my time. I'm ready to move on to the next challenge."

At this point, they expect the business to transition itself smoothly and still make the founders some money. They ask, "Are you the one who comes in here and looks after my interests?" I reply, "No. After the caretakers have come in and applied the wrong approaches to making something of your business, I'm the one who comes in afterwards, cleans up after the band aid surgery was applied and helps to re-start the business again."

Full-scope business planning is much more effective on the front end, helping business owners avoid the costly pitfalls attached to their losing interest and abdicating to the wrong activities. When "the fun" ends, the hard work begins. It is crucial for principals of the small business to follow their dreams, develop a cohesive strategic plan, find an effective working style, match the actions to the corporate culture and stay with the program sufficiently long enough to measure results.

Businesses usually stop growing because they have failed to make investments for future company success. Rather than plan to grow and follow the plan, they rationalize organizational setbacks, excuse poor service or quality, and avoid change, all the while denying the need for change and avoiding any planning. Too often, they rely upon what worked for them in the past, on buzzwords, and on incomplete strategies. We've all seen businesses in which a paralysis creeps in, keeping them from doing anything at all.

A growth plan or strategic plan is essential for any organization that intends to survive and thrive in today's rapidly changing business environment. Companies need to heed messages from the marketplace telling them of changing market conditions, new global business imperatives, new partnering concepts, recognition of new stakeholders, and other changes outside of their influence that may profoundly affect them.

Not only do they need to know where they are going, they need the tools to assess continually their plans in response to what the market is telling them. I have advised many businesses in their journey to the next plateau, or towards recovery after a setback, or as they attempt to change course.

Time and time again, I have found that companies spend so much time correcting or reshaping small pieces of their business puzzle – reacting to immediate concerns and crises—that they neglect the long-term. The cost of such a piecemeal approach (band aid surgery) is high, costing up to six times the price of planning on the front end.

My remedy is an approach to planning using a proprietary model I call The Business Tree™. Following it forces management to take a holistic approach to looking at their business and the marketplace, and developing their plans for growth.

The number seven appears frequently in this book. There are seven major parts to the tree. Seven is also the number of progressions toward meaningful growth.

This book series is all about creating and sustaining seven important business mindsets for your organization:

1. Look to craft innovative strategies to achieve steady, managed growth.
2. Analyze and fine-tune your product and process realignment.
   Collaborations are the most viable way to build sustainable business.
3. Human intelligence is the most important tool in your arsenal. You are in the credibility business. People are the company's most important resource and must be developed, reward and empowered.

4. Professional development, performance reviews, ethics, values, accountabilities and the court of public opinion all matter. All must be addressed in strategic planning.
5. Business is an honorable trust. Those who understand and utilize best practices will grow. Those who do not will fail.
6. Build a realistic and dynamic organization. The careful nurturing of your vision will yield results.
7. Never stop thinking, planning, dreaming and teaming.

Look at the Whole, Then at the Parts and Back to the Whole

The Business Tree is the centerpiece of this book, and through it, readers will learn to strategize and plan with the entire business in view.

I have spent 20 years in developing this model and overview philosophy of business. Most of the case studies in this book represent cases where this model, creative new thinking and new approaches to the business resulted in successes.

I decided upon a tree as a business symbol because it's something that we see everyday, in some form or other. The tree represents the organization as a whole. Each major branch then symbolizes a component or aspect of the company, including the core business, running the business, finance, people, business development, the organization's body of knowledge and where it is headed.

In spite of most organizations' inability to plan, forward-thinking people really do want things to operate effectively. They work towards goals, attend workshops, read books and seek out the best advice of consultants. They get discouraged when top management cannot recognize the paths of improvement that they see or recommend. They feel stuck and realize that inertia has set into their company or that management has settled for the status quo.

The process of periodic review and evaluation can help remedy the situation. All too often, management is caught in the daily grind and unfortunately believes that strategic planning is a luxury. The folks in the executive suites need to be gently reminded of what visionaries they could truly become. The review process looks at nuggets of gold and makes good companies great. That's what senior management must believe and model for employees in the new order of business.

In this book, I challenge readers to realize their companies' hidden strengths. I have learned again and again that the best opportunities come through periodic review and that nothing can grow without proper nurturing, care, and attention.

Any company or organization is like a tree. It seemingly looks the same each day but sheds leaves, lets its limbs rot and applies "band aid surgery" to its branches late in life. Therefore, it does not fully grow and bloom. Often, it dies an early death.

Give the organization the proper nourishment, and it will experience a growth process that is planned, steady, optimally profitable and a pleasure to watch it bloom.

Neglect it, and the tree (organization) will wither and eventually die. As the tree declines, it becomes a blight on the environment, harming its components and the neighboring grounds and flowers.

Understand the business in which you are really engaged. Trees seemingly look the same, but they're all different. They do not have the same purposes at comparable times in their developments. The nature of core business changes with time and should be steered, rather than evolve on its own.

Delineate how and why your organization operates. Trees are composed differently, with parts and structures relative to the environment in which they attempt to grow.

Perform multi-systemic therapy often. Without the proper care, trees (companies) will wither. Without continued care, they will die. With proper care, they indeed will blossom. If leadership addresses problems in every realm as they come up, rather than selectively ignore some, the growth process will be unhampered. With continued care, trees inevitably sprout deep roots and live a richer life.

The costs of remediation malnourishment, deterioration or damage are six times those of properly feeding the tree (organization) on the front end. Human beings being the way we are, few of us do everything perfectly on the front end. The art and skill with which we remediate difficulties—sooner rather than later— constitutes longevity in business.

Which branch am I on, one might ask. Most people working in large organizations do not fully understand each branch, the interrelationship of each branch to one or another or their own role as relating to the overall tree. For years, I've believed that if you shook the branches of the tree, people would fall out, land on the ground and then would climb back onto other branches, meaning that they would assume different jobs in different company niches.

The tree analogy applies to any kind of living, breathing organization, whether it is a corporation, health care institution, school, small business, non-profit agency, retailer, professional services firm, community volunteer group, professional association, partnership or collaborative joint venture.

Success Comes to Those Who Focus

Following the insightful examinations offered in this book, the ideal company would hopefully pursue a thoughtful strategic planning process. As a result, each company could make the following answers to questions posed above, per categories on The Business Tree:

1. **The business you're in.** You are in the best business and industry, produce a quality product or service and always lead the pack. Your customers get from you what they cannot really get elsewhere.

2. **Running the business.** The size of your company is necessary to do the job demanded. Operations are sound, professional and productive. Your standards, integrity and dependability assure customers and stakeholders that you will use your size and influence rightly. You employ state-of-the-art technology and are the leader in your industry.

3. **Financial.** Keeping the cash register ringing is not the only reason for being in business. You always give customers their money's worth. Your charges are fair and reasonable. Business is run economically and efficiently, with excellent fiduciary procedures, payables-receivables practices and cash management.

4. **People.** Your company is people-friendly. Your people are the organization's most valuable commodity. Executives possess good leadership skills. Your staff is empowered, likeable, competent and loyal to the overall tree (organization). Employees demonstrate initiative and use their best judgment, possessing and demonstrating the authority to make the decisions they should make. You provide a good place to work. You offer a

promising career and future for people with ideas and talent. Your people do a good day's work for a day's pay.

5. **Business Development.** You always research and serve the marketplace. Customer service is efficient and excellent, by your standards and by the publics. You are sensitive to customers' needs and are flexible and human in meeting them. Marketing is truthful and reflects the strategies that you have worked so diligently to nurture. You sell what you can deliver. Management decisions are made with the customers clearly in mind.

6. **Body of Knowledge.** There is a sound understanding of the relationship of each business function to the other. You maintain a well-earned reputation and are awake to company obligations. You contribute much to the economy. You provide leadership for progress, rather than following along. You develop and champion the tools necessary to changing with the times.

7. **The Big Picture.** You approach business as a Body of Work, a lifetime track record of accomplishments. You have and regularly update and benchmark strategies for the future, maintain a shared company vision, understand that ethics is good for business and "walk the talk."

In many companies, these things do not occur because people do not know the processes to enable them to occur. In some, a rigid adherence to egos and the old ways precludes success. Often, the wrong people are giving advice and have the ear of top management. Management is out of touch and ego-driven to lead without proper help or advice.

Oftentimes, the company does not feel that it needs to change…that change is something that others need, but not them. Perceptions of current success overshadow the hint that winds will shift in the marketplace. Assumptions are false and overshadow reality. Thus, the company is not really in the right business anyway. Management is afraid to think "outside the box." The company culture is based simply upon being afraid and paralyzed to do anything new, creative or pro-active.

Key Messages to Recall and Apply Toward Your Business
- Understand the Big Picture.
- Benefit from change.

- Avoid false idols and facades.
- Remediate the high costs of band aid surgery.
- Learning organizations are more successful.
- Plan and benchmark.
- Craft and sustain the vision.

Great Business and Life Lessons Learned

- Acquire visionary perception.
- Never stop learning, growing and doing. In short, never stop!
- Offer value-added service. Keep the focus on the customer.
- Lessons from one facet of life are applicable to others.
- Learn from failures, reframing them as opportunities.
- Learn to expect, predict, understand and relish success.
- Contribute to the Big Picture of the company and the bottom line, directly and indirectly.
- Prepare for unexpected turns. Benefit from them, rather than becoming victim of them.
- Realize that there are no quick fixes for real problems.
- It is not when you learn, but that you learn.
- The path of one's career has dynamic twists and turns, if a person is open to explore them.
- Learn to pace and be in the chosen career for the long-run.
- Behave as a gracious winner.
- Find a truthful blend of perception and reality, with sturdy emphasis upon substance, rather than style.
- Realize that, as the years go by, one's dues-paying accelerates, rather than decreases.
- Understand what you're good at. Be realistic about what you're best at. Concentrate on those areas where they intersect.
- Continue growing as a person and as a professional, and quest for more enlightenment.
- Be mentored by others. Act as a mentor to still others.
- One learns to become his/her own best role model.
- There is always a next plateau, when we seek it.

Chapter 4

THE PATH FROM PLEASURE TO SUCCESS

Stages in the Evolution of a Business
A Primer on Change Management

Every business, company or organization goes through cycles in its life. At any point, each program or business unit is in a different phase from others. The astute organization assesses the status of each program and orients its team members to meet constant changes and fluctuations.

Strategic Planning facilitates disciplined thinking about the organization, its environment and its future. It identifies conflicts, reinforces team building and serves as a vehicle for monitoring organizational progress.

The planning process is then translated into a company Vision. With that Vision, the organization will evolve steadily toward success. Without any kind of Vision, management will continually apply corrective techniques ("band aid surgery"), while the company stumbles and falls. The price tag for false surgery is six times that of front-end Vision...a concept that I call The High Cost of Doing Nothing™ .

I've talked with many entrepreneurs and founders of companies which rapidly grew from the seed of an idea they had. Most admitted enjoying the founding phase but lost interest shortly after giving birth. Over and over, they said, "When it stops being fun, I move on. "

After the initial honeymoon, you speak with them and hear rumblings like, "It isn't supposed to be this hard. Whatever happened to the old days? I'm ready to move on. This seems too much like running a business. I'm an idea person, and all this administrative stuff is a waste of my time. I should move on to other new projects."

When they come to me, they want the business to transition smoothly and still make the founders some money. They ask, "Are you the one who comes in here and makes this into a real business?"

I reply, "No. After the caretakers come in and apply the wrong approaches to making something of your business, I'm the one who cleans up after them and starts the business over again." The reality is that I'm even better on the front end, helping business owners avoid the costly pitfalls attached to their losing interest and abdicating to the wrong people.

Most companies enjoy the early stage of success…and wish things would stay as in the beginning. When "the fun ends," the hard work begins.

To "go the distance," the organization must complete all seven stages of evolution. There are no fast-forward buttons or skipping steps inn developing an effective organization, just as there are no shortcuts in formulating a career and Body of Work.

Stages in the Evolution of a Business

1. **Transient Pleasure.** Company founders are basking in the glow of initial achievements. There exists an excitement over mission and expertise, as they believe them to be. The founders' creative instincts are satisfied. Egos are inflated.

In the first year or two, the character of the organization has not changed yet. It reflects what they started with and the first wave of people coming into it. Unfortunately, the founders also brought along the excess baggage of the previous corporate cultures in which they worked. They don't want to be like company X, but, in swinging the pendulum in the opposite direction, they are more like the old company than they realize.

In the beginning, the founder projects his-her vision into others in the founding team. There is an exchange of egotisms from one person to the other. Pleasures are plentiful in the beginning because great responsibilities are to follow.

2. **Big Letdown.** The machinery of the company must now perform on its own. Imperfections start to reveal themselves, accompanied by dissatisfactions and the inevitable blaming of others for mistakes. The reality is that no fully compatible organization exists to handle growth at this point. Founders clingingly wish to return to the early moments of success, or at least the perceptions of victory.

3. **Crisis.** Principals recognize the end of the early illusions. Now, it's time to become more mature as an organization. Players must now determine if they are willing to make more sacrifices, in order to go the distance.

If management is willing to "stick it out," many strengths and an organizational character will soon be revealed. Founders must reaffirm their commitment toward themselves, the organization and the quest. They start seeing the company (mainly its people) as resources to be cultivated, not exploited.

4. **Pain.** Some prefer to bask in and try to relive the early experiences, not the current character of the organization that seems to be emerging. It's not fun anymore.

Now come the "band aid surgery" approaches that plague otherwise clear thinking. Management begins taking wrong courses of action. Certainly, "trial and error" is admirable and to be expected. Band aid surgeons usually pursue surface remedies for the pain.

Many people want quick, easy, flashy fixes…without doing the things necessary to maintain staying power. Thus, they move from venture to venture. The realities of doing business for the long-term have now set in.

5. **Semi-Permanent Joy.** Until they feel the pain and take steps to get through it, the organization will remain stuck. Those who think they are immune to pain and will remain in the pleasure mode are doomed to long-term failure, a fatal flaw of corporate thinking.

After enduring the crisis and realizing the extent of the pain, rational managers start to see the reasons why they went through this process. They achieve the knowledge and understanding that an evolution has just transpired. Effectively treating the pain and learning from it serves to reinforce the will and zest to achieve further.

6. **Assuring Future Success.** For long-term survival, it is important to give the seeds of creativity, planning and organizational vision enough time and nurturing to sow. Plan to grow the organization. Grow according to the plan. Craft a Vision from the frustrations, mistakes, failures, missed opportunities, short sightedness and self-sabotage.

7. **Understanding the Truisms to Navigate Your Journey.** Having worked with hundreds of CEOs (as clients, colleagues and friends), I've absorbed many nuggets of gold. Some of these were taught by me to them. Others were reality-based lessons from the marketplace. All steered them toward courses of success:

   • Organizations do not set out to go bad. They just don't "set out" (little or no planning). Thus, they go off course.
   • There is a difference between knowing a product-industry and growing a successful business. Understanding all seven components of a successful company is a concept that I call The Business Tree™.
   • Much of the wisdom to succeed lies outside your company. It must be called upon, sooner rather than later.
   • Much of the wisdom to succeed lies within. It must be fine-tuned and utilized.
   • People under-perform because they are not given sufficient direction, nurturing, standards of accountability, recognition and encouragement to out-distance themselves.

- Anybody can poke holes at an organization. The art-skill is to create programs and systems which do something constructive. That is a concept that I call Three Rights Offset a Wrong.
- Communicate abstract principles in concrete terms.
- The wheel of an organization must always move outward, establishing commonality and communicating with stakeholders.
- Counter balance left-brain precision for details with right-brain insights and creativity. There is a difference between knowing and feeling. The intellect (left brain) draws something to itself. The will-spirit (right brain) reaches out to something that it loves and aspires to do.
- People must continue to develop professionally, in order for the business to grow.
- Whenever the mind knows something that is below, it elevates the knowledge.
- When the mind confronts ideas and concepts which are above it, the inclination is to degrade them.
- When the will-spirit covets anything that is below itself, it is degraded. When people and organizations are obsessed with something beneath them (such as money and fame), the whole entity is pulled down.
- When the will has aspirations and visions above it, standards will rise. It is important to have the right kind of heroes and goals because role model status perpetuates throughout life and permeates organizations.
- It is possible for a company and its managers to know much about certain arts and sciences without having the will to pursue them.
- The level of achievement by a company is commensurate to the level and quality of its vision, goals and tactics. The higher its integrity and character, the higher its people must aspire.
- One learns three times more from failures than from successes. The lessons must be reinforced, studied and applied to future planning. That is a concept that I call The Fine Art of Failure.
- Organizations start to crumble when their people quit on each other.

- No organization can operate in a vacuum. Each needs bases of support, community goodwill and collaborative business partners.
- Unhealthy organizations will always "shoot the messenger," when changes and improvements are introduced.
- Healthy organizations absorb all the knowledge and insight they can… embracing change, continuous quality improvement and planned growth.

Truisms of a Healthy Business

There is a difference between knowing a product-industry and growing a successful business. It is possible for a company and its managers to know much about certain arts and sciences without having the will to pursue them.

Organizations do not set out to go bad. They just don't "set out" (little or no planning). Thus, they go off course.

Much of the wisdom to succeed lies within. It must be recognized, fine-tuned and utilized. Much of the wisdom to succeed lies outside your company. It must be called upon, sooner rather than later.

People under-perform because they are not given sufficient direction, nurturing, standards of accountability, recognition and encouragement to out-distance themselves. Organizations start to crumble when their people quit on each other.

Unhealthy organizations will always "shoot the messenger" when change and improvements are introduced. Healthy organizations absorb all the knowledge and insight they can…embracing change, continuous quality improvement and planned growth.

Anybody can poke holes in an organization. The art-skill is to create programs and systems which do something constructive. The level of achievement by a company is commensurate to the level and quality of its vision, goals and tactics. The higher its integrity and character, the higher its people must aspire.

Components of a Business-Organization

(with their percentages per role-function-activity on Hank Moore's Business Tree)

Branch 1. The business you're in (10%)
Rendering the service, manufacturing the products (5%)
Core business abilities, specialties, skills, expertise (5%)

Branch 2. Running the business (14%)
Administrative practices, procedures, operations, structure, review (4%)
Physical plant to produce products and services (3%)
Technologies (1%)
Equipment, supplies, systems (2%)
Distribution (4%)

Branch 3. Financial (10%)
Cash flow, forecasting, budgeting, tracking money trends (4%)
Equity and debt financing (1%)
Accounting and record keeping (4%)
Banking and investing (1%)

Branch 4. People (28%)
Recruiting, hiring and supervision (5%)
Human resources management (3%)
Empowerment, team building (7%)
Training, incentives, involvement (10%)
Professional-executive development (3%)

Branch 5. Business development (23%)
Corporate imaging (4%)
Perceptions and realities (1%)
Marketing (5%)
Sales (7%)
Promotional techniques, strategies (2%)
Tactical reviews, modifications (2%)
Marketplace sensitivities, adaptabilities (2%)
Category 6 (trunk). Body of Knowledge (8%)
Category 7 (roots). The Big Picture (7%)

Steps in the Corrective Action Process

The Corrective Action Process applies to all individuals operating in a business environment, divisions and entire companies. By employing these analytic tasks, problem solving may be turned into a marketplace advantage:

1. Identify customers for your goods or services, measuring their requirements…and problems incurred in delivering to the marketplace.
2. Prioritize problems.
3. Assign responsibilities for problem solving.
4. Apply appropriate problem-solving techniques, including checklists, process analysis, charts, diagrams and force field analysis.
5. Turn recommendations into implemented actions.
6. Review progress. Benchmark the accomplishments. Research serves as planning for the next project phase.

Analyze accomplishments in terms of overall organizational Vision and implications for successful achievement of long-term company objectives.

How Companies Develop Staying Power

Stick around by default. Some companies are One Hit Wonders. They have limited utility and don't have what it takes to go the distance. They live short lives because that's all they've got in them. Some One Hit Wonders stay around a little longer than they should have, not because they are doing right things but because they have just stuck around.

Needed for a Particular Niche. They don't try to be all things to all people. They have a specialized market.

Show Promise to Develop into a Longevity Company. Made an effort to justify their niche…not just to fill it by default. Take pride in being the best in their area of expertise. Do business with other quality-oriented companies.

Time Tested Products, Processes. They are good and plan to get better.

Willing to Do Things Necessary for Growth. Products and processes only represent one-third of a company's picture. Growth companies take risks and address the other two-thirds on a regular, systematic basis.

Earned Respect to Continue in Business. Dare to innovate. Commitment to Continuous Quality Improvement. Also look outward, rather than focusing all resources internally. View their products, processes and people as a holistic organization.

Contributions Beyond the Bottom Line. Understand other reasons for being in business than just the dollars. Make healthy profits, while creating the best products, being a learning organization, setting-upholding standards and continuing to justify leadership position.

Levels of Standards, Ethics

In order to progress and successfully navigate through the pains, changes and remedies, every organization has to develop its core values and a corporate culture. Though not a part of the initial pleasure phase, having standards and ethics will navigate the journey to success more forceful and surely. Here are seven progressive levels of standards and ethics:

Base Level. Just needing and attempting to get by. Basics of food, clothing and shelter. Knowing right from wrong. Trying to pursue a good life and aspire to something higher.

Lowest Common Denominators. Although knowing better, subscribing to prevailing philosophies and behaviors of others. This leads some to take advantage of the system, want more than one's share and fail to be accountable. Sadly, the common denominators are below what they used to be, and society continues to lower them. The mission of a successful person or organization is not to succumb quite that low.

Lessons from the School of Hard Knocks. Learning by experiences, trial and error, successes, life skills. Becoming more familiar with one's strengths, weaknesses, opportunities and threats. Understanding what an organization can and cannot accomplish, represent and become. Maximizing one's resources to the most practical advantage.

Launching a Quest. Striving to learn more and go further. Includes intellectual pursuits, professional realities, nurturing of people skills and executive abilities. At this point, people change careers, and organizations revisit their goals and crystallize new visions.

Standards. Set and respect boundaries. Many times, people and organizations will attempt to violate those standards or fail to acknowledge their existence. The test is how consistently one sets, modifies and observes one's own standards.

Values and Vision. No person or organization stands still. It is not enough to accept change but more importantly to benefit from it. It is not enough to see yourself on a higher plateau and quest for more. Success comes from charting a course, encompassing value systems and methodically reaching goals.

Code of Ethics. Fundamental canons, rules of practice, professional obligations, accountability-measurability, professional development, integrity, objectivity and independence. Commitment to uphold and enforce codes of ethics (yours and those of others) and the ethical responsibilities of members in business.

Change Management

Research shows that change is 90% positive and that individuals and organizations change at the rate of 71% per year.

Change is necessitated by a natural flow of events, stemming from changes already made and realized. Some changes are mandated by others in control, and others are necessitated by circumstances outside your control.

The worst blockages of change come from people who possess the "been there, done that" attitude. 87% of the time, they really haven't. Other preventers include middle managers who can't see the forest for the trees, don't want to see beyond the scope and are proud of it.

Young generations who grow up in the houses of the above group see and emulate the anti-change constituencies. They grow up not knowing any better , clinging to the status quos and acting out their limited scope in the classrooms, in social settings and in their early business careers (until they learn better).

Young people in the business world (up to age 40) tend to want instant results, instant gratification and the success of people their senior who have paid substantial dues. As they learn to benefit from change, they mellow into savvy business executives.

To those who block processes of organizational change, things will pass you by, with or without your efforts. Negative efforts will harm your potential for success. Mastering change sooner rather than later has beneficial effects, with no down side.

Styles and Approaches to Mastering Change

Low-Power:
    Maintain the status quo.
    Technical proficiency skills.
    Caution. Don't rock the boat.
    Dependency.
    Survival.
    Bureaucracy.
    Fulfill tasks, schedules.
    Live and let live.
    Learning.

Entrepreneur:
    Carve new opportunities.
    Develop to an art.
    Take bold steps to lead and create new things.
    Autonomy.
    Risk and expansion.
    Customer orientation.
    Honor-exceed commitments.
    Our corner of the world.
    Knowledge.

Innovator:
    Create future paths for others.
    Create new modules.
    Courage of convictions, ideologies.
    Self-reliant.
    Vision, philosophy, future of the business.
    Provide value-added.
    Leading-championing the marketplace.
    The global village.
    Wisdom.

Reasons to Embrace Change and Benefits Provided

People make voluntary and necessary changes everyday. Those who have learned to benefit from change retain a profound commitment to the process, reaping the benefits of continually changing opportunities.

The steps toward mastering change include:

1. Recognizing what has already occurred.
2. Perceiving new areas of change.
3. Prioritizing the work to be done.
4. Changing gradually and gracefully.
5. Behavior modification.
6. Quality management and orientation.
7. Commitment to furthering, monitoring, advocating and inspiring change.

To realize full benefits from change, be real with yourself about the changes. Confront what has been done to sabotage success. Be willing to make changes. Benchmark the changes.

Be accountable for fallout, by-products and after-effects of change. Advocate future changes…to yourself and others. Continually re-enact this process with other change management opportunities.

Changing with successful results beats the alternative. Organizations and professionals who become stuck in ruts and stubbornly cling to the past are dinosaurs, whom the marketplace will pass by.

Research shows that change is 90% beneficial. So why do people fight what's in their best interest? Change management is an art, not a death sentence.

Professionals, specialists and technicians owe their careers and livelihoods to change. Because they are educated and experienced at new techniques, they have market power.

Change is not as high-risk as some people fear. Failure to change costs the company six times more. Lost business, opportunity costs and product failures are signs of neglect, poor management, failure to plan-anticipate and grow the company.

Those who champion change will positively advance their companies and careers. It accelerates the learning curve and success ratio. Those who do not get on the bandwagon will not last in the company. Those who excel develop leadership skills, empowered teams and efficiencies.

Leaders who expose their teams to new territories helps them see how they adapt within that framework. Championing change can mark the next tier in an executive's development.

A well-intentioned person may want and try so hard to do the right thing that he-she makes mistakes and ultimately does the wrong thing. It is the mark of a great person to admit mistakes, correct the course and move on. Another mark of a great leader is to let his people lead too…and give them the reins to do so effectively.

Change helps you do business in the present and helps plan for the future. Without mastering he challenges of a changing world, companies will not be optimally successful.

The company-organization which manages change remains successful, ahead of the competition and is a business-industry leader. Meanwhile, other companies will have become victims of change because they stood by and did nothing.

Quotes on Change and Progress

"Nature's mighty law is change."
—**Robert Burns**, regarded as the national poet of Scotland

"Nothing's the same when you see it again."
— **Singer-songwriter Cat Stevens**, from his song "Portobello Road"

"Change is inevitable in a progressive society. Change is constant."
— **Benjamin Disraeli,** British statesman who
served twice as Prime Minister of the U.K.

"Change is not made without inconvenience, even from worse to better."
— **Richard Hooker**, 16th Century English theologian

"You can't step twice into the same river.
Everything flows, and nothing stays still."
— **Heraclitus,** pre-Socratic Greek philosopher

"The basic fact of today is the tremendous pace of change in human life."
— **Jawaharlal Nehru**, first Prime Minister of India

"He that will not apply new remedies must expect
new evils. For time is the greatest innovator."
— **ir Francis Bacon**, philosopher and Lord Chancellor of England

"All progress is precarious, and the solution of one
problem brings us face to face with another problem."
— **Dr. Martin Luther King, Jr.**

"Human progress is furthered, not by conformity, but by aberration."
— **H.L. Mencken**, essayist, satirist and scholar

"Chaos often breeds life, when order breeds habit."
— **Henry Brooks Adams**, historian, descended from two U.S. Presidents

Chapter 5

WHERE DO THEY GO TO GET BUSINESS ADVICE

Overview of Multiple Resources Available.

B usinesses operate at a pace such that they grab for help wherever it is available. More often than not, they reach toward the wrong resources, the untied advisors and sources that send them down rabbit holes.

It is lonely at the top. There are many demands upon entrepreneurs and senior management of companies. Each organization is confronted with challenges and opportunities, both real and perceived. It is tough to tackle all the obstacles and feel that substantial progress is being made.

Businesses spend so much time on momentary pieces of their puzzles that they neglect long-term Strategic Planning and miss potential successes. Costs of band aid surgery and make-good work cost six times that of planning for business on the front end.

The need exists for comprehensive business ideas and growth strategies. The need is ever-present for interfacing with senior executives and updating management skills, to avoid burnout and stimulate the seasoned professionals toward new heights.

Top management regularly needs the creative inspiration to take the company to new heights. Cutting-edge executives (the very top and those about to take the mantle) need seasoned advice and inspiration.

Here is where they go to get ideas, strategies and help, in the order where they commonly go. The lower numbers represent introductory resources. The highest numbers are where they should be reaching.

1. Hearsay and third hand sources:
    *   Comments heard at parties and networking functions
    *   Uninformed sources
    *   Friends of friends
    *   High participation networkers
    *   Research and surveys
2. Special and Vested Interests:
    *   Websites containing educational material as a way to sell services
    *   Surveys and their feedback
3. People Selling Stuff:
    *   Vendors who distract you, using expressions like "funding to grow your business."
    *   Online marketing firms
    *   Internet solicitors and sellers
    *   Website consulting
4. Internal Management in Companies:
    *   People you work with
    *   Mid-managers and supervisors
    *   Corporate leadership
5. Niche Experts and Business Consultants:
    *   Trainers
    *   Freelance consultants, per industry niche
    *   Banking, insurance benefits, human resources, etc.
    *   Technology consulting firms
    *   Researchers

6. Educational Programs:
   - Speakers
   - Seminars
   - Panels at forums
   - Workshops
   - Conferences
   - Webinars
   - Material published or broadcast in the media

7. Books and Publications:
   - Articles excerpted for meetings
   - Blog material posted online
   - Thin self-published books by people seeking to establish a platform
   - Online articles and blogs
   - Serious books in libraries
   - Cutting-edge books with original material

8. Advocacy Business Groups:
   - Business clubs
   - Chambers of commerce
   - People with whom you work in community and charity leadership roles
   - Boards of directors
   - The Better Business Bureau
   - SCORE
   - Small Business Development Center
   - Trade industry groups
   - Associations
   - Political action committees
   - Community alliances
   - Professional alliances
   - Consortiums of business
   - Cross-industry cooperative initiatives

9. Mentors:
   - Pier advisory groups such as Vistage, Silver Fox Advisors
   - One-on-one coaching

- CEO roundtables
- Programs such as Shark Tank, Fox Den, Ted Talks
- Leadership programs and Corporate heir apparent training

10. Senior Business Advisors:
   - Professional service firms, including lawyers, accountants, marketing, public relations, quality management

11. Major Business Gurus:
   - Track record experts with many years in advising strategically

7 Levels-Tiers of Qualifying Consultants and Senior Advisors
(with their percentages in the marketplace)

1. **Wanna-be consultants.** Vendors selling services. Subcontractors. Out-of-work people who hang out "consulting" shingles in between jobs. Freelancers and moonlighters, whose consultancy may or may not relate to their day jobs. (26%)

2. **Entry-level consultants.** Those who were downsized, out-placed, retired or changed careers, launching a consulting practice. Prior experience in company environment. (19.5%)

3. **Grinders.** Those who do the bulk of project work. Conduct programs designed by others. 1-10 years' consulting experience. (35.49%)

4. **Minders.** Mid-level consultants. Those with specific niche or industry expertise, starting to build a track record. 10-20 years' consulting experience. (13.5%)

5. **Finders.** Firms which package and market services. Most claim they have all expertise in-house. The more sophisticated ones are skilled at building and utilizing collaborations of outside experts and joint ventures. (3.5%)

6. **Senior level.** Veteran consultants (20 years+) who were trained for and have a track record in consulting. That's what they have done for most of their careers. (2%)

7. **Beyond the strata of consultant.** Senior advisor, routinely producing original knowledge. Strategic overview, vision expeditor. Creativity-insight not available elsewhere.

7 Tiers on the Corporate Ladder, Contexts for Service Providers and Consultants

Within every corporate and organizational structure, there is a stair-step ladder. One enters the ladder at some level and is considered valuable for the category of services for which they have expertise. This ladder holds true for managers and employees within the organization, as well as outside consultants brought in.

Each rung on the ladder is important. At whatever level one enters the ladder, he-she is trained, measured for performance and fits into the organization's overall Big Picture. One rarely advances more than one rung on the ladder during the course of service to the organization in question.

1. Resource. Equipment, tools, materials, schedules.
2. Skills and Tasks. Duties, activities, tasks, behaviors, attitudes, contracting, project fulfillment.
3. Role and Job. Assignments, responsibilities, functions, relationships, follow-through, accountability.
4. Systems and Processes. Structure, hiring, control, work design, supervision, decisions.
5. Strategy. Planning, tactics, organizational development.
6. Culture and Mission. Values, customs, beliefs, goals, objectives, benchmarking.
7. Philosophy. Organizational purpose, vision, quality of life, long-term growth.

7 Levels of Authority Figure

1. **Self Appointed, Flash in the Pan.** What they were doing five years ago has no relationship to what they're now marketing. They reap temporary rewards from momentary trends. They're here today, weren't an authority figure yesterday and likely won't be tomorrow. Yet, today, they're demanding your complete trust, respect and allegiance.
2. **Temporary Caretakers of an Office. Public officials.** Appointed agency heads in a government bureaucracy. Respect is shown to the temporary trust which they hold.

3. **Those Who We Think Control Our Destiny for the Time Being.** Caretakers of corporate bureaucracies, departmental supervisors, short-term clients, referral sources for business development and those who dangle carrots under people's noses.

4. **Those Who Remain Through the Peter Principle.** Supervisors and public servants who made fiefdoms by outlasting up-and-comers. Their longevity is due to keeping their heads down and noses clean, rather than excelling via special talents-achievements. Still living on past laurels.

5. **Those Who Really Empower People.** These are a rare breed, the backbone of well-run organizations. Some do what they do very well in poorly-run organizations. They may not be department heads, but they set exemplary standards and inspire others toward positive accomplishments. Category 2, 3 and 4 authority figures either resent them and try to claim credit for what they do…or are smart enough to place them in effective, visible roles. Some advance into management and encounter similar situations there too.

6. **Have Truly Earned Their Position-Respect.** They are also a very rare breed. They include those who excelled at every assignment given and each stage of their career. Never were too busy to set good examples, share ideas with others and help build the teams on which they played.

7. **Never Stop Paying Dues, Learning, Sharing Knowledge.** The rarest breed of all. Distance runners who created knowledge, rather than conveyed that of other people. Though they could coast on past laurels, for them, the best is yet to come.

7 Levels of Advice Given

1. **Answers to Questions.** There are 7 levels of answers which may be given, depending upon how extensive one wants: Easy and Obvious Ones, Knee-Jerk Reactions, Politically Correct, What People Want to Hear, Factual and Complete Explanations, Answers That Get Them Thinking Further and Deep Wisdom.

2. **Observations on Situations.** These take the forms of "When this happened to me, I did X," or "If this occurred with me, I would Y." It's often good to see things through someone else's perspective.

3. **Subjective Viewpoint.** Friends want what is best for you. This level of advice is usually pro-active and is influenced by the advisor's experiences with comparable situations.

4. **Informed Opinion.** Experts have core-business backgrounds upon which to draw. Advisors bring facts, analysis and methodologies of applying their solutions to your case. Niche consultants provide quality viewpoints…as it relates to their talents and skills. Carefully consider the sources.

5. **Researched Options.** Investments in research (formal, informal, attitudinal, demographic, sociological) will avert unnecessary band aid surgery expenses later. Research leads to planning, which is the best way to accomplish tasks and benchmark success.

6. **Discussion of Outcomes-Consequences.** Most actions and decisions in an organization affect many others. At this level, advisors recommend that sufficient planning be conducted…please take their advice. The more strategic and Big Picture in scope, then planning reaps long-term rewards.

7. **Inspiring Directions.** This gets into Visioning. Planning and going to new heights are stimulating. The mannerisms and substance by which any organization achieves its Vision requires sophisticated advice, deep insights and creative ideas.

Quotes on Advice and Counsel

"No one wants advice…only collaboration."
— **John Steinbeck**

"A good scare is worth more than good advice.
He that has no children brings them up well."
— Proverbs

"Advice is seldom welcome. Those who
want it the most always like it the best."
— **Earl of Chesterfield** (1748)

"Most people get advice. Only the few smart ones profit from it."
— **Daniel Webster**

*"Do not criticize your government when out
of the country. Never cease to do so when at home."*
— **Sir Winston Churchill**, British statesman

"Your business is to put me out of business."
— **President Dwight D. Eisenhower**

*"I intended to give you some advice but now I
remember how much is left over from last year unused."*
— **George Harris**, U.S. Congressman

"One gives nothing so freely as advice."
— **Duc de la Rochefoucauld**, 17th Century French writer

*"It's queer how ready people always are with advice in any real
or imaginary emergency. No matter how many times experience
has shown them to be wrong, they continue to set forth their
opinions, as if they had received them from the Almighty."*
— **Annie Sullivan,** teacher of the handicapped (1887)

"There is nothing we receive with so much reluctance as advice."
— **Joseph Addison** (1712)

"When we ask advice, we are usually looking for an accomplice."
— **Marquis de Lagrange**

Chapter 6

HOW TO PICK THE RIGHT
CONSULTANTS FOR YOUR COMPANY

S electing the most appropriate consultant for your company and optimizing
their expertise is the greatest challenge facing a decision maker.

It's lonely at the top. Certain kinds of objective information cannot come
from within your own camp. True expertise is a rare commodity, and the successful
company utilizes it on the front end, rather than on the costly back end.

Matching consultants with actual and emerging company needs is the corporate
leader's quest. With a wealth of expertise available via outsourcing, one can quickly
become a "kid in a candy shop," wanting whatever is readily available or craftily
packaged.

Too many consultants mis-state and over-represent what they do, stemming
from:

- Eagerness to get business.
- Short tenure in consulting, believing that recent corporate experience
readily translates to the entrepreneurial marketplace.

- Unfamiliarity with the actual practice of consulting at the executive level.
- Lack of understanding about business needs, categories, subtleties and hierachies.
- Failure to create service area niches and target clients.
- Professional rivalry with other consultants, resulting in the "I can do that" syndrome.

Everyone knows that dentists, nurses, social workers and respiratory therapists are all health care professionals. Yet, distinctions in their expertise lead consumers to discern and seek out specialists…or at least ask a general practitioner physician to make referrals for necessary services.

Niche consultants place emphasis in the areas where they have training, expertise and staff support for implementation…and will market their services accordingly. An accounting firm may suggest that an economic forecast is a full-scope business plan (which it is not). A trainer may recommend courses for human behavior, believing that these constitute a Visioning process (of which they are a small part). Marketers might contend that the latest advertising campaign is equivalent to re-engineering the client company (though the two concepts are light years apart).

Niche consultants believe these things to be true, within their frames of reference. They sell what they need to sell, rather than what the client really needs. Let the buyer beware.

Consultants Are Not All Alike

Distinctions must be drawn into three consulting categories (and percentages of their occurrence in the marketplace):

1. Vendors sell products which were produced by others. Those who sell their own multiply produced works are designated as subcontractors. (82.99%)
2. Consultants conduct programs designed by their companies, in repetitive motion. Their work is off-the-shelf, conforms to an established mode of operation, contains original thought and draws precedents from experience. (17%)

3. High level strategists create all knowledge in their consulting. It is original, customized to the client and contains creativity and insight not available elsewhere. (.01%)

As one distinguishes past vendors and subcontractors, there are six types within the 18% which constitute consultants (with their percentages in the marketplace):

1. Those who still lead in an industry and have specific niche expertise. (13.5%)
2. Those who were downsized, out-placed or decided not to stay in the corporate fold and evolved into consulting. (28%)
3. Out of work people who hang out consulting shingles in between jobs. (32%)
4. Freelancers and moonlighters, whose consultancy may or may not relate to their day jobs. (16%)
5. Veteran consultants who were trained for and have a track record in actual consulting. That's what they have done for most of their careers. (2%)
6. Sadly, there is another category…opportunists who masquerade as consultants, entrepreneurs who disguise their selling as consulting, people who routinely change niches as the dollars go. (8.5%)

99.9999% of actual management consultants come from five basic career orientations and fit onto one of the five branches of The Business Tree:

1. Technical or niche industry orientation.
2. Financial.
3. Entrepreneurial, small business management.
4. Academic, research.
5. Human resources management.

The remaining 1/10,000 of a percent of consultants is a rare breed, a Big Picture strategist, fitting onto Categories 6 and 7 (trunk and roots of The Business Tree).

The Corporate Strategist is an idea person who has run businesses, knows about all other categories, deals in concepts and policies, and possesses sophisticated understanding and insight.

What They Claim They Do

When they say they provide growth strategies, they're usually sales trainers.

When they say they provide company turnaround, they're usually marketers.

When they say they provide information for business solutions, they're usually accountants.

Choosing Consultants

These pointers are suggested in the selection of business advisors and consultants. Ask a true business strategist to help you to determine which consultants are needed, draft the requests for proposals, evaluate their credentials and recommend contracting options.

Understand what your company really needs and why. Don't pit one consultant against another, just to get free ideas. Don't base the business on "apples to oranges" comparisons.

Ask for case studies which were directly supervised by the person who will handle your business...not stock narratives from affiliate offices or a supervisor. Find out their expertise in creating and customizing for clients...rather than off-the-shelf programs which they simply implement. Determine their abilities to collaborate and interrelate with other consultants.

In budgeting for and pricing consulting services, budget for consulting at the start of the fiscal year, averaging 10% of gross sales. This does not include marketing, which should be another 10%.

See consulting as an investment (short-term and long-term), not to be short-changed. Every size of business needs consultants, just as your clients need your services. The company which makes the small investment on the front end (consulting) saves higher costs. Research shows that consulting fees foregone are multiplied six-fold in opportunity costs each year that action is put off.

Consulting fees are best compensated by the hour. The client who contracts a quantity of time may request a volume discounted fee. It is customary to pay for all consultations after the initial "get acquainted" session.

Out-of-pocket expenses are customarily passed through to clients, without markup. For project purchases, such as printing, graphic production, video production and materials creation, consultants customarily mark up slightly, to cover bank financing and handling costs.

Questions to consider in evaluating consultants include:

- Would you feel comfortable if they ran your company?
- What is their longevity? Were they consultants 10-20 years ago? Real consultants must have at least a 10-year track record to be at all viable as a judgment resource.
- What is their maturity level? Could they appear before a board of directors?
- How do they meet deadlines, initiate projects and offer ideas beyond the obvious?
- If one level of consultant sells the business, will this same professional service your account? Big firms usually bring in junior associates after the sale is made. Demand that consultants of seniority staff the project.
- How consistent are they with specific industries, types of projects and clients?
- How good a generalist are they? Consultants with too narrow a niche will not ultimately serve your best interests.

Professional status is important. Prospective clients should inquire about the consultant's respect among current and recent clients and reputation among affected constituencies within the business community. Look at their activity in professional development and business education. If they do not pursue a program of ongoing knowledge progression, they are obsolete and not valuable to clients.

Also examine potential consultants regarding their own track record at mentoring other business professionals. Check to see that they give beyond the scope of billable hours. Pro-bono community involvement is a factor because it indicates character, ethics and integrity. If they have done little or none, they are not worth hiring. Top professionals know the value of giving back to the community that supports them, becoming better consultants as a result.

The ideal consultant:

- Clearly differentiates what he/she does…and will not presume to "do it all."
- Is a tenured full-time consultant, not a recently down-sized corporate employee or somebody seeking your work to "tide themselves over."
- Has actually run a business.
- Has consulted companies of comparable size and complexity as yours.
- Has current references and case histories.
- Gives "value-added" insight…in contrast to simply performing tasks.
- Sees the scope of work as a professional achievement…rather than just billable hours.
- Pursues client relationship building…as opposed to just rendering a contract service.

Chapter 7

DANGLING CARROTS AND RABBIT HOLES

Cautionary Tales in Business Development
Guarding Your Time and Resources
Maximizing Real Business Opportunities

This chapter has taken 50,000+ hours of my life to write. From wasted and misspent time come perspective and wisdom. These pointers are offered to help manage time and resources.

The phrase "carrot and stick" is an expression for people who dangle business opportunities for other people. It implies a combination of reward and punishment to induce desired behaviors. When the incentive is given only by implying the offer of a reward, this is known simply as a "dangling carrot". The activity of the carrot dangling on a string gives an illusion of attainability and keeps the subject chasing it. Sometimes it suggests a choice between reward or punishment as a means to alter behaviors of the person being dangled.

Intelligence tradecraft is getting people to do what you want them to do, often without them knowing it. The concept of rewards coming after actions was built into us in childhood. Dangling carrots to business people who are seeking more business puts them in tough situations.

Carrots being dangled might put the unwitting businesses in jeopardy because expectations are high and disillusionment is deep. Then, reality sets in and one sees the rabbit holes they have traveled in search of promises.

Research shows that more than half of all promises made are broken. 90% of consumers say they will switch providers as a result of broken promises. Companies with track records of broken promises find it 2-6 times as hard to repair the damage as it would have been to make and keep promises made.

This essay is a cautionary tale about setting boundaries and not jumping through every hoop every time. Having spent thousands of hours going down rabbit holes in the name of business development, I saw the lengths that some people will go to wasting your time, getting hopes up and causing frustration.

There are people who will judge you and try to entice you on the basis of your performance, possessions and popularity.

7 Levels of People Who Dangle Carrots:
1. Don't know any better.
2. Desperate for business.
3. Think that this is a norm to be expected.
4. Copy-cat the activities of others.
5. Organized intents to defraud.
6. Part of a pattern of using people.
7. Playing into their hubris.

They want you to do things for them, make introductions for them and give your ideas that they may later call their own. Such people are taking from you what you cannot get back: time, intellectual property, contacts, influence and reputation.

The cautionary recommendation is to analyze tough situations and avoid them the next time. Cutting wasted time gives you more energy to put into pro-active work in support of the business.

Recommendations:
- Avoid falling for carrots so often.
- Understand the angles of their dangles.

- Those who dangle carrots are also the victims of others who dangle them.
- Better futures depend on the work you are doing today, not false promises.
- When you promise something, remember it and keep it.
- Concentrate your energy on the good work you are doing.
- Aspire to higher standards, not the arbitrary premises of others.
- Associate yourself with others of purpose.
- Cut the weeds.

Rabbit Holes

Rabbit holes are euphemisms for bizarre and confusing paths that you take seemingly in the name of progress. The term originated in Lewis Carroll's "Alice in Wonderland." Alice fell down a rabbit hole and faced a series of confusing twists and turns in her journey to get back on course.

Internet rabbit holes are everywhere. You do a search and get a quick link, then finding another on that page, then clicking another link to another page, which gives you the idea to search for something else, that makes the process repeat again. Rabbit holes go from one point to another with no clear route or how one got there.

Life detours are unexpected and intentional. These will detour your path to success: perception, confusion, emotion and freedom. There are turns on the course and turns that are caused by the influence of others. Rabbit holes are confusing or nonsensical situations, making it difficult from which to extricate oneself.

These are the characteristics of rabbit holes:

- The pace changes and accelerates.
- So-called quick fixes send you elsewhere.
- Wastes of your time tend to get multiplied.

Some people know how to get you to do or respond as they wish. They want you beholding to them or at their service to perform services. Dangling of carrots results in rabbit hole creations. They ask open-ended questions on texts. They use Facebook as a message board. They barrage you with questions at networking functions, without offering material of their own. They refer friends to you for free use of your time. They rarely thank or acknowledge your expenditure of time.

These are some results of following rabbit holes:

- You get too much bad information.
- False starts get you frustrated, thus following more rabbit holes to get out.
- They leave paper trails that may catch up with you later.
- You develop a dependence upon the behaviors of others.
- There is an expectations that further distractions will occur.
- You try to do things that are not ingrained in your skill set.
- You do things against your better judgment.

Following paths of rabbit holes leaves you more vulnerable to other kinds of distractions. It leaves cultures of distraction hanging over business situations.

These are the styles of dogging and harassing others that have changed over the years:

- Desperation, economic recession.
- Age discrimination, as if to say that you owe it to us to give your time.
- Who do you know who.
- Internet scams.
- Robo calls.
- E-mail hoaxes.
- Social media junk messages and putting you into groups without your permission.
- Supposed charitable appeals.
- Combinations of techniques.

Things that you need to examine to avoid following so many rabbit holes going forward:

- Understand why we take the paths that we take.
- Reflect how other people's egos, wants and demands are forcing you needlessly to follow rabbit holes.

- Realize that one cannot please everyone. One must be more selective with time allocation.
- Call out the bad information. Fact-check what others say.
- Avoid being railroaded into group environments where further issues occur.
- Avoid teaming with the wrong people on nebulous situations.
- See situations that put you in ethical danger if you keep following paths.
- Understand how you send yourself on rabbit holes.
- Prioritize your energies and time management.
- Limit distractions. Recognize cultures of distraction that exist.
- Plan your next plateau of success.
- Celebrate the successes that occurred without following rabbit holes.

People Who Hog Your Time

- You hear their appeals quite often:
- I need just a minute of your time.
- Let's meet for coffee.
- X says we need to meet.
- Please complete this survey.

Toxic people will pick at or bully others to make themselves seem superior. They make pick at the physical appearance of others or obsess about things that bring others down. Their goal is to make other people feel bad about themselves. They pick on self-aware and accomplished people to get them feeling doubtful.

Their dialog will reveal what levels of hurt and pain they feel about themselves. Toxic people are to be avoided. Counter them by thanking them for their opinion without showing that they got under your skin. Another way to disarm them is to say, "Thank you. You may be right." A person cannot hurt you unless you let them. You don't need someone else's approval.

These are the categories of toxic people:

- Those who refer others for you to help but do not reciprocate.
- Dangling their charities at you
- They try to get you to pay for their marketing.

Some try to get you to buy services they are selling:

- Act as though you are technologically savvy if you do business with them.
- Extort participation in schemes.
- Try to steal portions of your identity.
- Sell this extorted information to others.
- Repeatedly harass you.

There are countless Internet solicitations. You get an e-mail with the message "X's friend (someone you've never heard of) would like to share referrals." These people are trying to steal your contact lists and use your name to approach others top get their contact lists.

There are many online scams designed to appeal to your vanity or desire to market. They may tell you that you can purchase your own page on Wikipedia, when in fact no listings are sold. They may say that you've been elected into some kind of Who's Who organization, asking for a donation and your sensitive information. They may say that you're invited to a fee based consulting assignment, but you have to wire funds and submit your information. It is vital to see online scams for what they are and not open their e-mails.

There are those who try to get you to pay them for services, many of them not equipped to deliver. Talent agents exploit families to pay to get their kids modeling jobs. Some dangle the promise of speaking engagements in order for you to pay them for "marketing expenses." They like your Facebook posts to make it look like they are promoting you. Then, there are those websites who say that your advertising on their portal will bring you riches, glamor and prestige.

These are the kind of harassing e-mails that they send:

- Meeting request.
- Quick follow-up.
- I was hoping we could connect sometime next week to discuss your current phone system and future plans. Would that work for you?
- Do you have enough people checking out your sales page?
- Want more people checking out your branding page?
- Your friends thought we should meet.

- Reminder of event. Checking to see if you are coming to it.
- And then there are those who try to steamroll you into service for their cause. They act as though you are obligated to them.

Recommendations for Leaders

Research shows that 72% of employees admit to not giving it their all on the job, with 77% of managers agreeing. Employers dangle carrots to their staff in order to boost productivity. They include cash incentives, gift cards, family gifts, days off and lower insurance premiums for participating in a wellness program. Some offer to pay you tomorrow for extra work done today.

Managers should actually:

- Offer recognition and respect.
- Stop dangling carrots by coalescing common dreams and aspirations.
- Evaluate appropriate incentives to offer.
- Have a compensation plan, rather than just random payments.
- Focus employees as they contribute to the company's big picture.
- Offer leadership, not just process management.
- Prepare each employee to succeed.

Rather than carrots and sticks, exhibit motivating factors that exhibit:

- Passion.
- Understanding.
- Respect.
- Potential.
- Opportunity.
- Support.
- Empowerment.

It is important for organizations and individuals to

- Make promises.
- Keep promises.

- Exhibit behaviors that are respectful and consistent with best practices.
- Pursue activities that align with corporate culture and best practices.
- Advocate ethical practice to others.
- Benchmark your success in keeping promises.
- Inspire younger business associates toward paths of excellence.
- Make quality commitments.
- Ask for commitments from others.
- Focus upon processes.
- Realize commitments that come with new and expanded roles.
- Continually monitor for contradictions between promises and commitments.

This chapter is not to discourage networking. Instead, it stimulates questions about your own wants, desires, experiences, gains, losses and changing perspectives in the game of "give and take."

Networking can be and should be a wonderful thing. In theory, you meet people, share ideas and grow richer for the experience. Indirectly, it enhances the climate in which business is done. Ostensibly, all participants benefit from the synergy.

If one is growing from networking and all parties benefit, it works well. Unfortunately, one can get caught in a trap of being on the short end of the equation. One can wake up, realize their energy has been zapped and experience setbacks in their business because he-she was spending disproportionate time on networking.

These are important questions to ask about networking:

- Is the person making the request a true friend, a business associate or just an acquaintance? Who are they to you, and what would you like for them to be?
- Will there be outcomes or paybacks for the other person? Will there be outcomes or paybacks for you? If there's a discrepancy in these answers, how do you feel about it?

- Are there networking situations that are beneficial for all parties? If so, analyze them, so that you can align with those situations, rather than the fruitless ones?
- What types of "wild goose chases" have you pursued in your networking career? Analyze them by category, to see patterns.
- Is the person requesting something of you willing to offer something first?
- Are the people truly communicating when they network? Or, are hidden agendas the reason for networking? Without communicating wants, it is tough to achieve outcomes.
- How much time away from business can you take? How does it compare with the business you can or will generate?

Concluding Thoughts on Networking:

- Networking is a Two-Way Proposition. Associate with those who feel similarly.
- Show and demonstrate respect for each other's time.
- Be careful not to pro-bono yourself to death.
- See your time for networking and volunteering as a commodity. Budget it each year. Examine and benchmark the reasons and results. Set boundaries, and offer your time on an "a la carte" basis.

By curbing old behavior patterns, you may feel less used and get more out of future networking. By analyzing the true motives for networking (yours and other people's), one can avoid hurt feelings and letdowns. By approaching the process with a realistic attitude, positive outcomes of future efforts will pay better dividends.

Chapter 8

KICK THE CAN, CHECK THE BOX

Pop Culture Terms, Slang and Jargon Used in Business

Y ou hear phrases and labels used everyday. People use terms that they have heard second-hand or afterward. Terms are often used out of context. The catch phrases are repeated, they get into the public psyche. People say things out of habit, often when more applicable terms could be used.

The purpose of this chapter is to sift through slang and jargon terms. They are believed to represent different things. These terms are about language in general.

Slang is colloquial and is used in informal situations. It is fun and creates a feeling of belonging. Slang often is used in ways that are unkind or cruel, so as to exclude others. It involves creating new meanings for existing words and terms. It is characteristic of certain social groups. Slang does not stay in the language for long periods of time and tends to come back later, often with expanded meanings. Slang is usually spoken and should not be used in professional and formal settings.

Jargon is language common to trades, per industry and niche. It is special language that conveys its own ideas. Sometimes jargon is a form of showing off that leads to confusion. Such code expressions vary over time and may not be understood out of context. Jargon is written and spoken, usually used in professional contexts. Over time, many jargons become understood by larger segments of the population.

Slang and jargon often morph into each other. Pop culture adapts to usage, and people often intercept terms, often using them out of context. A lot of words and terms can be very confusing.

Kick the can: People kick the can down the road to delay actions and shirk responsibilities. This causes a chain reaction of other things not getting done and threatens the consequences of actions. There are costs and side effects of kicking cans, included distorted outcomes, lost business and forcing others to alter their activities.

Check the box: On paper forms, we check boxes to designate categories. On forms, boxes may signify ethnicity, category of business function, markets served, conditions held and other declarations. Often, "check the box" refers to how people tick off obligations in order to prove that they did something. Businesses often seek contenders for services, often checking the box that they did a search process, when in fact they had a predetermined decision. Boxes often give the appearances that concerns were addressed, quotas were met and that important issues were addressed.

Moving parts: So much in business is at play, and the components change. Moving parts are factored into the seven branches-parts of my Business Tree model. These include core business, running the business, financial, people, business development, body of knowledge (relation of all components to each other) and the big picture (where each company is going and how they get there).

Bite the bullet: To accept something difficult or unpleasant. In the days, when doctors were short on anesthesia or time during war, they would ask patients to bite down on a bullet to distract from the pain. The first recorded use of the phrase was in 1891.

Low culture is a term for forms of popular culture that have mass appeal. It has been said by culture theorists that both high culture and low culture are subcultures. The boundaries of low culture and high culture blur, through convergence. Low-context culture is a term used by anthropologist Edward T. Hall in 1976 to describe a communication style that relies heavily on explicit and direct language.

Tone deaf: A person who lacks the ability to correctly hear something they do not believe in. Such people also turn a deaf ear or blind eye to dissenting information or viewpoints.

Out of step: Not conforming to what others are thinking. Not being aware of others' beliefs.

Over the top: To an exaggerated or excessive degree.

Outside of the box: Thinking differently, creatively or outside the perimeters. Novel approaches to old problems.

In the pocket: When music is in the groove, then players function well together as an ensemble.

Off the table: A proposed decision or action has been removed from consideration.

Yin and yang: Seemingly opposite forces may be complimentary. Opposites can work well together. Two can be together as a single force.

Let's rock n' roll: Ready to start a process or commence activity.

Witch hunt: In the 17th and 18th centuries, the practice of convicting dissidents as witches took place in Europe. In modern times, it signifies a campaign directed against people holding unpopular or unorthodox views.

Love fest: An expression of goodwill, praise and affection. Where multiple sides can come together. Mutual admiration and appreciation.

Weakest link: Any strong team can be hurt by having one participant not playing their parts.

Good, fast and cheap: People say they want all three in buying services. The reality is that one can only get two. Something has to be sacrificed.

Slush fund: Aboard a sailing ship, slush is waste fat from the galley, which is used to grease the masts. All extra slush may be sold by the cook, and he does not have to account for the money made. In business and government, a slush fund is money that need not be accounted for and maybe had not better be.

Bigwig: In Great Britain, it was long the custom for men of importance to wear wigs. A person of extreme importance wore a big wig and was called one.

Good to go: Being ready or prepared for something.

Be-all and end-all: The line first appeared in William Shakespeare's "Macbeth" in 1606.

Blow your mind: Something extraordinary that will affect someone strongly.

Lock, stock and barrel: There are three parts to a gun: the barrel, the stock and the firing mechanism, known as the lock. This reaffirms the totality of the entity or enterprise.

Maverick: In 1840, Samuel Maverick began raising cattle in Texas. He failed to brand any of the calves, which led to the wholesale rustling of Maverick stock. Unbranded animals came to known as mavericks. This term today refers to someone who is independent, goes his/her own way and takes unique approaches to things.

Sit on one's hands: From the theatre, if the audience does not wish to applaud, it sits on its hands. In business, it signifies people who choose to do nothing or fail to commit to something.

Fire and water: In early times, a method of proving one's innocence was to suffer trial by ordeal. One was by fire, where the person walked barefooted through hot coals. Another was by water, where the person plunged his hand into a pot of boiling water. Those who suffer extreme hardships are though to be worthy of heroism.

Sayings, Meanings and Interpretations

This chapter uses grammar as an analogy for looking new ways at how business is conducted. Strategy development requires the mining the gold within any organization and seeking new outcomes via creative applications of ideas.

Times of crisis and economic downturn get people thinking differently about the conduct of business. Organizations say that they need to re-evaluate and get back to basics, that nothing is guaranteed. They realize that the old ways of doing business will no longer work. They seek to better themselves as professionals and to rethink the business models.

Changing times require new perspectives. For some, these are stark new approaches. This is the reality in which the small business and entrepreneurial worlds have always experienced. Welcome to the paradigms that many of us have operated under for some time.

Accepting change as a positive guiding principle, one then seeks to find, analyze and apply fresh approaches toward addressing the old problems. For many, times of crisis mandate that they think boldly and get used to doing business that way henceforth.

This essay is an exploration into the creativity, the opportunities and the potential rewards of reflecting differently upon business. Our intention and the experiences of many companies who have followed the model presented here is that organizations must now learn how to paint their own "big pictures" of business, rather than focusing upon certain niches. They benefit from change, while the non-change stagnates become additional casualties.

Fish is one of those rare multi-purpose words that is used as a noun, verb, adjective and adverb. Examples include: Let's have fish for dinner. Are you fishing for an answer? This has a fishy taste. Something smells fishy.

The word "bar" has numerous meanings and is used as a noun, verb, adjective, adverb and preposition. Examples include:

- Raise the bar. (increased standards of quality, measurement)
- Stand by the bar. (piece of furniture, a counter)
- Visit the bar. (place of business where alcohol is served, nightclub)
- Pass the bar exam. (qualification to practice in the legal profession)
- Bar someone from doing something. (ban, prohibit, exclude or prevent)
- Bar coding. (price verification, inventory control)
- Bar none. (unlike any other, unsurpassed)
- Bar in the courtroom. (railing that encloses the judge)
- Bar bells. (weights for physical training)
- Bars as accent materials. (used in construction)
- Bars of music. (contents of notes and accents)
- Put someone behind bars. (sentenced to jail)
- Bars on a uniform. (metal strips, connoting military service)
- Bars on the windows. (metal pipes, for safety and protection from intruders)

Business Meanings Via the Perspectives of Words

Marketing can be either inward or outward. Companies undergo marketing campaigns to promote products and services to potential customers. Those same consumers do their own marketing when they shop at grocery stores.

People define music according to their personal tastes, experiences and backgrounds. What may be entertainment to one person may be noise or objectionable content to another. Music to one's ears is defined as what they want to hear or choose to acknowledge.

Service is a term that constitutes more hype than actual practice. Companies say they pride themselves on customer service. In reality, they see service as a sales vehicle or an add-on product. When customers ask for non-paid service (politeness, consideration, follow-up, manners), that's a totally different situation, and they are often disappointed. Sadly, customer service in business is poor, declining or nonexistent, per company.

Change is a wonderful phenomenon that people hate and fight to their detriments. Research shows that change is 90% positive and that people and organizations change at the rate of 71% per year. Yet, out of fear, they fight, resist and are combative toward change and to those who are change agents. It is inevitable, and one should benefit from change, rather than become a victim of it.

When some people hear the term consultant, they run. Research shows that only 2% of all consultants are really veteran business advisors. Most consultants are vendors who sell packages of products and services, displaced executives, computer vendors or people in transition. There really is an art to quality consulting, which requires years of experience, finesse, discipline and talent to amass, and few have it.

Futurism is seen as an esoteric term. Some say they have no control over their destiny. In reality, thoughtful planning for future eventualities enables one to prevent tragedies 85% of the time. Futurism is a series of thinking and reasoning skills, backed by planning. To deny, ignore or fight the future is foolhardy. To prepare for it means steady growth and success.

Diversity is a concept that encompasses ideas, cultures, philosophies and behaviors. Sadly, some people see diversity as a punishment, when associated with training. To the contrary, it is a gift because all of us are living examples of diversity.

Technology is a tool of the trade, not an ideology or a mantra. Some people mistakenly believe that technology creates the future, or they are willing to abdicate control of their own destinies to outside forces. Such an extreme position is not fair to technology because it sets up mechanical processes to get blamed later for thinking not done today. Thought processes need many avenues in which to be successful. Thereafter, tools of the trade (including technology) may be applied.

Avoid the Tired, Trite Terms

Words count. Put together, they reflect corporate culture. Used out of context, words become excuses, gibberish, rationales and basically wastes of energy.

When people hear certain words and expressions often enough, they parrot them. Rather than use critical thinking to communicate, many people often gravitate to the same old tired catch phrases.

I sat in a meeting of highly educated business executives. The presenter was dropping the term "brand" into every other sentence. The word had lost its power and came across as a fill-in-the-blank substitution for a more appropriate though. Many people used to do the same thing with the word "technology," using it far from its reasonable definitions.

These clichés do not belong in business dialog, in strategic planning and in corporate strategy. These expressions are trite and reflect a copy-cat way of talking and thinking:

- "Solutions" is a tired 1990's term, taken from technology hype. People who use it are vendors, selling what they have to solve your "problems," rather than diagnosing and providing what your company needs. It is a misnomer to think that a quick fix pawned off as a "solution" will take care of a problem once and for all. Such a word does not belong in conversation and business strategy, let alone the name of the company.
- The "brand" is a marketing term. The strategy, culture and vision are many times greater and more important.
- "So…" In the 1960's, TV sitcom writers began every scene with "So." After enough years of hearing it, people lapse that dialog into corporate conversations. It is intended to reduce the common denominator of the discussion to that of the questioner. It is monotonous, and there are more creative ways to engage others into conversation aside from minimizing the dialog.
- "Value proposition" is a sales term and is one-sided toward the person offering it. It implies that the other side must buy in without question.
- "Right now" is a vendor term for what they're peddling, rather than what the marketplace really needs. Expect to render good business all the time.

- "Customer care" means that customer service is palmed off on some call center. "Customer experience" comes right out of marketing surveys, which rarely ask for real feedback or share the findings with company decision makers. That is so wrong, as customer service must be every business person's responsibility. Service should not be something that is sold but which nurtures client relationships.

Many of these stock phrases represent "copywriting" by people who don't know about corporate vision. Their words overstate, get into the media and are accepted by audiences as fact. Companies put too much of their public persona in the hands of marketers and should examine more closely the partial images which they put into the cyberspace. Our culture hears and believes the hype, without looking beyond the obvious.

Here are some examples of the misleading and misrepresenting things one sees and hears in the Information Age. These terms are judgmental and should not be used in marketing, least of all in business strategy: Easy, Better, Best, For all your needs, Perfection, Number one, Good to go, Results, World class, Hearts and minds, Cool, The end of the day, Virtual, Right now, Not so much and Game changing.

Street talk, misleading slogans and terms taken out of context do not belong in the business vocabulary. Business planning requires insightful thinking and language that clearly delineates what the company mission is and how it will grow.

These are the characteristics of effective words, phrases and, thus, company philosophy:

- Focus upon the customer.
- Honor the employees.
- Defines business as a process, not a quick fix.
- Portray their company as a contributor, not a savior.
- Clearly defines their niche.
- Say things that inspire you to think.
- Compatible with other communications.
- Remain consistent with their products, services and track record.

Yesterdayism

People are interesting combinations of the old, the new, the tried and the true. Individuals and organizations are more resilient than they tend to believe. They've changed more than they wish to acknowledge. They embrace innovations, while keeping the best traditions.

When one reflects at changes, he-she sees directions for the future. Change is innovative.

7 Levels of Yesterdayism. Learning from the Past. Sources of Insights:
1. Think They've Been There…Haven't Yet Fully Learned from It.
2. Saw It Happen…Understand It.
3. Participated In It.
4. Been There…Learned from It.
5. Teach, Understand and Interpret It.
6. Innovated It…and Teach You Why.
7. Innovative Then and Now…Still Creating.

7 Applications for Yesterdayism…How to Shape the Past into the Future:
1. Re-Reading…Reviewing…Finding New Nuggets in Old Files.
2. Applying Pop Culture to Today.
3. Review case studies and their patterns for repeating themselves.
4. Discern the differences between trends and fads.
5. Learn from successes…and three times more from failures.
6. Transition your organization from information down the branches to knowledge.
7. Apply thinking processes to be truly innovative.

Chapter 9

COLLABORATIONS, PARTNERING AND JOINT-VENTURING

T he biggest source of growth and increased opportunities in today's business climate lie in the way that individuals and companies work together.

It is becoming increasingly rare to find an individual or organization that has not yet been required to team with others. Lone rangers and sole-source providers simply cannot succeed in competitive environments and global economies. Those who benefit from collaborations, rather than become the victim of them, will log the biggest successes in business years ahead.

Just as empowerment, team building and other processes apply to formal organizational structures, then teaming of independents can likewise benefit from the concepts. There are rules of protocol that support and protect partnerships... having a direct relationship to those who profit most from teaming.

Definitions of these three terms will help to differentiate their intended objectives:

Collaborations—Parties willingly cooperating together. Working jointly with others, especially in an intellectual pursuit. Cooperation with an instrumentality with which one is not immediately connected.

Partnering—A formal relationship between two or more associates. Involves close cooperation among parties, with each having specified and joint rights and responsibilities.

Joint-Venturing—Partners come together for specific purposes or projects that may be beyond the scope of individual members. Each retains individual identity. The joint-venture itself has its own identity…reflecting favorably upon work to be done and upon the partners.

Here are some examples of Collaborations:

- Parties and consultants involved in taking a company public work together as a team.
- Niche specialists collectively conduct a research study or performance review.
- Company turnaround situation requires a multi-disciplinary approach.
- A group of consultants offer their collective talents to clients on a contract basis.
- The client is opening new locations in new communities and asks its consultants to formulate a plan of action and oversee operating aspects.
- Professional societies and associations.
- Teams of health care professionals, as found in clinics and hospitals.
- Composers and lyricists to write songs.
- Artists of different media creating festivals, shows and museums.
- Advocate groups for causes.
- Communities rallying around certain causes (crime, education, drug abuse, literacy, youth activities, etc.).
- Libraries and other repositories of information and knowledge.

Here are some examples of Partnering:

- Non-competing disciplines create a new mousetrap, based upon their unique talents, and collectively pursue new marketplace opportunities.

- Widget manufacturing companies team with retail management experts to open a string of widget stores.
- A formal rollup or corporation to provide full-scope professional service to customers.
- Non-profit organizations banning resources for programs or fund-raising.
- Institutions providing startup or expansion capital.
- Managing mergers, acquisitions and divestitures.
- Procurement and purchasing capacities.
- Corporations working with public sector and non-profit organizations to achieve mutual goals in the communities.
- Private sector companies doing privatized work for public sector entities.
- Organ donor banks and associations, in consortium with hospitals.
- Vendors, trainers, computer consultants and other consultants who strategically team with clients to do business. Those who don't help to develop the business on the front end are just vendors and subcontractors.

Here are some examples of Joint-Venturing:

- Producers of energy create an independent drilling or marketing entity.
- An industry alliance creates a lobbying arm or public awareness campaign.
- Multiple companies find that doing business in a new country is easier when a consortium operates.
- Hardware, software and component producers revolutionizing the next generation of technology.
- Scientists, per research program.
- Educators, in the creation and revision of curriculum materials.
- Distribution centers and networks for retail products.
- Aerospace contractors and subcontractors with NASA.
- Telecommunications industry service providers.
- Construction industry general contractors, subcontractors and service providers in major building projects.

- Group marketing programs, such as auto dealer clusters, municipalities for economic development, travel and tourism destinations, trade association and product image upgrades.
- International trade development, including research, marketing, relocation, negotiations and lobbying.

Situations Which Call for Teams to Collaborate

1. **Business Characteristics:** Most industries and core business segments cannot be effectively served by one specialty. It is imperative that multiple disciplines within the core business muster their resources.
2. **Circumstances:** People get thrown together by necessity and sometimes by accident. They are not visualized as a team and often start at cross-purposes. Few participants are taught how to best utilize each other's respective expertise. Through osmosis, a working relationship evolves.
3. **Economics:** In today's downsized business environment, outsourcing, privatization and consortiums are fulfilling the work. Larger percentages of contracts are awarded each year to those who exemplify and justify their team approaches. Those who solve business problems and predict future challenges will be retained. Numerically, collaboration contracts are more likely to be renewed.
4. **Demands of the Marketplace:** Savvy business owners know that no one supplier can "do it all." Accomplished managers want teams that give value-added, create new ideas and work effectively. Consortiums must continually improve, in order to justify investments.
5. **Desire to Create New Products and Services:** There are only four ways to grow one's business: (1) sell more products-services, (2) cross-sell existing customers, (3) create new products-services and (4) joint-venture to create new opportunities. #3 and 4 cannot be accomplished without teaming with others.
6. **Opportunities to Be Created:** Once one makes the commitment to collaborate, circumstances will define the exact teaming structures. The best opportunities are created.
7. **Strong Commitment Toward Partnering:** Those of us who have collaborated with other professionals and organizations know the

value. Once one sees the profitability and creative injections, then one aggressively advocates the teaming processes. It is difficult to work in a vacuum thereafter. Creative partnerships don't just happen…they are creatively pursued.

This is what collaborations are NOT:

- Shrouds to get business, where subcontractors may later be found to do the work.
- Where one partner presents the work of others as their own.
- Where one party misrepresents his-her capabilities…in such a way as to overshadow the promised team approach.
- Where one partner treats others more like subcontractors or vendors.
- Where one participant keeps other collaborators away from the client's view.
- Ego fiefdoms, where one participant assumes a demeanor that harms the project.
- Where cost considerations preclude all partners from being utilized.
- Where one partner steals business from another.
- Where non-partners are given advantageous position over ground-floor members who paid the dues.
- Where one or more parties are knowingly used for their knowledge and then dismissed.

Who Wants to Collaborate

- Those who have not stopped learning and continue to acquire knowledge.
- Those who are good and wanting to get progressively better.
- Those who have captained other teams and, thus, know the value of being a good member of someone else's team.
- Those who do their best work in collaboration with others.
- Those who appreciate creativity and new challenges.
- Those who have been mentored and who mentor others.
- Those who don't want to rest upon their laurels.
- Those who appreciate fresh ideas, especially from unexpected sources.

Who Does NOT Want to Collaborate

- Those who have never had to collaborate, partner or joint-venture before.
- Those who don't believe in the concept…and usually give nebulous reasons why.
- Those who think they're sufficiently trained and learned to conduct business.
- Those who want only to be the center of attention.
- Those who fear being compared to others of stature in their own right.
- Those who think that the marketplace may not buy the team approach.
- Those who are afraid that their process or expertise will not stand the test when compared with others.
- Those who had one or two bad experiences with partnering in the past…usually because they were on the periphery or really weren't equal partners in the first place.

Characteristics of a Good Collaborator

- Already has a sense of self-worth.
- Has a bona fide track record on their own.
- Have a commitment toward knowledge enhancement.
- Walk the Talk by their interactions with others.
- Supports collaborators in developing their own businesses, offering referrals.
- Have been on other teams in the past…with case studies of actually collaborations.
- Has a track record of successes and failures to their credit…with an understanding of the causal factors, outcomes and lessons learned.

Stages of Relationship Building for Business Partners

1. **Want to Get Business:** Seeking rub-off effect, success by association. Sounds good to the marketplace. Nothing ventured, nothing gained. Why not try!
2. **Want to Garner Ideas:** Learn more about the customer. Each team member must commit to professional development…taking the program

to a higher level. Making sales calls (mandated or voluntarily) does not constitute relationship building.

3. **First Attempts:** Conduct programs that get results, praise, requests for more. To succeed, it needs to be more than an advertising and direct marketing campaign.

4. **Mistakes, Successes & Lessons:** Competition, marketplace changes or urgent need led the initiative to begin. Customer retention and enhancement program requires a cohesive team approach and multiple talents.

5. **Continued Collaborations:** Collaborators truly understand teamwork and had prior successful experiences at customer service. The sophisticated ones are skilled at building and utilizing colleagues and outside experts.

6. **Want and advocate teamwork:** Team members want to learn from each other. All share risks equally. Early successes inspire deeper activity. Business relationship building is considered an ongoing process, not a "once in awhile" action or marketing gimmick.

7. **Commitment to the concept and each other:** Each team member realizes something of value. Customers recommend and freely refer business to the institution. What benefits one partner benefits all.

Evaluating Collective Working Relationships

I have observed the greatest successes with collaborations, partnering and joint-ventures to occur when:

- Crisis or urgent need forced the client to hire a consortium.
- Time deadlines and nature of the project required a cohesive team approach.
- The work required multiple professional skills.
- Consortium members were tops in their fields.
- Consortium members truly understood teamwork and had prior successful experiences in joint-venturing.
- Consortium members wanted to learn from each other.
- Early successes spurred future collaborations.

- Joint-venturing was considered an ongoing process, not a "once in awhile" action.
- Each team member realized something of value.
- The client recommended the consortium to others.

My own disappointments with previous collaborations include:

- Failure of participants to understand—and thus utilize—each other's talents.
- One or more participants have had one or a few bad experiences and tend to over-generalize about the worth of consortiums.
- One partner puts another down on the basis of academic credentials or some professional designation that sets themselves apart from other team members.
- Participants exhibit the "Lone Ranger" syndrome…preferring the comfort of trusting the one person they have counted upon.
- Participants exhibit the "I can do that" syndrome…thinking that they do the same exact things that other consortium members do and, thus, see no value in working together, sharing projects and referring business.
- Junior associates of consortium members want to hoard the billing dollars in-house…to look good to their superiors, enhance their billable quotas or fulfill other objectives that they are not sophisticated enough to identify.
- Junior associates of consortium members refuse to recognize seniority and wisdom of senior associates., tilizing the power of the budget to control creative thoughts and strategic thinking of subcontractors.

Here are the reasons to give the concepts of Collaborating, Partnering and Joint-Venturing a chance:

- Think of the "ones that got away" …the business opportunities that a team could have created.
- Think of contracts that were awarded to others who exhibited a team approach.

- Learn from industries where consortiums are the rule, rather than the exception (space, energy, construction, high-tech, etc.).
- The marketplace is continually changing.
- Subcontractor, supplier, support talent and vendor information can be shared.
- Consortiums are inevitable. If we don't do it early, others will beat us to it.

The benefits for participating principals and firms include:

- Ongoing association and professional exchange with the best in respective fields.
- Utilize professional synergy to create opportunities that individuals could not.
- Serve as a beacon for professionalism.
- Provide access to experts otherwise not known to potential clients.
- Refer and cross-sell each others' services.
- Through demands uncovered, develop programs and materials to meet markets.

These are the truisms of collaborations, partnering and joint-ventures:

- Whatever measure you give will be the measure that you get back.
- There are no free lunches in life.
- The joy is in the journey, not in the final destination.
- The best destinations are not pre-determined in the beginning, but they evolve out of circumstances.
- Circumstances can be strategized, for maximum effectiveness.
- You have got to give to get. Getting and having are not the same thing.
- One cannot live entirely through work. One doesn't just work to live.
- As an integrated process of life skills, career has its place.
- A body of work doesn't just happen. It's the culmination of a thoughtful, dedicated process…carefully strategized from some point forward.
- The objective is to begin that strategizing point sooner rather than later.

Quotes on Teamwork, Collaborations and Partnering

"All for one, one for all."
— **Alexandre Dumas**

"Never ask that which you are not prepared to give."
— Apache law

"Tsze-Kung asked, saying, 'Is there one word which may serve as a rule of practice for all one's life?" The Master said, "Is not Reciprocity such a word? What you do not want done to yourself, do not do to others."
— **Confucius** (551 BC-479 BC)

"Whose bread I eat, his song I sing."
— German proverb

"A chain is no stronger than its weakest link. Union is strength. United we stand, divided we fall."
— Proverbs

"It takes more than one to make a ballet."
— **Ninette de Valois**, choreographer

"What I want is men who will support me when I am in the wrong."
— **Lord Melbourne**, 19th Century British statesman

"There are only two forces that unite men…fear and interest."
— **Napoleon Bonaparte**

"When bad men combine, the good must associate. Else they will fall, one by one, an unpitied sacrifice in a contemptible struggle."
— **Edmund Burke**

"One man alone can be pretty dumb sometimes, but for real bona fide stupidity, there ain't nothin' can beat teamwork."
— **Edward Abbey**

"The finest plans have always been spoiled by the littleness of those that should carry them out. Even emperors can't do it all by themselves."
— **Bertolt Brecht**, German dramatist

Chapter 10

THE HIGH COST OF DOING NOTHING

Why good companies go bad
How to avoid troubles and assure success

Each year, one-third of the U.S. Gross National Product goes toward cleaning up problems, damages and otherwise high costs of doing either nothing or doing the wrong things.

On the average, it costs six times the investment of preventive strategies to correct business problems (compounded per annum and exponentially increasing each year). In some industries, the figure is as high as 30 times, and six is the mean average.

The old adage says: "An ounce of prevention is worth a pound of cure." One pound equals 16 ounces. In that scenario, one pound of cure is 16 times more mostly than an ounce of prevention.

Human beings as we are, none of us do everything perfectly on the front end. There always must exist a learning curve. Research shows that we learn three times more from failures than from successes. The mark of a quality organization is how it corrects mistakes and prevents them from recurring.

Running a profitable and efficient organization means effectively remediating damage before it accrues. Processes and methodologies for researching, planning, executing and benchmarking activities will reduce that pile of costly coins from stacking up.

Doing nothing becomes a way of life. It's amazing how many individuals and companies live with their heads in the sand. Never mind planning for tomorrow, and they will just deal with problems as they occur. This mindset, of course, invites and tends to multiply trouble.

There are seven costly categories of doing nothing, doing far too little or doing the wrong things in business. They result in:

1. **Cleaning Up Problems:** Waste, Spoilage. Poor controls. Down-time. Lack of employee motivation and activity. Back orders because they were not properly stocked. Supervisory involvement in retracing problems and effecting solutions.

2. **Rework:** Product recalls. Make-good for shoddy or inferior work. Poor location. Regulatory red tape. Excess overhead.

3. **Missed Marks:** Poor controls on quality. Fallout damage from employees with problems (For example, a substance abuser negatively impacts 20 people before treatment is applied.) Under-capitalization. Unsuccessful marketing. Unprofitable pricing.

4. **Damage Control:** Crisis management. Lawsuits incurred because procedures were not upheld. Affirmative action violations. Violations of OSHA, ADA, EEOC, EPA and other codes. Disasters due to employee carelessness, safety violations, oversights, etc. Factors outside your company that still impede your ability to do business.

5. **Recovery and Restoration:** Repairing ethically wrong actions. Empty activities. Mandated cleanups, corrections and adaptations. Employee turnover, rehiring and retraining. Isolated or unrealistic management. Bad advice from the wrong consultants. Repairing a damaged company reputation.

6. **Retooling and Restarting:** Mis-use of company resources, notably its people. Converting to existing codes and standards. Chasing the wrong leads, prospects or markets. Damage caused by inertia or lack of progress.

The anti-change "business as usual" philosophy. Long-term expenses incurred by adopting quick fixes.

7. **Opportunity Costs:** Failure to understand what business they're really in. Inability to read the warning signs or understand external influences. Failure to change. Inability to plan. Over-dependence upon one product or service line. Diversifying beyond the scope of company expertise. Lack of an articulated, well-implemented vision.

7 Primary Factors of The High Cost of Doing Nothing

1. Failure to value and optimize true company resources.
2. Poor premises, policies, processes, procedures, precedents and planning.
3. Opportunities not heeded or capitalized.
4. The wrong people, in the wrong jobs. Under-trained employees.
5. The wrong consultants (miscast, untrained, improperly used).
6. Lack of articulated focus and vision. With no plan, no journey will be completed.
7. Lack of movement really means falling behind the pack and eventually losing ground.

What Could Have Reduced These High Costs

1. Effective policies and procedures.
2. Setting and respecting boundaries.
3. Realistic expectations and measurements.
4. Training and development of people.
5. Commitments to quality at all links in the chain.
6. Planning.
7. Organizational vision.

"They can't hang you for saying nothing," quipped President Calvin Coolidge in the 1920's. He spent more time doing chores at his farm and taking long naps than taking care of the nation's business. Coolidge prided himself upon doing little and, thus, failed to see crises brewing during his presidency. This "keep your head in the sand" mentality is prevalent of people who move on and let others clean up the damage.

High Cost Case Studies

An outsourced prison management firm was charged with unnecessary violence against inmates in a prison. Films of brutal beatings and unleashed dogs on the prisoners made the national news. The State of Missouri cancelled its contract with the state. Other states began investigating how their monies were spent in outsourcing prison management. The actions of one contractor put the concept of privatized law enforcement under question.

At a university campus, 200 cases of food poisoning were reported. Hospitalized students made the news. The university spent time and resources on damage control and investigation, with the possibilities of litigation and decreased development support in mind. Alas, it was determined that one employee failed to wash his hands and transmitted bacteria into the food that was consumed by the 200 students and then some. The employee failed to obey the university's health code.

A city council was fined $150,000, based upon the over-zealousness of one council member. Her efforts to set limits against multi-family dwelling construction were found to deny the right by one builder to do business. The court ruling said the builder was unfairly denied right to the marketplace due to prejudicial specifications.

When heavy flooding occurs, residents are forced to evacuate and are charged with millions of dollars to repair property. Property owner groups charge county flood control districts with responsibility. Their public outcries and class action suits charge that sufficient planning could have averted much of the damage.

A recent audit of a county hospital district stated that more than $20 million has been spent over five years on a computer contract that is so vague and poorly monitored that county auditors say it cost taxpayers hundreds of thousands of dollars.

The 1999 trial and conviction for a racist killing put a strain on that tiny town's treasury. To pay the $500,000 costs for justice being reached, the state contributed $100,000, and every Jasper resident was assessed an increase in property taxes by $40 per year.

It costs $55 per day to house prison inmates. Additional costs are $177 to overhead expenses. The average lethal injection costs $1 million, counting the costs for arrest, investigations, lawyers, trials, appeals and all other actions before the convicted felon is executed.

During 1999 bombings in Yugoslavia, a misdirected mission caused the accidental bombing of a Chinese embassy. To make amends, the U.S. government paid $4.5 million for the rebuilding of the destroyed structure.

When the federal government sued IBM for antitrust violation, in 1972, the process dragged on 13 years and cost both sides hundreds of millions of dollars. Joint federal-state antitrust actions against Microsoft promise to be equally costly to both sides.

The Exxon Valdez oil spill in Alaska cost millions to clean up. Worse, it put most oil companies under a cloud of public distrust. Some companies spent large sums of money in proclaiming their points of difference. Others simply did nothing and continued business as usual. Handling of other oil disasters is continually compared to the Valdez, as the benchmark. Public confidence in energy firms has been shaken ever since the Valdez incident.

Union Pacific Railroad and Southern Pacific Railroad merged. The promise, like most mergers, was greater operating efficiency. Predictably, cost-cutting measures were enacted. Service decayed, complicated by several derailments. The gridlock stunted service, costing customers millions of dollars. At one point, shipments were backed up as much as 30 days. Investigations showed that it would take up to five years to get service back to where it was before the merger.

A study was conducted concerning the economic impact of new stadiums and sports franchises upon major city economies. The conventional wisdom of course is that such things are good for local economies…the bars, hotels, transporters, peanut vendors, etc. all get a piece of the action. The study found, though, that in the great majority of cases, there was little if any economic benefit once all things were considered…community division, costs of promoting, financing, construction, damage control, etc.

An abandoned paint factory was deemed to be a severe environmental hazard, due to emissions and its effect on the neighboring water supply. The owners had been previously cited by the Environmental Protection Agency but eluded without being arrested. It cost the EPA $1.2 million in taxpayer funds to clean up the mounting debacle.

31% of young people imprisoned for crime said that they imitated acts seen on television and in the movies.

The costs of other high-profile strikes (to customers and to the economy): 1997 British Airways strike, $200 million.

A power failure occurred in San Francisco, CA, at the height of the rush hour on December 8, 1998. It cut service to more than one million people, leaving train commuters stranded under San Francisco Bay, stalling electric buses in the streets and forcing businesses, some schools and the stock exchange to shut down. This disaster resulted in the death of a 75-year-old woman who was crossing the street. Hundreds were trapped in elevators. Hospitals canceled elective surgeries. Most computer-effected operations were shut down.

It was caused because a construction crew at a transmission station in San Mateo County forgot to remove the ground wire after completing maintenance on a substation switchboard, causing a blowout and triggering a chain reaction that knocked two generators off-line. Human error was blamed. Cost of this "human error" to the San Francisco economy was in millions of dollars and lost productivity hours.

A handful of band members from two rival universities got into a skirmish on the football field, resulting in suspensions from the conference and negative publicity. Both schools had to take expensive and time-consuming steps to apologize, show remorse and save face, stemming from poor behavioral choices by a few students.

Things Business Does Not Address, until costs pile up:

Accountabilities.
Habits.
Processes.
Actions.
Learning curve.
Quality control.
Assumptions.
Operations.
Research.
Attitudes.
Opportunities.
Rumors.

Consequences.

Outcomes.

Skills.

Corrections.

People.

Strengths.

Egos.

Policies.

Successes.

Erroneous information.

Problems.

Threats.

Getting informed advice.

Procedures.

Weaknesses.

Levels of Doing Things:

1. Partial or Distorted.
2. Not Well Thought Out.
3. Popular or Politically Correct.
4. The Only Recourse.
5. The Right Thing to Do.
6. Correct and Accurate.
7. The Best Thing to Do.

Motivations for Doing Things:

8. Do by Direction.
9. Do by Default. Things done because it was the only choice.
10. Need to.
11. Want to.
12. In our best interest to do so.

13. Should, would and could do.
14. Committed, energized and eager to do or achieve.

Levels of Doing the Wrong Things:

1. Actions-Inactions.
2. Wrong, Inaccurate and Biased Information.
3. Inappropriate Choices and Judgments.
4. Poor Timing-Response.
5. People Skills Flaws.
6. Cover-ups, Denial and Scapegoating.
7. Fighting Change.

The High Cost of Not Listening to Advice:

1. Bad Advice.
2. Wrong Advice.
3. Buying Someone's Bill of Goods.
4. Doing What Will Spin Well.
5. Actions That Get Artificial Results.
6. Perpetuates the Cycle of Management by Crisis.
7. Long-term Irrecoverable Costs.

Chapter 11

ACHIEVING THE BEST BY PREPARING FOR THE WORST

Crisis Management and Preparedness

Just as we gain wisdom from the business failures and corporate scandals, we can learn equally valuable lessons from crisis situations that were successfully handled. The insightful companies examine their own backyards, applying the discussions and applicability to how they will better manage in the future.

For many years, we will be measuring how loss of corporate credibility has tainted all facets of business, in terms of remediation, replacement, litigation, make-good, rework, damage control, recovery process, settlements to victims, decreased stock market value and sagging retail sales. The Enron scandal alone has cost each taxpayer twelve dollars.

Some of those events that had profound impacts upon us recently included corporate fraud, accounting irregularities, earnings misstatements, hiding expenses, Enron, Arthur Andersen, the dot.com bubble burst, Worldcom, Tyco, Qwest, Imclone, Martha Stewart and Global Crossings.

It's not enough just to handle a crisis effectively. The follow-through and crisis preparedness planning process helps to divert other crises from transpiring. Recommendations for crisis management and preparedness as part of macro planning are offered.

Every organization and community in America is presently at a crossroads. There exist two current options. Business can be seen and known as a dynamic community that addresses its problems and moves forward in a heroic fashion…as a role model to the rest of the world. Or, the organization can bury its head in the sand and hope media attention dies down…thus becoming a generic tagline for troubled communities.

Purposes and expected benefits of reviewing business crises include:

- Understanding the difference between good and bad handling of crises.
- Comparing crisis follow-ups that help heal and rebuild, versus those that fester and bring destruction to cities.
- Preparing the community to utilize the concepts of bridge building and problem remediation.
- Implementing methodologies to address problems sooner, rather than later.
- Creating cause-related marketing opportunities, so that local businesses can sponsor the community healing process.
- Benchmarking the progress made and communicate it outside the community.
- Rebuilding the community image.
- Involving the widest base of support in pro-active change and growth.
- Establishing safeguards against future trouble.
- Putting more emphasis upon the positive ingredients and happenings in the community.
- Taking hold of the future.

Some of those events that had profound impacts upon us recently, examined in this chapter, include examples of crises that were handled well, thus increasing public trust and respect.

Actions During the Crises

In times of crisis, business does what it should have done earlier: study, reflect, plan and manage change. Sadly, business adopts a "head in the sand" mentality when the crisis seemingly passes. Many rationalize that they dodged the bullet.

In the aftermath of Three Mile Island and the Exxon Valdez crisis, companies increasingly became scrutinized under the public microscope., hus affecting its Wall Street book value, reputation in the marketplace and employee morale. It became incumbent to communicate openly to media about the crisis and what was being done. Companies had to overcome the poorly handled crises, as well as mount their own proactive strategies.

In times of crisis, advisors are called upon more frequently. Crisis Management and Preparedness has been one of my areas of expertise for many years. Among the types of crises that I advised clients through were government reorganizations, plant explosions, contaminated food and drugs, school shootings, executive kidnappings, plant bombings, hostile company takeovers, natural disasters and problematic employee behaviors. I have learned that strategic planning for crises can avert them 85% of the time.

There have been far-reaching business after-effects from the attacks on September 11, 2001. 1.5 million jobs were affected. The events of September 11, 2001, were attributed as costing New York City 83,000 jobs and negatively impacting its economy by $1 billion.

As new security procedures at the nation's airports has significantly increased ground time for airline travel, interest in business aviation also increased as companies were drawn to the productivity, efficiency, safety and security of business aircraft.

K-Mart closed 617 of its under-performing department stores and filed for Chapter 11 bankruptcy reorganization in 2002. K-Mart, long the dominant discount chain, had gotten comfortable with its leads over competitors. During the years while K-Mart did not plan for change, Target and Wal-Mart did plan, change and established defined marketplace niches.

K-Mart had become the odd retailer out but still kept 1,500 stores for its reorganization. Inevitably, when retailers contract, they blame poor performance upon bad locations.

Usually, the criteria for retail stores opening is the availability of property, not marketplace studies and strategies. That's why so many chains rapidly expand and subsequently contract so frequently. Real estate consultants are not business strategists, but the retail system gives them the say-so in establishing community presence. This is yet another example of niche consultants skewing the client in the wrong directions. Similarly, it is poor business to suddenly wake up one day and wonder why the marketplace passed you by. Retail stores are about more than just storefront locations.

In 1999, the U.S. economy spent one trillion dollars fixing and treating the so-called Y2K Bug, which we now know was a manufactured "crisis" by technology consulting companies. Certainly, aspects of the bug were treated successfully, and troubles were averted because of professional actions. Overwhelming public hype contributed to a "sky is falling" mentality that made computer consultants rich.

Among the lessons which we learned from the Y2K Bug exercise were:

- When they want to do so, company leadership will provide sufficient resources to plan for the future, including crisis management and preparedness (of which computer glitches are one set of "what ifs.")
- When they are compelled to do so, company leadership will provide leadership for change management and re-engineering, two of the many worthwhile concepts that should be advocated every business day.
- People are the company's most valuable resource, representing 28% of the Big Picture. Today's work force will need three times the amount of training that it presently gets in order for the organization to be competitive in the millennium.
- Change is good. If you like change, then don't fear it. Change is 90% positive. Without always noticing it, individuals and organizations change 71% per year. The secret is to benefit from change, rather than become a victim of it.
- Pro-active change involves the entire organization. When all departments are consulted and participate in the decisions, then the company is empowered.

- Fear and failure are beneficial too. One learns three times more from failure than from success. Failures propel us toward our greatest future successes.
- When we work with other companies and the public sector, we collaborate better. All benefit, learn from each other and prepare collectively for the future.
- In the future and in order to successfully take advantage of the future, make planning a priority…not a knee-jerk reaction.

What Causes Crises

Crises can have many liabilities upon companies, including loss of profits and market share. Inevitable spin-offs include government investigations, public scrutiny, and a tarnished image. This causes loss of employee morale and, as a result, company productivity.

Based upon research and experience with hundreds of client situations, I have found that seven types of crises exist:

1. **Those Resulting from Doing Nothing.** The biggest problem with business, in a one-sentence capsule: People exhibit misplaced priorities and impatience…seeking profit and power, possessing unrealistic views of life, and not fully willing to do the things necessary to sustain orderly growth and long-term success.
2. **Doing Things as We Always Have.** Resulting from inflexible conditions, obsolete policies-procedures, procrastination, attitude, resistance to innovation, failure to change.
3. **Those We Bring Upon Ourselves.** Don't have sufficient management skills or resources to do something well. Ignore small problems when they occur. Won't listen to advice.
4. **Circumstances Beyond Our Control.** Miscalculations, manmade disasters, natural disasters, shifting resources, changing marketplaces, regulations, bureaucracies.
5. **Bad Work, Poor Planning.** Damage control for what someone else did wrong, sub-standard, behind schedule, in poor taste, without regard for quality or ill-prepared.

6. **Averted.** 85% of the time, planning and forethought will avert the crisis. So, why don't organizations and individuals remediate trouble by planning on the front end?

7. **Intervention.** Getting past the current crisis does no good unless you take steps to assure that it does not recur. Planning is necessary to remediate current and future problems.

Crisis management and preparedness can minimize negative impacts of any emergency. Going through the planning and implementation is a quality assurance process that strengthens any company. Crisis communications means banking goodwill for those times when the plan is called to the test.

Effective Crisis Handling, Case Studies

Crises can and will happen to good organizations. Most often (85% of the time), they can be heeded, planned for averted. There is an art to Crisis Preparedness. It must be included as part of a formal Strategic Planning and Visioning process. So also should diversity, branding, quality, marketing, re-engineering and other important processes. No single facet of planning should be done out of sync with the others.

There will also be those unplanned crises that nobody could have predicted. The same planning process that nurtures Crisis Preparedness can and must also accommodate for Crisis Management. Many of the elements of planning strategies can be taken off the shelf and implemented when extreme danger presents itself.

The City of New York had conducted planning for multiple contingencies. Having done so put the city in the position of responding to the unthinkable on September 11, 2001.

Some of those events that had profound impacts upon us recently are examined in this chapter. In this section are examples of crises that were handled well, thus increasing public trust and respect for their organizations.

Product Recall, Tylenol. Several deaths occurred as a result of tampered Tylenol capsules. The company's swift recall of product from the shelves and the timely response of the company CEO were part of the crisis plan that was in place well ahead of the tragedy. Johnson & Johnson quickly put its crisis plan into action and subsequently drew good reviews for its open communication with the public.

Tylenol mobilized public support, with the company also positioned as the victim. Seeking to facilitate U.S. Food and Drug Administration approval of the tamper-proof caplet, a public awareness campaign was waged. The next phase in restoring public credibility to Tylenol was the reintroduction of new product to the shelves, done in such a way as to restore consumer confidence and increase market share. This is regarded as a premiere textbook case of quality crisis management.

Product Contamination-Damage. Unrelated cases but both well handled involved Perrier Water and the Girl Scouts of America. Ground substances in localized batches of Girl Scout Cookies were contained effectively, thus having no adverse effect on the organization's fund raising activities. Contaminated quantities of liquid resulted in a worldwide recall of product. Activities included crisis communications, grassroots lobbying, dealer relations, issues management, and the recently-completed successful market reintroduction of the product. Perrier utilized media opportunities to advocate for environmental protection and sought to educate consumers about product purification processes.

Reclaim Company's Good Name, Chrysler bankruptcy. Going to the government and asking for bailout loans is quite chancy, as the airlines have learned recently. Automaker Chrysler was at an impasse in the late 1970s, facing competition and marketplace dominance from imported autos. From top to bottom, the corporate culture was overhauled. Fresh approaches were taken to getting out of the hole, putting emphasis upon quality in workmanship and moving the company forward. When so many companies today put forward a "branding campaign" and call it a change in focus, I laugh. Chrysler was one of the few to totally rethink and retool. Their success should be a beacon to companies striving to make the long way back.

Saccharine. In 1977, the federal government banned saccharine, claiming that it caused cancer. Producers of the product teamed together to form the non-partisan Calorie Control Council of America. Its members included physicians, researchers, diabetes support groups and nutritionists. The coalition fostered healthy lifestyles, rather than attack the government bad directly.

The national credibility restoration campaign included crisis management, re-educating the public on the need for artificial sweeteners as part of healthy diets and government relations activity. By organizing business groups with citizens into CCC, this effort coalesced grassroots support, which caused Congress to overturn a U.S. Food and Drug Administration ban on saccharine, thus restoring the product to the market. Research denying its link to cancer and other promotional health aspects of the campaign served to return saccharine to credible common usage and create a wider market share for its uses as artificial sweeteners.

Maquiladoras. In the early 1980s, Laredo, Texas, was faced with a 28% unemployment rate. Devaluation of the Mexican peso and slumps in energy and ranching economies had taken tolls on a city whose population was losing faith. The decision was made to unify the community and actively go after manufacturers to relocate to the area.

Maquiladora is a Spanish word which means "made by hand." The program offered tax advantages to assembly line manufacturers who either left northern factories or added additional installations on the Mexican border.

This unified business community effort, in response to a dire economic crisis, resulted in 63 major factories being built in Laredo, Texas, and Nuevo Laredo, Mexico, occupied by General Motors, Ford, Sony, Hitachi, JVC, 3-M, Stokeley Foods and others. The Maquiladora program lowered the unemployment rate from 28% to 13%. This industrial development program carried the theme, "You Can Believe/Puede Creer."

Columbine. Following shootings at Columbine High School, the City of Littleton, Colorado, was in the media spotlight. Still a relatively new community, its right hand and left hand still were not fully acquainted. Uniting to bravely face the tragedy, the community found inner strengths and mounted a visioning program. Infrastructures were put in place. Quality of life issues were addressed. Economic development and community stewardship programs emerged. Out of the ashes of a school massacre came a community that created and nurtured strategies for the future.

Thinking Through the Strategies

Crisis management is so much more than handling of the media. A major oil company had a plant explosion and proceeded to do a good job of communicating afterwards. Unfortunately, the follow-through never transpired after the media coverage died down. Thus, lawsuits flew in the company's face.

My client (a different chemical company) later had a similar explosion. The chief legal counsel called and stated that we did not want the fallout as from the other company. We therefore mounted a full-scope crisis management initiative that focused heavily on after-the-crisis help for the victims and their families. The goal was to keep litigation from occurring, which was met. At a later news conference, OSHA announced that it was assessing its smallest fine, as a result of the forthright way in which my client had handled the crisis.

Another energy industry client operated coal mines. The irresponsible actions of two employees thrust sludge from the mines and into the Cumberland River, which subsequently contaminated the water supply of three cities. The State of Kentucky filed suit, seeking criminal charges against the company.

Working closely together with legal counsel, our recommended crisis program posed an alternative to a worst-case sentence. The program, approved by the judge, consisted of TV and newspaper apology statements, plus the assurance that safety-environmental training would be provided to employees. An investment of $50,000 effected a reduction of the fine from $2 million to $500,000 and reduction of the charges from criminal to civil. Sustained follow-up communication with employees, customers, the court, regulators and opinion leaders ensued.

Another client was a large urban shopping center. Rapes occurred in the parking lot during the Christmas shopping season. Neighboring offices began e-mailing their friends, concerned that the center was unsafe.

Our strategy to address the crisis was three-fold. We engaged senior citizen volunteer corps and criminal justice students to wear Santa hats and serve as holiday escorts, assuring safety but not appearing as armed guards. Secondly, we initiated safety training that expanded to help home owners avoid accidents. Thirdly, the communications process served to glean research data that we needed to upgrade the center, its tenant mix and security issues. The common denominator was open communications with customers, where other retail centers try to stifle mention of incidents.

The process of strategy development is not esoteric. It is common sense, with an emphasis upon ideas that work and are easy to communicate. You always draw upon successful elements of other client crises. I had a restaurant chain attacked by an auto incident. Its family customer base was uneasy for their safety. We took the shopping center escort idea and translated it to senior citizen door greeters, armed with friendliness and the latest serving suggestions. Coupled with armed guards in parking lots, the approach was to reiterate the friendly, homey atmosphere, in contrast to the stereotype of sterile chain eateries.

There are three aspects to Crisis Management and Preparedness. First, qualified business advisors conduct Crisis Communications Audits. This securing and evaluation of programs needed or in-progress has enabled corporate management to make informed decisions, take swift action and avoid possible litigation.

Next comes Crisis Planning. This becomes a coordinated committee, with multiple departments and professional disciplines represented. What-if scenario planning is similar to the processes utilized in overall company strategic planning and visioning. The crisis plan must be part of the bigger process, not an adjunct or afterthought.

Finally comes Crisis Training. Activities include media-spokesperson training, field and operations staff training, coordination of corporate response and message points, community liaison, collateral materials writing-production, video archiving-production, media relations, monitoring and expert testimony. The crisis teams need to be prepared.

Crisis planning and strategies should be intertwined with security issues, financial goals, workforce empowerment and many other corporate dynamics. Elements which Crisis Management and Preparedness Plans should address, per categories on The Business Tree™, include:

1. **The business you're in (core business).** Protection of intellectual property, materials, business continuity and core business production information. Prevention of theft, leaks in proprietary information and delays in deliverables.

2. **Running the business.** Protection of physical plants, equipment, office files and other supplies. Prevention of unnecessary downtimes, spoilage, stoppage in processes and theft.

3. **Financial.** Protection of fiduciary responsibilities and financial assets. Prevention of theft, embezzlement, accounting fraud and overpayments.

4. **People.** Protection of human capital, knowledge bases of workers, executives, company safety and the work environment. Prevention of unnecessary employee burnout.

5. **Business development.** Protection of company reputation, partnerships and alliances, marketplace intelligence and customer interests and relationships. Prevention of leaks in customer information and losses in company market position.

6. **Body of Knowledge.** Protection of status and utilization of organizational working knowledge, management's activities and relationships with regulators. Prevention of strains in company relationships with others and attacks from outside the organization.

7. **The Big Picture.** Protection of the overall organization, compliance standards in the organization. Prevention of loss in quality, purpose or vision.

In times of crisis, take assessment of damages, and investigate the truth. Never exaggerate, speculate, or withhold information. No statements should be "off the record." Provide complete answers, and respond to media requests for additional information in a timely manner. Failure to return calls implies something to hide. Maintain accurate records of all inquiries and news coverage.

The best way to build bridges is to seek out community opinion leaders and stakeholders before times of crisis. Educate them of your activities. Offer tours or community visitations to facilities. Provide printed information on your business… and a video, if at all affordable.

Test crisis plans during simulated drills, using qualified outside strategic planning consultants to evaluate results. Company officials should take these simulations seriously. The military does, terming them "war games."

Part of being prepared is being engaged in routine activity. Have a plan in force, and be sure that every employee has a copy. The binder containing the plan should include easy-to-read fact sheets and backgrounders on company operations, current phone numbers, and a delineated line of authority (from company resource people to the spokesperson)

Crises can have many liabilities upon companies, including loss of profits and market share. Inevitable spin-offs include government investigations, public scrutiny, and a tarnished image. This causes loss of employee morale and, as a result, company productivity.

Crisis management and preparedness can minimize negative impacts of any emergency. Going through the planning and implementation is a quality assurance process that strengthens any company. Crisis communications means banking goodwill for those times when the plan is called to the test.

Crises of one sort can and will happen to every company. They can be turned from disasters into opportunities to project corporate strengths. The manner in which a crisis is handled often wins praise for companies whose positions are improved in the public eye. Those who are prepared will survive and thrive.

Volatile business contractions, uneasy economic climate, plant explosions, health care crises, hostile corporate takeovers, governmental shakeups, and financial failings are crises that upset the routine of business life.

Some jolting incident puts every organization into a reaction mode. The consequences of miscommunication in a crisis can be devastating to all involved. By dealing with the unexpected, preferably before it occurs, companies can bank public goodwill that may be useful later. Playing catch-up means that you have lost the game.

It is the responsibility of corporate management to practice effective Crisis Management and Preparedness. Management must study practical experiences of what can go wrong, put a crisis team into place, understand the workings of news media, identify community opinion leaders, and predict potentially harmful or controversial situations. Learn from those who were successful, those who failed to achieve the desired effects, and those whose corporate credibility was damaged by inaction or the wrong actions.

Quotes on Courage During Times of Crisis

"Courage is resistance to fear, mastery of fear—not absence of fear."
— **Mark Twain**

"Courage is the price that life exacts for granting peace."
— **Amelia Earhart**, 20th Century aviator

"We could never learn to be brave and patient.
If there were only joy in the world."
— **Helen Keller** (1890)

"In the dark days and darker nights when England stood alone,
and most men save Englishmen despaired of England's life, he
mobilized the English language and sent it into battle."
— **President John F. Kennedy**, upon proclaiming
Sir Winston Churchill a honorary U.S. citizen, April 9, 1963

"I was not the lion. But it fell to me to give the lion his roar."
— **Sir Winston Churchill**

"Courage and perseverance have a magical talisman, before
which difficulties disappear and obstacles vanish into air."
— **President John Quincy Adams** (1767-1848)

"Courage is the ladder on which all the other virtues mount."
— **Clare Booth Luce** (1903-1987)

"Life shrinks or expands in proportion to one's courage."
— **Anais Nin** (1903-1977)

"I wanted you to see what real courage is, instead of getting
the idea that courage is a man with a gun in his hand. It's
when you know you're licked before you begin but you begin
anyway and you see it through no matter what."
— **Harper Lee**, "To Kill a Mockingbird"

"Every human being on this earth is born with a tragedy, and it isn't
original sin. He's born with the tragedy that he has to grow up. That he
has to leave the nest, the security, and go out to do battle. He has to lose

everything that is lovely and fight for a new loveliness of his own making, and it's a tragedy. A lot of people don't have the courage to do it."
— Actress **Helen Hayes**

"Discouragement is simply the despair of wounded self-love."
— **Francois de Fenelon** (1651-1715)

"Difficulties are meant to rouse, not discourage. The human spirit is to grow strong by conflict."
— **William Ellery Channing** (1780-1842)

"The bravest thing you can do when you are not brave is to profess courage and act accordingly."
— **Corra Harris**

"When you meet your antagonist, do everything in a mild and agreeable manner. Let your courage be as keen, but at the same time as polished, as your sword."
— **Richard Brinsley Sheridan** (1751-1816)

"If you explore beneath shyness or party chit-chat, you can sometimes turn a dull exchange into an intriguing one. I've found this to be particularly true in the case of professors or intellectuals, who are full of fascinating information, but need encouragement before they'll divulge it."
— **Joyce Carol Oates**

"Have courage for the great sorrows of life and patience for the small ones; and when you have laboriously accomplished your daily task, go to sleep in peace."
— **Victor Hugo** (1802-1885)

"Never discourage anyone who continually makes progress, no matter how slow."
— **Plato**

"You gain strength, courage and confidence by every experience in which you really stop to look fear in the face. You say to yourself, I have lived through this horror. I can take the next thing that comes along. You must do the thing you think you cannot do."
— **Eleanor Roosevelt**

"Keep your fears to yourself, but share your courage with others."
— **Robert Louis Stevenson**

"Discourage litigation. Persuade your neighbors to compromise whenever you can. As a peacemaker the lawyer has superior opportunity of being a good man. There will still be business enough."
— **President Abraham Lincoln** (1809-1865)

"Have patience with all things, but chiefly have patience with yourself. Do not lose courage in considering you own imperfections but instantly set about remedying them. Every day begin the task anew."
— **Saint Francis de Sales**

"Courage is doing what you're afraid to do. There can be no courage unless you're scared."
— **Eddie Rickenbacker** (1890-1973)

"It is curious that physical courage should be so common in the world and moral courage so rare."
— **Mark Twain** (1835-1910)

"Courage is being scared to death…but saddling up anyway."
— **Actor John Wayne** *(1907-1979)*

Chapter 12

DIVERSITY IS IMPORTANT FOR BUSINESS

D iversity is the lifeblood of business, the economy and quality of life. Specialized positioning and communications are necessary for social harmony and a global economy. We are a diverse population, and the same ways of communicating do not have desired effects anymore.

Diversity is about so much more than human resources issues. It means making the most of the organization that we can. It means being anything that we want to be. Diversity is not about quotas and should never be perceived as imposed punishment. By taking stock and planning creatively, then we can and will embody diversity.

The premise of multicultural diversity is ambitious and necessary to achieve. It is a mindset that must permeate organizations from top-down as well as bottom-up. If not pursued in a sophisticated, sensitive way, good intentions will be wasted.

The following pointers are offered to companies who communicate with niche publics:

- Seek and train multi-cultural professionals.
- Contribute to education in minority schools…assuring that the pipeline of promising talent can rise to challenges of the workforce.

- Design public relations programs that embrace multicultural constituencies, rather than secondarily appeal to them after the fact.
- Interface with community based groups, sharing in activities and civic service…to learn how communications will be received.
- Realize that minority groups are highly diverse. Not every Asian knows each other, nor speaks the same language. There are as many subtle differences in every ethnic group as the next. Thus, multicultural communicating is highly customized.
- Realize that multi-cultural communications applies to all. Black professionals do not just participate in African American community events. Cultivate communicators toward cross-culturization.
- As media does a good job of showcasing multicultural events, note it positively. If thanked enough, media will continue to shine the light on multicultural diversity.
- Sophistication in the gauging of public opinion will result in a higher caliber of communicating. The demands of an ever-changing world require that continuous improvement be made. Attention paid to writing and graphics quality will enhance the value of multicultural communications.

The old theory was that society is a Melting Pot. That philosophy evolved to the Salad Bowl concept. In either, one element still sinks to the bottom. We must now see it as a Mosaic or Patchwork Quilt. Each element blends and supports others. Diversity is a continuing process where we keep the elements mixed.

People believe that they are now thinking differently and creatively about diversity issues. In truth, they are really rearranging their existing prejudices. To be diverse and united, societies must be sealed with common purposes.

We can be diversified and unified at the same time. We can remain culturally diversified. We still can and should work together as a society. We all hold cultural values. One set is not better than another.

Look at the issues and how they affect the total person. Actions are always required. Good intentions and political correctness are not enough.

It is important to acknowledge changes in society. It is good business to recognize opportunities for practice development. In the Chinese culture, every crisis is first recognized as a danger signal and always as an opportunity for overcoming obstacles.

Every professional must embrace a set of ethics:
- Things for which each professional holds himself/herself accountable.
- Holds benchmarks for Continuous Quality Improvement.
- Realistically attainable goals.
- Contains mechanisms to teach and mentor others.
- Continually re-examines and adds to the list.

There are many good reasons why diversity relates to your livelihood:
- Society will make increasing demands that you address these issues.
- It makes good business sense.
- It opens your services to additional market niches.
- It embodies the spirit of open communications, the basis of winning companies.
- This process creates more job opportunities for multicultural professionals.
- And it is the right thing to do.

Quotes About Diversity

"What is food to one is to another bitter poison."
— **Lucretius**

"Variety's the very spice of life, that gives it all its flavor."
— **William Cowper**, The Task

"Letting a hundred flowers blossom and a hundred schools of thought contend is the policy."
— **Mao Tse-tung** (1956)

"No pleasure lasts long unless there is variety to it."
— **Pubililius Syrus**

"It were not best that we should all think alike.
It is difference of opinion that makes horse races."
— **Mark Twain**

"Everyone is a prisoner of his own experiences.
No one can eliminate prejudices. Just recognize them."
— **Edward R. Murrow** (1955)

"Diversity is the one true thing we all
have in common. Celebrate it every day."
— Proverb

"When power leads man towards arrogance, poetry reminds
him of his limitations. When power narrows the area of man's
concern, poetry reminds him of the richness and diversity of
his existence. When power corrupts, poetry cleanses."
— **President John F. Kennedy** (1917-1963),
honoring poet Robert Frost at Amherst College

Chapter 13

THE MEDIUM IS THE MESSAGE

Understanding the Nuances
Communicating in Multigenerational Society

Marshall McLuhan studied communications and introduced break-through concepts at a conference in Vancouver in 1958. He wrote a book about it in 1964, "The Extensions of Man."

The McLuhan premise, research and publication said, ""the medium is the message."

The concept is based upon several conditions:

- The manner in which information is communicated has more of an effect on the person receiving the message, rather than the message itself.
- Each new medium is to be seen in terms of behaviors that it creates or inspires.
- The medium is an environment of services and disservices.
- The message is the change of scale or pace or pattern that a new invention or innovation introduces into human affairs.

- Changes affect the ability for many people to notice change. And noticing change is crucial.
- A medium is any extension of ourselves.
- The content of any medium binds us to the character of the medium.
- When the channel supersedes the content, then many people overlook the content.
- We know the nature of a medium by the changes that we create or adhere to.
- Noticing change in our societal or cultural ground conditions indicates the presence of new messages.
- We can identify the new medium before it is obvious to everyone.
- Control over change would enable moving ahead of it, rather than behind it.
- Anticipation gives the power to deflect and control force.
- The way that something is conveyed affects the way in which the meaning is conveyed.
- Technologies are extensions of human capacities.
- Mass media entices people into accepting marketing messages.
- Personal and social consequences of a medium result from the new scale that is introduced into our affairs by each extension of ourselves and by new technologies.
- Whatever medium we use, it is always the people in the media who bring the message.
- Context is more significant than the message itself.
- Mass communications has changed the dynamics of life. Understanding these extensions of ourselves is important for society to cope and move forward.

Updating Medium is the Message in the 21st Century

The biggest problem with business in our society, in a capsule sentence, is:

People with one set of experiences, values, wants and perceptions make mistargeted attempts to communicate with others in trying to get what they want and need.

Success is just in front of our faces. Yet, we often fail to see it coming. Too many companies live with their heads in the sand. Many go down into defeat because it was never on their radar to change.

One of the biggest cop-outs that businesses in denial use is the term Messaging. They say, "We're in the right business. We only need to improve our messaging." That's a rationalization to avoid confronting key strategic issues.

7 Biggest Communication Obstacles:
1. Lack of people skills, manners
2. Wrong facts
3. Denial-avoidance of the real issues
4. Non-communication
5. Saying the wrong things at the wrong times, for the wrong reasons
6. Failure to pick up subtle clues
7. Failure to master communication as an art

7 Levels of Communicating:
1. Sending out messages we wish-need to communicate.
2. Sending messages which are intended for the listener.
3. Communicating with many people at the same time.
4. Eliciting feedback from audiences.
5. Two-way communication process.
6. Adapting and improving communications with experience.
7. Developing communications as a vital tool of business and life.

Lack of communication is symptomatic of fear, which is the biggest handicap for any company. Because of fear, productivity suffers, turnover increases and profitability drops. There are four main fears in the business environment:

- Reprisal. This includes disciplining, termination, transfer to an undesirable position. When employees fear reprisal, more effort is spent on affixing blame to others than achieving pro-active progress.

- Non-communication. Rather than risk going out on a limb, employees either don't learn or use their communication skills. This stymies employees' professional development and hampers company productivity.
- Not knowing. Rather than admit areas where information is lacking, employees often cover up, disseminating erroneous data, which comes back to hurt others. The wise employee has the building of knowledge a part of their career path…sharing with others what we most recently and most effectively learn.
- Change. Managers and employees with the most to lose are most fearful of change. Their biggest fear is the unknown. Research shows that 90% of change is good. If people knew how beneficial that change is, they would not fight it so much.

Each member of the organization should understand and covet the position they play. It is just as important how, when and why we communicate with each other:

- Shows that the company is a seamless concept, an integrated team working for the good of customers.
- Indicates sophistication by each representative that every team player knows how to utilize each other for mutual benefit.
- Reminds customers that the company is detail-focused and quality-oriented, with an eye toward continually improving.
- Underscores how internal communications are comparable to the way we will interface with customers.

Communications are nuanced by various factors:
- How things change meanings.
- How things are said.
- How they are heard.
- How they are passed on to others.
- Code language.
- People's susceptibility to believing distortions and lies.
- Physical behaviors that send messages.

Each medium has its own characteristics, usage practices and protocols:

Signs

Billboards

Books

Newspapers

Radio

Television

Newsletters

Faxes

E-mails

Telephone service

Telephone advertising

Direct mail

Internet

Social media

Fake news

Spam, scams and phony communications

Music media

Video media

Challenges for Communications in the Digital Age

There are lots of communications and endless distractions. Users have the control to select media and content. There are now too many media choices. Content is conveyed in real-time and is ever-present. There are very few editors and filters, causing a wave of unedited opinion. Interactive communications distill data and offer narratives, causing information of varying worth and applicability.

In modern society, there are negative ways in which media present stresses, challenges and problems for the rest of us. Examples include:

- Organizations that force their software and reporting programs on others.
- Companies that hide behind call centers and never really facilitate good customer service.
- Human resources departments that pass paper and do not seek to understand people.

- People who never talk to you on the phone and hide behind texts.
- People who discriminate against others by talking in code around them.
- Communications used to be one-way focused. Now, it is interactive, and many opposing forces are conflating messages.

Paying careful attention to Communications as part of The Big Picture of Business should address:

- Generational takes on communications.
- The Multigenerational Workforce: How Communication Styles Impact Office Culture.
- Bridging the communication gap between the Baby Boomer generation and Millenials: Include them in future focused conversations. Mentor them. Embrace differences.
- Study communicating with machines, including the voices of Siri and Alexa.
- Communicating with people with attention deficit.
- Communicating with people with disabilities.
- Recognizing that many people hear without listening.

Pictures are Symbolic of Corporate Culture

One of the hottest and most accessible vehicles is the photograph. With cameras now on phones, people are snapping more pictures than ever before. Some get distributed on the internet, through social media and in direct transfer to friends.

This resurgence in photography comes after a conversion of the industry from film to digital. Photography is presently at an all-time high in terms of societal impact. The irony is that its principal corporate contributor (Eastman Kodak) fell by the wayside, a victim of changing technologies. The same fate had fallen the electronics industry, whose innovator (the Thomas Edison Electric Company) fell behind others in leading the trends and usage.

Photographs convey thoughts, ideas and experiences. Hopefully, their usages represent thoughtful communications. Organizations can see photography as a boon to their business, if utilized properly.

Every business person and company needs a website and social media presence. Photographs convey what you're doing new. They're indicative of the scope of your business activity.

Use photography to personify the company. Pictures draw relationships to the customers. Think of creative ways to show employees doing great work. Show customers as benefiting from the services that you offer.

Most companies would do well to devote a portion of its homepage to its charitable involvements. Show employees as being engaged in community activities. Promote and graphically portray your company's designated cause-related marketing activities. Interface with outside communities tends to grow your stakeholder base.

Don't just view photography as something that everyone does. Establish company ground rules for the usage of pictures. Tie activities to customer outcomes (the tenet of Customer Focused Management).

Nourish Communications Skills

There are 7 stages of communications strategy for companies:

1. **Basic.** There is more information available now than ever before. Most of it is biased and slanted by vendors with something to sell. There exists much data, without interpretation. Technology purveys information but cannot do the analytical thinking.

2. **Limited and guarded.** Appearance of data leads to initial perceptions, usually influenced by the media in which the information exists. To many people and organizations, perception is reality because they do not delve any further. Thus, learning stops at this point.

3. **Brand, not strategy.** Determined more by events-processes than words. Verbal statements are more important when people are suggestible and need interpretation from a credible source. Does not anticipate emergencies… only reacts to them. Many perceptions and opinions are self-focused and affected by self-esteem. Once self-interest becomes involved, opinions do not change easily.

4. **Ideas and Beliefs.** Formulated ideas emerge, as people-organizations learn to hold their own outside their shells. Two-way communication ensues…opinion inputs and outputs craft ideas and beliefs. As people become more aware of their own learning, they tally their inventory of

knowledge. Patterns of beliefs emerge, based upon education, experiences and environment.

5. **Systems of Thought and Ideologies.** Insights start emerging at this plateau. Connect beliefs with available resources and personal expertise. Measure results and evaluate outcomes of activities, using existing opinion, ideas and beliefs. Actions are taken which benchmark success and accountability to stakeholders.

6. **Core value, direct.** Shaped by ideas, beliefs, systems of thought and ideologies. Becomes what the person or organization stands for. Has conviction, commitment and ownership. Able to change and adapt. Behavioral modification from the old ways of thinking has transpired.

7. **Committed to Excellence and Vision.** An informed plateau that few achieve. Able to disseminate information, perceptions and opinions for what they really are. Wisdom focused…an evolving flow of philosophies. A quest to employ ideologies and core values for benefit of all in the organization. Committed to and thriving upon change.

It is important to generate ideas and suggestions via writing memos, E-mail messages and internal documents. Their succinctness and regularity of issue have a direct relationship to your compensation and the company's bottom line.

Before presenting ideas to a customer or prospect, consider organizing your approach:

- Predict reasons why someone might oppose your suggestions.
- Seek out supporters, early-on.
- Determine goals. Is the objective to get the idea accepted or get credit for it?
- Understand your audience. Understand differing personality types of your audiences.
- Think of yourselves as leaders, who are good communicators.
- Listen as others amplify upon the idea, which shows their buy-in potential.
- Determine as much accuracy in others' perceptions to your ideas. Don't fool yourself or be blind-sighted to opposition.

- Throw out decoy ideas for others to shoot down, so they don't attack your core message.
- Use language that is easily understood by all. Avoid technical terms, unless you include brief definitions.
- Don't over-exaggerate in promises and predictions.

Other pointers in effectively communicating include:
- Speak with authority.
- Make the most of face-to-face meetings, rather than through artificial barriers.
- Remember that voice inflection, eye contact and body language are more important than the words you use.
- Charts, graphs and illustrative materials make more impact for your points.
- Don't assume anything. If in doubt about their understanding, ask qualifying questions. Become a better listener.
- Sound the best on the phone that you can.
- Use humor successfully.
- Get feedback. Validate that audiences have heard your intended messages.
- Attitude is everything in effective communications.

Messaging in the Millennium

In many professions, the idea of full-scope, sophisticated positioning has been foreign up until now. Business development has occurred primarily by accident or through market demand. Because of economic realities and the increased numbers of firms providing comparable services, the notion of business development is now a necessity, rather than a luxury.

Competition for customers-clients is sharpening. The professions are no longer held on a pedestal, a condition mandating them to portray or enhance public images. As companies adjust comfort levels and acquire confidence in the arena of business development, there is a direct relationship to billings, client mix diversity, market share, competitive advantage, stock price and levels of business which enable other planned growth.

Public perceptions are called "credence goods" by economists. Every organization must educate outside publics about what they do and how they do it. This holds for corporate operating units and departments. You must always educate corporate opinion makers on how you function and the skill with which you operate.

Gaining confidence is crucial, as business relationships with professionals are established to be long-term in duration. Each organization or should determine and craft its own character and personality, seeking to differentiate from others. That appeals to professionals within your own staff, those professionals whom your firm would like to attract and clients.

Top management must endorse corporate imaging and other forms of practice development, if your company is to grow and prosper. Few companies can even sustain present levels of sales without some degree of business development. Some people in your organization will devote much time to promotions, public relations, marketing and advertising. This quality should be recognized and rewarded, since professionals with a sense of business direction play an important part in company growth.

Be it a "necessary evil" or not, corporate imaging activity can be accomplished with skill and success, provided that organizations follow the advice of professional communicators.

Organizations must maintain a delicate balance between seeking new business, replacing lost clients and nurturing client relationships. Operating units and departments must schedule and follow a program to market their worth to their companies. No matter what time allocation basis is selected by the organization, it is vital that some basis exists in writing and in execution. The organization that evokes a caring image and backs it up with service will be more successful.

In image building, the following ideas should be considered:

- Your company and profession fill essential needs of society.
- Each key staff member represents a learned profession.
- Qualities include skill, expertise, objectivity and independence.
- Work and abilities of your employees are diverse and creative.
- Your key management team is dynamic, in terms of business issues.

- The marketplace is rapidly expanding and is an excellent career choice for young people.
- Your team encompasses multi-dimensional professionals...concerned with much more than the immediate responsibilities of the work at hand.
- Recognize the role of professional communicators. Seek qualified counsel.

Words count. Put together, they reflect corporate culture. Used out of context, words become excuses, gibberish, rationales and basically wastes of energy.

When people hear certain words and expressions often enough, they parrot them. Rather than use critical thinking to communicate, many people often gravitate to the same old tired catch phrases.

These are the characteristics of effective words, phrases and company communications:

- Focus upon the customer.
- Honor the employees.
- Defines business as a process, not a quick fix.
- Portray their company as a contributor, not a savior.
- Clearly defines their niche.
- Say things that inspire you to think.
- Compatible with other communications.
- Remain consistent with their products, services and track record.

Quotes on Communications, Fame and Corporate Image

"It is a heavy burden to bear a name that is too famous."
— Voltaire

"Fame, if you win it, comes and goes in a minute.
What is the real goal that life brings?"
— Lyrics from the song "Make Someone Happy,"
from the musical "Bye Bye Birdie"

"As an adolescent I aspired to lasting fame, I craved factual certainty, and I thirsted for a meaningful vision of human life—so I became a scientist. This is like becoming an archbishop so you can meet girls."
— **M. Cartmill**

"Some for renown, on scraps of learning dote, and think they grow immortal as they quote."
— **Edward Young** (1683-1765), "Love of Fame"

"It is just the little touches after the average man would quit that make the master's fame."
— **Orison Swett Marden** (1850-1924)

"When Alexander the Great visited Diogenes and asked whether he could do anything for the famed teacher, Diogenes replied: 'Only stand out of my light.' Perhaps some day we shall know how to heighten creativity. Until then, one of the best things we can do for creative men and women is to stand out of their light."
— **John W. Gardner**

"Rather than love, than money, than fame, give me truth."
— **Henry David Thoreau** (1817-1862)

"He who pursues fame at the risk of losing his self is not a scholar."
— **Chuang-tzu** (369 BC-286 BC), The Great Supreme

"Loyalty to petrified opinion never yet broke a chain or freed a human soul."
— **Mark Twain** (1835-1910), inscription beneath his bust in the Hall of Fame

"Wisdom alone is true ambition's aim. Wisdom the source of virtue, and of fame, obtained with labor, for mankind employed, and then, when most you share it, best enjoyed."
— **Alfred North Whitehead** (1861-1947)

*"Fame comes only when deserved, and
then is as inevitable as destiny, for it is destiny."*
— **Henry Wadsworth Longfellow**

Chapter 14

OXYMORON'S OF BUSINESS

Studies in conflicting terminology

We hear them everywhere, especially in business. Things are said and believed to be true. Organizations which perpetuate myths and inconsistencies set themselves up for failure.

This chapter, both for fun and sophisticated insight, puts forth several contradictory terms and business ideologies.

The dictionary's definition of oxymoron: "A combination of contradictory or incongruous words. Pointedly foolish."

Judge for yourself the realities of each term and cliché phrase in business usage.

Courtesy booth. Picture of perfect health. One size fits all.

Common sense. Free money. Cruel kindness.

Responsible behavior. Neighbors who know you. Gentle giant.

Low-cost provider. Economy car. Planned serendipity.

Child-like qualities. The Great American Novel. Rest room.

Family values. Public servant. Computer logic.

Low bidder. Military orderliness. Get rich quick.

White House crisis. Special commission. Executive privilege.

Profit motive. Youthful maturity. Pointedly dull.

Careful listening. Good scissors. Genuine imitation.

Best on Earth. Sales quotas. Good for you.

Public spirited. Law and justice. Low-salt.

Service station. Bank draft. Low cholesterol.

Efficiency in government. Equal opportunities. Fair and just.

Liked by everyone. Hated by everyone. Gift of gab.

Plan as you go. Perfect marriage. Popular boss.

Quick fixes. Ease and convenience. Justice for all.

Matter of life and death. An hour-long TV show. Free earth.

Good music. Constructive criticism. Just like the rest.

Doctors' bedside manner. Bring out the big guns. Dead to right.

Oxymoron's in the Business World

- Sales and service as equal corporate priorities.
- Organization that doesn't need to grow any further.
- Saying everything that needs to be said.
- People knowing what is expected of them in their jobs.
- Business that puts environmental concerns first.
- Simple solutions for business problems.
- Customer friendly service.
- Micro-niche professionals who become company leaders.
- Personal attention from an automated telecommunications system.
- This page intentionally left blank.
- People whom you think can and will do things as well as you can do them.
- Outside-the-box management thinking.
- Companies with flexible rules-policies.
- Low-cost insurance that covers everything.
- Nothing to hide.
- Fixing problems for free.
- Temporary tax increase.
- Objective planning by internal people.

- Interim financing.
- Lotteries benefiting the taxpayers.
- Re-engineering.
- Seeing from the customer's point of view.
- Work party or crew.
- Born with leadership potential.
- One-man work crew.
- All-inclusive concept or policy.
- Partially completed.
- People-friendly products.
- Clearly misunderstood.
- Doing things for all the right reasons.
- Random logic (fuzzy logic).
- Responsible discord.
- Free publicity.
- Knowing the facts all they need to know.
- The perfect plan.
- Having it all together.
- Original thinking.
- Unlimited resources.
- Mandatory option.
- Designed with you in mind.
- Global village.
- Quality at the lowest cost.
- Free legal advice.
- Mid-managers taking risks.
- Original copy.
- Fully developed listening skills.
- Exact estimate.
- Equipped to handle any situation.
- Committee decision.
- Having all the answers.
- Artificial intelligence.
- Payment for performance.

- Say what you mean, and mean what you say.
- All the opportunities in the world.
- Veteran consultant.
- Walk the talk.
- Taught them all they know.
- Amateur expert.
- Living in the real world.
- Good, fast and cheap.
- Affordable health insurance.
- Budget shortfall.
- Fast results with little effort.
- Unacceptable solution.
- User friendly computer.
- Fast track bureaucrat.
- Full control.
- Idiots' work.
- Knowing exactly how someone feels.
- Creative accounting.
- Have them eating out of your hand.
- The best is none too good for someone.
- Government planning and strategy.
- Job security.
- Working vacation.
- Standard deviation.
- Flexible freeze (economics term).
- Advanced basic standard.
- Faster, cheaper and better.
- Computer learning.

Other Oxymoron's

Act naturally Government organization Sanitary landfill
Airline food Great Depression Scheduled spontaneity
Almost exactly Green forest Second best
Alone together Guest host Secret FBI Files

Athletic scholarship Half-full, half-empty Silent music

Baby grand (piano)Heart healthy gourmet food Silent scream

Bad sex Holy war Singular relationship

Black light Honest crook Small crowd

Brief survey Hopelessly optimistic Software documents

Broadcast journalism Hospital food Sounds of silence

Butt head Ideal situation Student teacher

Buyer's market In-depth TV reports Sure bet

Child-proof Industrial park Sweet sorrow

Children's encyclopedia Irate patient Synthetic natural gas

Civil War Jumbo shrimp Taped live

Classic novel Junk food Terribly nice

Clean waterways Lean pork Terribly pleased

Code optimization Legally drunk Tight slacks

Computer jock Light Heavyweight Turbo diesel

Computer security Live on tape, live recording12-ounce pound cake

Concise dictionary Living dead White chocolate

Congressional ethics Marijuana initiative

Criminal justice Medium-Large

Criminal lawyer Metal woods

Deafening silence Mild Abrasive

Death benefits Military Intelligence

Deficit spending Minor disaster

Definite maybe Mobile home

Diet ice cream Mobile station

Divorce court Natural childbirth

Down elevator-escalator New classic

Dry wine New wave of nostalgia

Efficiency in government No-good do-gooder

Elementary calculus Non-stop flight

Evaporated milk "Now, then…"

Even odds Old news

Extra time Organized mess

Family vacation Passive aggression

Fast idle Peace force

Fat-free Peacekeeper missile

Fat-free ice cream-margarine Perfect idiot

Found missing Plastic glasses

Freezer burn Political correctness

Fresh frozen Political science

Friendly argument Political will

Friendly fire Pretty ugly

Golf fashions Resident alien

Good grief Safe sex

Gourmet pizza Same difference

Oxymoron's of Humor

- Why do you need a driver's license to buy liquor when you can't drink and drive?
- Why isn't phonetic spelled the way it sounds?
- Why are there interstate highways in Hawaii?
- Why are there flotation devices under plane seats instead of parachutes?
- Why are cigarettes sold in gas stations when smoking is prohibited there?
- Have you ever imagined a world with no hypothetical situations?
- How does the guy who drives the snowplow get to work in the mornings?
- If a convenience store is open 24 hours a day, 365 days a year, why are there locks on
- the doors?
- If a cow laughed, would milk come out of her nose?
- If nothing ever sticks to Teflon, how do they make Teflon stick to the pan?
- If you're driving in a vehicle that is going at the speed of light, what happens when you turn on the headlights?
- You know how most packages say Open here. What is the protocol if the package says, Open somewhere else?
- Why do we drive on parkways and park on driveways?
- Why is it that when you transport something by car, it's called a shipment, but when you transport something by ship, it's called cargo?

- Why is it that when you're driving and looking for an address, you instinctively turn down the volume on the radio?

Oxymoron's of Business Logic

- Surveys show that change is 90% positive. So, why do people and organizations fight what is most in their best interest?
- Why do organizations think about planning process only when they are deep in trouble?
- Why is it that large numbers of seasoned professionals do not have sufficient training in communications and leadership skills.
- Why do companies grow rapidly without first studying the marketplace, processes to deliver the goods and management styles of key players?
- How are sales quotas determined?
- How are managers of employees trained and measured on their people skills?
- Which criteria determine who are the true team players in an organization?
- If everyone worked as though "their name were on the door," how much better would business function?
- If everyone were paid what the customers thought they were worth, how much better would they perform their jobs?
- Why do aggressive sales-driven companies proclaim their commitment to customer service?
- Why is it that progressive organizations are the ones to embrace and exemplify quality management tenets, when those who need it the most do not acknowledge the concepts?
- Why do some professionals live in the past, fight change and stagnate, when others pride themselves on reinventing themselves and evolving?
- Why do people hold jobs without clear understanding of the company's mission?
- Why do many companies operate without a clear mission and vision?

Making Your Business More Than an Oxymoron

Futurism is not an esoteric concept that relates to others. It is not driven by external forces against your will. Futurism is your ability to understand and capitalize upon change. People and organizations change successfully every day. Those who excel are most adept at thinking and reasoning their way through change.

The past is the greatest weapon in the arsenal of Futurism. The past indicates opportunities to succeed and those that were not utilized. Learning from others' shortsightedness gives us the advantage. The past repeats itself, in many ways. Reapplying past knowledge to the future is the best way to stay ahead of the pack. Futurism converts past occurrences to tomorrow's realm.

It is said that each person has three careers. Actually, it's about seven. Being a student of life and all those youthful dues-paying jobs constituted phenomenal careers. Few people stand completely still. Realizing how far we've come inspires us to persevere harder. The next career will encompass all the previous ones.

The concept of a well run organization appeals to more than just the pocketbook. It appeals to the heart and gut...wanting to achieve something that nobody else could. It appeals to the mind...learning and creating more than others could. Any organization wants to be much more than outsiders may think or perceive.

Individuals who conduct their jobs well do so because of factors far beyond the written job description. Rewards are far beyond financial. The effective worker has pride in achievement, value in the services utilized and knowledge that he-she did the best possible. A good worker is his-her strongest critic and continually strives to improve.

Chapter 15

WHY THE FUTURE MUST MOVE

T he public does not react to any crisis until it is big enough and far-reaching to affect their daily lives. When business news gets on Page 1 of every day's newspaper and every evening TV newscast, then the public notices and cares.

Business and organizational stories do not hit the public consciousness until there is a crisis. People decry the scandals and rest assured that such doings are not happening in their companies.

Often, it is assumed that some protector or regulator will adequately address the issues. When the outcomes are of high magnitude, the outcry becomes larger. As people see the events as having a direct effect on the economy and their livelihood, they take notice and follow the stories more thoroughly.

Corporate scandals of 2001-2004 exploded myths and presumptions about business. Formerly sainted icons went down in disgrace. Tactics deemed as "standard operating procedure" for some companies were exposed and ridiculed by others. A few whistle blowers were lauded in the efforts, though others were scapegoated as the perpetrators of the chaos shuffled aside.

One must ask many simple and pertinent questions:

- How did business get this far?
- Why did the scandals and corporate disrepute occur?
- What are the implications of Enron and other corporate scandals upon business?
- Where are the next trends and opportunities?
- How do we cope in the new environment?
- What beacons of opportunity do we look for?
- What will it now take to succeed and fail?
- How do we react to and benefit from changes, rather than become victims of them?
- Do we still take band aid approaches (such as buying enterprise software)? Or, do we now see the need and importance to embrace longer-term approaches?
- How far will we go to excel?
- How creative must we become in the New Order of Business?
- How far-reaching are business practices?
- How much further should we extend ethics?
- Where will the pendulum swing next?

Business in the 21st Century is changing. Yesterday's strategies simply do not work anymore. Many of the old assumptions which business previously held have proven untrue and unworkable. We really must examine what we assumed before and what we can assume now. Business is at a juncture and needs new focus.

After corporate scandals, the term CEO was recently held in disfavor. We decry CEOs for the same reasons that we formerly sainted and canonized them. People are envious of the power, status and wealth of company heads. Yet, most CEOs were never trained on how to be CEOs, with all the responsibility, people skills, leadership and ethical management that must go along with the job.

Every organization in the world must reexamine how we will keep score in the New Order of Business. Continuing to justify blind spots will blur accountability. Having maintained too much of a myopic focus is what got so many companies in trouble already.

Most of the downfalls, stumbles, false starts and incorrect handling of situations stemmed from business' lack of focus on the macro…and over-emphasis upon certain micros, to the exclusion of other dynamics.

What we do with fear and uncertainty determines who we are. It is time for fresh thinking, heightened ethical behavior and a shift to a macro focus. Rules and responsibilities within each sector of companies are changing. Each of us must ask what we can contribute and our roles in adapting to the crises.

High Costs, Scandals and Learning Curves

Corporate scandals of 2001-2004 cost the U.S. economy more than $200 billion in lost investment savings, jobs, pension losses and tax revenue. The scandals resulted in one million job cuts. 401(k) plans dropped $13 billion as a result of these events alone. Recent corporate scandals have cost good businesses in reputation, credibility and support, by virtue of being lumped with some bad apples. Thus, consumer confidence dipped, and it will take years to fortify the trust in business.

Losses from 401(k) investment accounts alone totaled $175 billion, making them worth 30% less than they were two years ago. Public pension funds nationwide lost at least $6.4 billion as the stock market plummeted, amid a crisis of investor confidence. More than a million workers lost their jobs at the affected companies, while company executives cashed out billions of dollars of their stock.

There are 25 million small businesses in America, all affected in some way by corporate scandals.

As settlements in investigations, eight Wall Street investment banking firms agreed to pay $1.4 billion in fines. They were charged with conflicts of interest and giving out false information to investors.

For four years, the average citizen paid $4.81 on the maintenance of parks and $12.00 per person to cover the government's litigation costs of the Enron debacle.

Steroid scandals periodically rocked the sports world. The public decries the use of steroids but secretly supports the results that they yield (athletic records being set). The steroids usage norm in some team sports has the effect of institutionalizing breaking the rules, even though the health of some is seriously endangered. Temptations to break the rules for the hope of future financial gain are at the heart of corporate arrogance, greed, deceptions and double-dealings, as well as in the minds of some sports promoters.

Operational Statistics

One out of every 12 businesses fails. 90% of all e-businesses will fail. 99% of internet websites do not make a profit.

Retailers make 70% of their earnings in the fourth quarter of each year. That is why holiday sales are vital to their bottom line and, thus, the economy.

Airport screeners fail to detect fake bombs and guns 24 percent of the time.

52% of all high school students know someone who brought a weapon to school. 61% of those students did nothing about it. 52% of all high school students know someone who made a weapon-oriented threat. 56% of those students did nothing about it.

The Pentagon says that it cannot account for 25% of what it spends.

Shoplifting costs American retail business $10 billion per year.

Airlines say that delays caused by air traffic controllers cost them a combined $4 billion per year. For every 1-cent reduction in the cost of jet fuel, the airlines save $170 million.

Cargo theft costs the U.S. economy $6 billion per year. The victimized companies pass their recoveries from losses along to the customers. For example, $125 of the cost of each new personal computer goes to reimburse companies for previous thefts.

Consumers are cheated at gas pumps of self-serve marts each year in excess of $1 million because of faulty computer chips.

On any given day in the United States, over 100 convenience stores are robbed. Every day in the U.S., people steal $20,000 from coin-operated machines.

The average bank teller loses about $250 every year.

One third of our nation's Gross National Product is spent in cleaning up mistakes. Yet, only 5.1% is spent on education, which is the key to avoiding mistakes on the front end.

Fires cost more than $150 billion per year in damage. Most fires are caused by carelessness: overloading electrical sockets, smoking in bed, failure to turn off kitchen burners, malfunctions with space heaters, allowing trash to accumulate, failure to repair electrical wiring and electrical breaker explosions. Electricity-related incidents account for half of all fires.

A member of the U.S. Forestry Service was on patrol in June, 2002. She burned a letter from her estranged husband at a campfire site, thus starting a wildfire that spread to 100,000 acres. This damaged dozens of homes and displaced countless residents of Colorado. The Forestry worker had previously served 20 years in volunteer firefighting service and should have known better. Cost to U.S. taxpayers for containing the wildfire that she started was $50 million.

These are representative costs of wars, adjusted for inflation: Afghanistan, $3 billion. Somalia, $1.5 billion. Gulf War, $72 billion. Vietnam, $517 billion. World War II, $4.3 trillion. These figures do not include aid and restoration to countries following the wars.

The trial of Timothy McVeigh, mastermind of bombing the federal building in Oklahoma City, OK, cost U.S. taxpayers $15.1 million.

Learning the Lessons and Moving Forward

The U.S. Congress enacted the Sarbanes-Oxley Act, corporate reform legislation, in 2002. The bill delineated new regulations, in response to the accounting scandals at WorldCom, Enron, Tyco and other large companies that left thousands of employees without retirement savings and investors with worthless stock shares.

The bill was intended to prevent malfeasance, restore investor confidence and crack down on corporate cheaters. It set up new regulations for corporate auditing practices and creates strict penalties for executives who hide debt in accounting tricks. It was the largest reform since changes were made to halt the Depression-era slide into bankruptcy.

Sarbanes-Oxley instituted extensive corporate governance reforms, including standards for advisors representing public companies and their nonpublic subsidiaries. Under it, business leaders are expected to embrace both the letter and spirit of the bill and other existing laws, designed to protect investors, employees and other stakeholders.

In moving forward, one must review those junctures where leaders and their companies recognize when a business is in trouble. These are the high costs of neglect, non-actions and wrong actions, per categories on The Business Tree™:

1. **Product, Core Business.** The product's former innovation and dominance has somehow missed the mark in today's business climate. The company does not have the marketplace demand that it once had. Others have

streamlined their concepts, with greater success. Something newer has edged your company right out of first place.

2. **Processes, Running the Company.** Operations have become static, predictable and inefficient. Too much band aid surgery has been applied, but the bleeding has still not been stopped. Other symptoms of trouble have continued to appear...often and without warning.

3. **Financial Position.** Dips in the cash flow have produced knee-jerk reactions to making changes. Cost cutting and downsizing were seemingly ready answers, though they took tolls on the rest of the company. The overt focus on profit and bean counter mentality has crippled the organizational effectiveness.

4. **Employee Morale and Output.** Those who produce the product-service and assure its quality, consistency and deliverability have not been given sufficient training, empowerment and recognition. They have not really been in the decision making and leadership processes, as they should have been. Team members still have to fight the system and each other to get their voices heard, rather than function as a team.

5. **Customer Service.** Customers come and go, at great costs that are not tallied, noticed or heeded. After the percentages drop dramatically, management asks "What happened?" Each link in the chain hasn't yet committed toward the building of long-term customer relationships. Thus, marketplace standing wavers.

6. **Company Management.** There was no definable style in place, backed by Vision, strategies, corporate sensitivities, goals and beliefs. Whims, egos and momentary needs most often guided company direction. Young and mid-executives never were adequately groomed for lasting leadership.

7. **Corporate Standing.** Things have happened for inexplicable reasons. Company vision never existed or ceased to spread. The organization is on a downslide...standing still and doing things as they always were done constitutes moving backward.

These situations are day-to-day realities for troubled companies. Yes, they brought many of the troubles upon themselves. Yes, they compounded problems by failing to take swift actions. And, yes, they further magnify the costs of "band aid surgery" by failing to address the root causes of problems.

Each year, one-third of the U.S. Gross National Product goes toward cleaning up problems, damages and otherwise high costs of failing to take proper action. On the average, it costs six times the investment of preventive strategies to correct business problems). 92% of all problems in organizations stem from poor management decisions.

7 Most Significant Things that Managers Are Not Taught on Their Way Up

1. **Know Where You Are Going.** Develop, update and maintain a career growth document. Keep a diary of lessons learned but not soon forgotten. Learn the reasons for success and, more importantly, from failure.
2. **Truth and Ethics.** If you do not "walk the talk," who will? Realize that very little of what happens to you in business is personal. Find common meeting grounds with colleagues. The only workable solution is a win-win (or as close to it as can be negotiated).
3. **Professional Enrichment.** Early formal education is but a starting point. Study trends in business, in your industry and, more importantly, in the industries of your customers. There is no professional who does not have one or more "customers." The person who believes otherwise is not a real professional.
4. **People Skills Mastery.** There is no profession that does not have to educate others about what it does. The process of communicating must be developed. It is the only way to address conflicts, facilitate win-win solutions and further organizational goals.
5. **Mentorship and Stewardship.** We are products of those who believe in us. Find role models and set out to be one yourself. To get, you must give.
6. **Going the Distance.** Career and life are not a short stint. Do what it takes to run the decathlon. Set personal and professional goals, standards and accountability.
7. **Standing for Something.** Making money is not enough. You must do something worth leaving behind, mentoring to others and of recognizable substance. Your views of professionalism must be known.

Cliches and Terms That Do NOT Belong in Strategic Planning and Corporate Strategy:

Solutions Easy

The brand Better, Best

Technology For all your needs

Value proposition Handle problems

Perfection Do the math

Number one Good to go

Sales leader Customer experience

Customer care Results

Learning organization Perfection

World class Capitalism

Hearts and minds Cool

The end of the day Best in breed

Virtual Game changing

These expressions are trite, meaningless and reflect a copy-cat way of thinking.

"Solutions" is a tired 1990's term, taken from technology hype. People who use it are vendors, selling what they have to solve your "problems," rather than diagnosing and providing what your company needs. It is a misnomer to think that a quick fix pawned off as a "solution" will take care of a problem once and for all. Such a word does not belong in conversation and business strategy, let alone the name of the company.

Street talk, misleading slogans and terms taken out of context do not belong in the business vocabulary. Business planning requires insightful thinking and language which will clearly delineate what the company mission is and how it will grow.

Chapter 16

SMALL BUSINESS GUIDEBOOK

Business Partnerships

C oaching industries are growing rapidly because self-styled experts are creating pockets of business for themselves. Demands have long existed for quality service, with few seasoned business advisors available. Thus, niche consultants served the business.

New generations of entry-level consultants are hanging out shingles as "coaches" without backgrounds in guiding people, organizations and processes. Most business coaches used to be something else and are turning to "coaching" in their downsized career period.

Training programs for coaches are available, some good and some nothing more than multi-level marketing. There's presently more marketing to the concept of business coaching than substantive track record.

The hot new idea is to focus on depth-and-substance...not on flash-and-sizzle. Those who proclaim that hot ideas make good coaches, then they are vendors selling flavors of the month...not seasoned business advisors. If coaching is based only on hot ideas, it is nothing more than hucksterism. Coaching must be a thorough process of guiding the client through the levels of accomplishment.

There are 7 Levels at Which Mentors are Utilized:

1. **Resource.** Equipment, tools, materials, schedules.
2. **Skills and Tasks.** Duties, activities, tasks, behaviors, attitudes, contracting, project fulfillment.
3. **Role and Job.** Assignments, responsibilities, functions, relationships, follow-through, accountability.
4. **Systems and Processes.** Structure, hiring, control, work design, supervision, decisions.
5. **Strategy.** Planning, tactics, organizational development.
6. **Culture and Mission.** Values, customs, beliefs, goals, objectives, benchmarking.
7. **Philosophy.** Organizational purpose, vision, quality of life, ethics, long-term growth.

There are 7 Levels of Business and Organizational Mentoring:

1. **Conveying Information.** Initial exposure to the coaching process. One-time meeting or conference between mentors and mentees. The coach is a resource for business trends, societal issues, opportunities. The coach is active listener, coaches on values, actions.
2. **Imparting Experiences.** The coach becomes a role model. Insight offered about own life-career. Reflection strengthens the mentor and shows mentee levels of thinking and perception which were not previously available to the mentee.
3. **Encouraging Actions.** The coach is an advocate for progress, change. Empowers the mentee to hear, accept, believe and get results. Sharing of feelings, trust, ideas, philosophies.
4. **Paving the Way.** The coach endorses the mentee…wants his-her success. Messages ways to approach issues, paths in life to take. Helps draw distinctions. Paints picture of success.

5. **Wanting the Best.** Continuing relationship between the coach and mentee. Progress is envisioned, contextualized, seeded and benchmarked. Accountability and communication by both sides are essential.

6. **Advocating, Facilitating.** The coach opens doors for the mentee. The coach requests pro-active changes of mentee, evaluates realism of goals, offers truths about path to success and shortcomings of mentee's approaches. Bonded collaboration toward each **other's success.**

7. **Sharing Profound Wisdom.** The coach stands for mentees throughout careers, celebrates successes. Energy coaching and love-respect for each other continues throughout the relationship. Mentor actively recruits fellow business colleagues to become mentors. Lifelong dedication toward mentorship…in all aspects of one's life.

Third Party Building Affects Business Climate

Everyone needs a friend to speak periodically upon their behalf. Especially when things get tough, it's nice to have someone to count on.

Companies—like individuals—must bank support. Times to call for endorsements inevitably arise. The time to build bridges is today…not when crisis strikes.

In selling goods and services, third party support may include past and present clients, suppliers and industries affected by your customers.

In affecting policies and disposition toward your doing business, liaisons must be established with elected officials, the judiciary, regulatory agencies, the public sector, advocate groups and private sector opinion makers.

Most companies realize the impact of special-publics community support, including various socio-economic and ethnic groups. Cause-related marketing, environmental sensitivity and meaningful "giving back to the community" are essential for the coming years.

These recommendations are offered for gaining and maintaining third party endorsements:

- Make lists of your company's current friends and enemies. Update them regularly.

- Determine why friends support you…and what would happen if their backing was lost.
- Understand why some people and groups oppose you. Ascertain what would have prevented their objections and what it would take to turn them around.
- List whom you want to win as friends and with whom you are most afraid of becoming enemies.
- Analyze what your competitors are doing to win friends and build coalitions.
- Foresee what would happen if you sat still and did nothing.
- Project the financial and other benefits of pro-active building of credible third party endorsements.
- Make this initiative a primary responsibility for top management.
- Retain outside counsel with demonstrated expertise in issues management and forecasting, community relations, cause-related marketing, minority relations, government relations and grassroots constituency building.

Third party support can move mountains when you need it the most…or it can wreak havoc on your bottom line and the future in which you do business. Be honest about your current status. Take stock of opportunities. Make decisive actions, and reap future rewards.

Business Advisory Boards

Every company needs objective input on the business climate. With informed perspective, management can chart future growth and compete in a changing marketplace.

Non-profit organizations learned long ago the importance of assembling collective expertise. Boards, advisory councils, development committees and other volunteer structures contribute to organizational effectiveness. Successful non-profits seek to routinely upgrade the caliber of resources and to maximize their use.

Similarly, the private sector can muster ideas via Business Advisory Councils.

Some corporations form committees, with regular meetings. Business leaders from industries significant to company success are recruited. Honorariums are paid for participation: by the hour, deal-effecting ability or agreed retainer for advice and counsel.

Small and mid-sized businesses collect independent thought by retaining management consultants. Qualified public relations counsel brings that expertise. PR counsel can then assemble others "spheres of influence," including community and business leaders.

Business Advisory Councils must be chartered with defined purposes: strategic planning, product development, marketing, staff development, joint venturing, industry dominance or otherwise. Choose feasible goals in the beginning. Expand council scope as results are realized.

Everyone needs support. No business is an island unto itself.

The Big Picture of Small and Emerging Businesses

82% of all the companies in America are small and emerging businesses. 98% of all new business starts are small and emerging businesses.

The primary categories of emerging businesses are: (1) Retail. (2) Build a new mousetrap. (3) Clone mousetraps. (4) Pursue a dream that was started elsewhere. (5) Transition company…nurturing to grow and then sell to someone else. (6) Just for the bucks. (7) Professional services.

The realistic life expectancies are that 66.7% of all businesses cannot grow any further than they are now. 44.1% of all companies should not grow into large organizations. 36.2% have limited life expectancies and are destined to be acquired by a larger organization.

It is crucial for principals of the emerging business to follow their dreams, develop a cohesive Strategic Plan, find a niche and stay with the program sufficiently long to measure results.

These are the mindsets that will sabotage the success of small businesses:

1. Categorically don't want to grow.
2. Growth is all that matters.
3. Company leaders are not good at networking.
4. Company representatives can sell well but follow through delivery suffers.

5. Take the unrealistic premise technology is all that matters.

6. Executives don't like to sell…but need to realize that every executive must contribute to business development.

These are the 7 Basics of Small Business Growth Strategy, per categories on my trademarked business concept, The Business Tree™:

1. **The business you're in.** Clear understanding of what the business really is and why you've got what the target marketplace needs and wants.

2. **Running the business.** Core industry people must learn how to be managers. Give administrative team enough rein-resources to do their jobs. Insist upon a holistic relationship to the rest of the tree-organization.

3. **Financial.** Financial managers-personnel-consultants must focus beyond their own niche. Profit cannot be the only driving force. Show-measure full accountability.

4. **People.** The largest, most overlooked branch of the tree-organization. Employees must be empowered. Management must develop people skills. Job descriptions, evaluations and advancements are documented-communicated. Train regularly.

5. **Business Development.** Do all things necessary to capture-maintain market share. Maintain sales, marketing, advertising, public relations, research and product development programs…which must interact cohesively with each other.

6. **Body of Knowledge.** Understand the relationship of each branch to the other. Research-know what's going on outside your doors. Develop the tools to change.

7. **The Big Picture.** Business cannot grow without a holistic relationship to all parts of the tree-organization…what benefits one department benefits all. Keep existing roots living and sprout deeper, healthier ones (long-term planning). Master change. Shared Vision must be crafted, articulated and followed.

These are the 7 biggest roadblocks to Emerging Business Growth, per categories on The Business Tree™:

1. **The business you're in.** Not clear about the business you're really in, much less how-when-why to grow. Growth just for the sake of growth can ruin what you've built.

2. **Running the business.** Not properly trained or equipped to handle rapid influxes of business. Production, deliverability strained already…and it gets worse.

3. **Financial.** Increased revenues, new sales and heightened profits are the only driving forces, without understanding how to protect the business you already have.

4. **People.** Employees are taught that corporate growth is the most important objective. Not empowered to make decisions or take risks. Management appears distant, with limited people skills. Employees don't really associate with company Vision because they're not sure what it is or what's in it for them.

5. **Business Development.** Customer service suffers the most. Company is likely to be killing the goose that laid the golden egg.

6. **Body of Knowledge.** Management doesn't take the time to understand how the company has grown or analyze the relationship of each branch to the other. Setting themselves up to avoid change…yet grow without a Vision.

7. **The Big Picture.** Business will not grow because no Big Picture ever existed. Cannot truly grow without a crafted Vision for the future.

Demons Which Thwart Strategic Planning

Dealing with problematic behaviors. Dysfunctional strategies.

Little or no work ethic. Working without benchmarks.

Blunders, cover-ups and excuses. Mediocrity. Complacency.

Looking too much inward. False sense of security.

Myths, hype & over-generalizations. Addictions to failing.

Marketing hype for the status quo. Addictions to not trying.

Addictiveness to band-aid surgery. Fear.

Abdicating too easily to others' values. Ignorance.

Not seeing the warning signs. Believing the hype.

The "what's hot right now" syndrome. Fear of success

What If These Things Occur, per categories on The Business Tree

1. The business you're in.
    *   You are really in the correct business-industry.
    *   The product-service is really the best it can be.
    *   Customers get from your company what they cannot get elsewhere.
2. Running the business.
    *   The company is properly structured to do the job demanded.
    *   Operations are sound, professional and productive. Technology is used wisely.
    *   The physical plant is enough to do the job and can accommodate growth.
    *   Products-services are delivered on schedule.
3. Financial.
    *   Keeping the cash register ringing is not the only reason for being in business.
    *   You always give customers their money's worth. Your charges are fair and reasonable.
    *   Business is run economically and efficiently. Employees have fiduciary responsibility.
4. People.
    *   Your company is people-friendly.
    *   Executives possess good people skills.
    *   Staff is professional, empowered, likeable and competent.
    *   Employees demonstrate initiative and use their best judgment, with authority to make the decisions they should make.
    *   You provide a good place to work. You offer a promising career and future for people with ideas and talent. Your people do a good day's work for a day's pay.
5. Business Development.
    *   The company always researches and serves the marketplace.
    *   Customer service is efficient and excellent. You are sensitive to customers' needs and are flexible and human in meeting them.
    *   You don't market or sell anything that is not true or can be delivered.
    *   Sales and company operations communicate with each other.

- Your company and its products-services really do have a Point of Difference.

6. Body of Knowledge.
   - You develop-champion the tools to change.
   - There is a sound understanding of the relationship of each business function to the other.
   - You maintain a well-earned reputation and are awake to company obligations.
   - You provide leadership for progress, rather than following along.

7. The Big Picture.
   - The organization and its components approach business as a Body of Work, a lifetime track record of accomplishments.
   - You have and regularly update-benchmark a strategy for the future, shared company Vision, ethics, Big Picture thinking and "walk the talk."

In the average company, many of these things do not occur because:

- People do not know the processes to enable them to occur.
- Rigid adherence to egos and the old ways precludes success.
- The wrong people are giving advice and have the ear of top management.
- Management is out of touch and ego-driven to lead without proper help or advice.
- The company does not feel that it needs to change…that change is something that others need, but not them.
- Perceptions of current success overshadow the hint that winds will shift in business.
- Assumptions are false and overshadow reality.
- The company is not really in the right business anyway.
- Management is afraid to think "outside the box."
- The company culture is based simply upon being afraid…and paralyzed to do anything new, creative or pro-active.

Every business, company or organization goes through cycles in its life. At any point, each program or business unit is in a different phase from others. The astute organization assesses the status of each program and orients its team members to meet constant changes and fluctuations.

Strategic Planning facilitates disciplined thinking about the organization, its environment and its future. It identifies conflicts, reinforces team building and serves as a vehicle for monitoring organizational progress.

The planning process is then translated into a company Vision. With that Vision, the organization will evolve steadily toward success. Without any kind of Vision, management will continually apply corrective techniques ("band aid surgery"), while the company stumbles and falls. The price tag for false surgery is six times that of front-end Vision…a concept that I call The High Cost of Doing Nothing™.

To "go the distance," the organization must complete all seven stages of evolution. There are no fast-forward buttons or skipping steps inn developing an effective organization, just as there are no shortcuts in formulating a career and Body of Work.

Quotes on Trust, Relationship Building

"If I have the public trust, then anything is possible.
If I don't have it, then nothing is possible."
— **President Abraham Lincoln**

"A friendship founded on business is
better than a business founded on friendship."
— **John D. Rockefeller**

"The body is shaped, disciplined, honored, and in time, trusted."
— **Martha Graham** (1893-1991)

"I know God will not give me anything I can't handle.
I just wish that He didn't trust me so much."
— **Mother Teresa** (1910-1997)

"Trust men and they will be true to you; treat them greatly, and they will show themselves great."
— **Ralph Waldo Emerson** (1803-1882)

"Love all, trust a few. Do wrong to none."
— **William Shakespeare**

"Just trust yourself, then you will know how to live."
— **Johann Wolfgang von Goethe** (1749-1832)

"Put more trust in nobility of character than in an oath."
— **Solon** (638 BC-559 BC)

"Never trust the advice of a man in difficulties."
— **Aesop** (620 BC-560 BC)

"Love God and trust your feelings. Be loyal to them. Don't betray them."
— **Robert C. Pollock**

"If you wish in this world to advance, your merits you're bound to enhance. You must stir it and stump it, and blow your own trumpet, or trust me, you haven't a chance."
— **W. S. Gilbert** (1836-1911)

"Do not trust all men, but trust men of worth. The former course is silly, the latter a mark of prudence."
— **Democritus** (460 BC-370 BC)

"A human being is only interesting if he's in contact with himself. I learned you have to trust yourself, be what you are, and do what you ought to do the way you should do it. You have got to discover you, what you do, and trust it."
— Singer **Barbra Streisand**

Chapter 17

TRADE SHOWS

T he number of companies participating in trade shows increases each year. While sales objectives are most common, trade shows may also be behavior, product, distribution or marketing oriented.

Booth exhibitions at trade shows are viable and cost-effective sales tools to:

- Achieve new customers, in order to grow and increase profits.
- Introduce new products. Most of the visitors come to see what's new.
- Target a select group of visitors.
- Allow your staff to interface with the public.
- Perform informal market research.
- Educate the public about what your company and your industry do.
- Enhance your company's image.
- Assess competition and the overall business climate.

Trade shows generate sales leads at a lower cost per contact than a typical sales call. Research shows that industrial sales calls costing $252 to reach a prospect, with 4.6 follow-up calls necessary to book an order = $1,158. At a trade show, you might spend $133 to reach a prospect, with .8 follow-up calls necessary to book an order = $334.

Exhibits can be designed to appeal to all the senses: sight, sound, touch, smell and taste. Research shows that 75% of what show visitors recall after expos is what company representatives told them.

Exhibiting in business-to-business shows requires different skills and approaches. The objective should be qualifying prospects, rather than selling. One meets more business prospects in a faster period of time at a trade show.

Today's customers are becoming increasingly complex and more difficult to identify. They are knowledgeable, sophisticated and have increased expectations about what they want. Customers are now under more pressure to act immediately.

These pointers are offered to prospective exhibitors before the show:

- Determine your correct mission for participating.
- Evaluate each trade show for what it contributes to your sales objective
- Determine who you want as key prospects.
- Delineate other categories of visitors, and develop a strategy for maximizing your time with key prospects.
- Develop action plans for accomplishing your goals and getting the right people to visit with your company at the show.
- Be sure that booth personnel understand what they are responsible for… and what they are selling. Untrained staff can lose qualified prospects and leads.
- Employ professional counsel to format your exhibit, thus maximizing your investment.
- Keep labor costs to a minimum.
- Be sure that every member of your company is aware of the exhibit. Encourage all to invite prospects and to attend themselves, even if not involved in exhibiting.
- Market your presence at the show in advance via mailings, distribution of VIP tickets and inclusion of your booth in advertising. Invite your current clients to visit your booth. Most attendees go to the shows in response to invitations to visit specific exhibitors.

- Notify your trade media that you will participate.
- Work closely with the show's management. They too are interested in the same audiences as you: attendees and the media. Invite the board of the sponsoring organization to visit your booth.

These pointers are offered in order to maximize the way in which you should exhibit the product-service:

- Graphically describe and show what you do. Don't expect the product to show itself. Don't expect people to know about you already. This is a fresh opportunity for you to communicate.
- Keep your focus upon your products, rather than pretentious displays.
- Keep the booth simple, clean and organized.
- Give facts and simple explanations of your products. Since many visitors may be unfamiliar, don't assume that they know what you do.
- Ask questions and listen. Don't concentrate on giving a sales pitch.
- Good lighting, decoration and booth dress are always relevant to the product.
- Show a maximum number of products.
- A good demonstration convinces visitors that your product is all you claim it is.
- Show what the product can do for them and what it has done for others.
- Give samples, if possible.
- Encourage audience participation.
- Distribute professionally-produced, factual literature, or don't give out any literature.
- Use video as interactive demonstration elements, augmented by signage.
- Collect business cards, as the basis for follow-up activities.
- Make appointments to have in-depth presentations to serious prospects.
- Trade show selling requires high energy levels. Booth people must be pro-active, greet all prospects and learn how to qualify.
- Approach large numbers of people within short periods of time, determining how to best process each contact.

Research shows that trade show booths that have dishes of candy tend to draw twice the number of visitors than those without candy. The value of premium giveaways lies in lasting impressions, increased name identification and paves the way for faster follow-ups with prospects.

These observations and recommendations are made for booth exhibit personnel:

- Booth personnel must be equipped to give precise, detailed information on your product.
- Train booth attendants for show duty. If possible, stage a dress rehearsal. Follow procedures for literature distribution, trash cleanup, conversation and public demeanor.
- Work out approach statements in advance. Have talking points in writing. Follow a step-by-step process.
- Staff with a technical representative, as well as a greeter. You can never have enough well-trained people at the show.
- Avoid the high-pressure approach.
- Do not smoke, drink or eat in the booth.
- Booth personnel should look and act the part. Stand up straight. Keep your hands out of your pockets. Use approachable body language. Do not sit down unless you are with a client.
- Dress conservatively.
- Keep small talk with other booth personnel to a minimum.
- Arrange and follow duty schedules. Keep staff alert and on their toes.
- Make booth visitors feel welcome at all times.

Lead collection and follow-ups must be treated seriously. After the show is over, don't forget to follow through on details, promises and intentions:

- Send follow-up letters to each visitor who left a business card.
- Send out requested additional materials within one week after the show.
- Set a lead follow-up program, since early response is vital. Follow up on sales leads for at least two years after the show.
- Evaluate your results.

Your company's commitment to participate in trade shows represents a big step. You should always want to improve the exhibit each time, thus insuring a return on the investment. The process of strategizing your exhibit relates directly to your company's promotional and business development philosophy. This process inevitably makes every company's marketing position much stronger.

Chapter 18

THE REQUEST FOR PROPOSAL PROCESS

Tips for Effective Writing and Soliciting of RFPs

R equests for Proposals for professional services are often sent by companies who need specific talents. Few RFPs are worded in such a way that gleans the best available information. Thus, companies make decisions for professional services based upon responses to questions that may not be appropriate.

Companies often find themselves comparing apples to oranges and may lose the best available firm because the questions were not designed to "read between the lines."

Especially when you will not interview all firms and make preliminary decisions based upon the subjective reading of RFPs, some pointers are offered:

- Consult one or more other companies in your industry (or respected peers in related companies) on their RFP process. Ask to see sample RFPs.

- Call one reputable professional service firm, even if they are one that you intend to ask for a bid. If they agree to offer ideas for your proposed search and will send you samples of RFPs that they answered for other companies, then they are providing you a valuable service. You should seriously consider that firm as a contender.

- Include lots of "fill in the blank" sections, so that you can compare answers to identical questions. Do not let your RFP skew to subject areas that respondents want to answer. • Include essay-type questions in key areas: sticking with budgets, accountability and delivering what they promise.

- If you have a budget and project concept, state it. Ask how they would handle the project that you envision. Do not go on a fishing expedition for ideas in an RFP, when you already have an idea of what you want.

- Since full-service professional service firms yield efficiencies and economies that solo practitioners cannot, address that issue in the RFP. Ask why they differ from one-person shops and how that stands to benefit you.

- Require biography sketches of persons who will actually service your business. Differentiate between who sells and who services the work. If a respondent's seasoned practitioner or company CEO really will be working on your account, that is a plus.

- Inquire about awards won for client work, if applicable to their industry. If they have not won any awards, then you should wonder why.

*Ask for references, both for client work and for community standing. Inquire as to their reputation within their own profession. Inquire about their civic leadership.

You get what you pay for. See through low-ball bids and people who will say or do anything to get the business, thus edging out a better firm who may have submitted a slightly higher bid. That is why your RFP should announce a fee.

Service firms should be considered as your long-term partners. The more thoroughly that you investigate the pool of applicants, the larger the pool you have to call upon again, even firms not awarded the current project. Too often, companies reinvent the wheel with Requests for Proposals for professional services. It does not have to be that way.

These pointers are designed to help you compare apples to apples. Get the best available information, in order to positively impact your projects.

Chapter 19

WHY GOOD ORGANIZATIONS CLICK

Nostalgic Excursions Through Memories and Culture

Think of any organization or business as being analogous to a successful and highly entertaining television variety show or situation comedy series. To better understand and improve your organization, remember the most successful TV series and the elements that made them work.

1. **The Host-Star.** Great TV variety show hosts made their presence known, without overshadowing the scope of the show. The best ones showcased talent, were viewer-friendly and did what it took to make the show a continuing and lasting force. The perennial ones were strategically positioned to last, rather than just appearing and staying.

Perry Como prided himself in being able to perform ensemble singing with ease. Certainly a great headline singer, he knew that singing as part of a harmonious group required a different vocal delivery than the opening number he would deliver at the top of the show and in his "spotlight" medley.

A fundamental element of variety shows was the duet. After the guest star delivered a song or two, the host would make lively patter, and the two would croon together. Many guest stars were actors, comics or other performers. However, all got the opportunity to duet with the boss…most performing nobly. Next to Dinah Shore, Patti Page or Andy Williams, any and all performers sounded their best and gave that "extra something."

There were group production numbers. Garry Moore had a segment, "That Wonderful Year." He narrated and occasionally sang, but this segment was designed to showcase his ensemble (Carol Burnett, Durward Kirby, Marion Lorne) and guest stars.

Then, there were the hosts that were good administrators. They did not perform but had a sense of timing, mixing the right ingredients, vision for the show and production values. Media veteran Ed Sullivan knew these elements better than anyone and had the longest running TV variety show (series, 1948-1971; specials, 1971-1974; "best of" compilations still running).

The sitcom star knew that the on-screen family had an obligation to showcase both the whole and each of the parts. Superstars like Mary Tyler Moore, Lucille Ball and others had the ability to shine and also become the spotlight that pointed toward the talents of others.

There were ensemble shows like "Cheers," "Family Ties," "The Addams Family," "The Golden Girls," "The Beverly Hillbillies," "Full House" and others. No part of the ensemble could have functioned only on his or her self. In these, the team is always the star, with rotating parts featured.

2. **Regular Cast, Setting and Other Constants.** The ensemble is what makes the show succeed or fail. Remember the "Dick Van Dyke Show," "Make Room for Daddy," "Adventures of Ozzie & Harriet," "Lucy Shows," "Night Court," "Father Knows Best" and others.

Think of favorite long-lasting series and what made them memorable. Each season's batch of episodes represented the following:

- Each cast member interacted with the other.
- The star was pivotal to the ensemble but was also a part of it.

- Each character got their own lead storylines during the course of each season.

- Each character played a supportive role to another's lead storyline.

- Not every character appeared in every storyline, every week. Some were occasionally absent because they did not figure into the story at hand.

- Guest stars appeared but were not the "make or break" ingredient.

- The sets and settings had audience appeal. They were believable within the context of the series premise.

- Some storylines were predictable. Others broke new ground. And a few were dramatic changes of pace, for emphasis, including the trips to new locations.

3. **The Guest Stars.** All the top stars guest starred on each other's shows. That was a way to assure big names and allow those headliners to do things they necessarily could not do on their own shows. The most successful "guest shots" had diversity in performance, rather than the same old schtick.

Ed Sullivan finally got to perform sketch comedy on Red Skelton's and Flip Wilson's shows. Broadway and opera headliners sported new dimensions when clowning with the likes of Danny Kaye or Spike Jones.

The longest lasting stars were the ones who were equally good at being guest stars, as they were successful headliners. Lucille Ball was the quintessential guest star. Stars like Kathie Lee Gifford ably fulfill that versatility nowadays.

The business analogies here are to effective partnering, collaborations and joint venturing. One is a better member of other people's teams if he or she has captained their own. The art of doing business on other turfs enables the executive to expand, grow and become proficient at diverse talents.

4. **Breadth of Material, Backup Production Techniques and Company.** The best remembered shows were strategically planned. Writing was consistently good. Subject topics referred to each show's premise and the integrity of its characters.

What goes on behind the camera is more important that what is in front. A star does not make a show. The team does. Successful series learned the value of loyal crews, technicians who voluntarily went the distance and supervisors who saw the team holistically.

5. **The Time Slot—Marketplace Advantage.** Scheduling is everything in mass entertainment. A good show in the wrong time slot inevitably is cancelled because it fails to build enough audience. Having the right lead-in and follow-up show help deliver the viewership.

Sitcoms always work best in the first hour, the "family hour." Variety shows and specials always work best in the second hour, the "median mark of the evening." Third hours are always reserved for prestige dramas, containing deep material, adult content and a thought provoking edge to their narratives.

One cannot produce a product or service without regard to their intended marketplace. Studying demographics and continually benchmarking is imperative. Too many companies keep manufacturing products after the demand has ebbed.

6. **The Opposition—Competition.** In TV, the only way to measure up to a seasoned hit is to break new ground (i.e. build a better mousetrap).

Even the nature of competition is changing. In the old days, three major television networks competed against each other. With the advent of expanded TV channels, cable, video rentals and VCRs, the number of alternatives keep the industry and the consumers from staring at test patterns.

Too many companies think the public will beat a path to their doors. They're blind sighted by the competition and fail to properly consider the alternatives held by prospective customers.

Business must research and comprehend every external influence upon the marketplace. Though most are beyond the company's concern, each constituency, problem and opportunity must be predicted, studied and acted upon. Businesses can no longer perform out of sync with everything else around them.

7. **Societal Factors During Their Run.** Radio and the phonograph were toys in the 1920s. Within 20 years, they had mainstreamed into the primary artistic media showcases.

Television, though developed for years, signaled the post-World War II era of wonderment and renewed hope. In the early years, the public accepted everything that the box had to offer, without questioning why...and still clamoring for more. The earliest TV series reflected the public's insatiable appetite for anything that sang, danced or joked.

Television grew as an art form and business in the 1950s. Its cultural beacons encompassed the next decades. The seemingly calm years of the 1950s were an undercurrent of social upheaval. Thus, popular entertainment reinforced traditional values while gradually evolving contemporary issues.

The 1960s were transition years, as extreme artistic expressions began to emerge. The emerging youth culture became the largest target of advertisers and, thus, network executives. The 1970s shocked society with stark reality amidst the entertainment genre.

In the 1980s, videotape enabled viewers to watch what they wanted, when they wanted. With tape rentals, pay-per-view and stockpiling private libraries with tapes, consumers became their own programming executives.

Niche marketing hit its zenith in the 1990s. Cable channels (like magazines and radio stations before them) narrowcast each audience and demographic within. New media (CD rom, the Internet) emerged to create alternative information and entertainment resources.

Business has paralleled milestones in the entertainment industry. Additional societal factors include multicultural diversity, workplace literacy, global markets, environmental concerns, political correctness, ethics and values, the changing nature of employee bases, virtual corporations, collaborative joint-venturing and putting the customer first...which comes full-circle to the way business started out to be.

What Motivates People to Work and Achieve

Per each category of Hank Moore's Business Tree™:

1. The business you're in
   Doing good work, with standards of professionalism.
   Producing products/services that make a difference
2. Running the business
   Maintaining high productivity
   Ability to control and influence
   Making correct decisions
3. Financial
   Receiving adequate compensation
   Maintain standards of accountability
4. People
   Being accepted and acknowledged
   Being part of a motivated team
   Receiving praise, recognition and advancement
   Having a certain amount of freedom on the job
   Learning new things
   Enjoying work relationships and having fun with the job
   Achieving balance in life, thus becoming a more valuable employee
   Working with good managers and leaders
   Being perceived as a role model
5. Business Development
   Direct involvement in important projects
   Doing work that empowers customers
   Integrity, with customers and ourselves
6. Body of Knowledge
   Exemplifying standards of quality
   Remaining confident about work
   Exemplifying value and excellence
   Need for personal and professional growth
7. The Big Picture
   Feeling like you've made a positive contribution
   Accomplishing worthwhile things
   Being in an organization that makes a difference

Conclusion

Organizations, which click and sustain a track record, must realize the same lessons, which its leaders gleaned as consumers of mass media programs:

- There is nothing more permanent than change.
- Change is 90% beneficial. So, why do people fight what's in their best interests?
- Learn from the past.
- Avoid repeating the same mistakes.
- There exists more knowledge in failure than through repeated successes.
- "Saving face" is not the most important thing.
- Many cancelled TV shows have won prestigious awards. Some were just "too good" to be ratings hits.
- Becoming part of an organization involves commitment and responsibility from each of its members.
- Put the customer first, and they will keep you first.
- Get advice from the best consultants, not the wanna-be's.
- Never stop planning.
- Never stop changing.
- Never stop improving.
- Continually research, study, understand and communicate what works well.
- Loyalty and consistency pays off.
- Learn that the guest star should sound better in the song duet than you do.
- Thank the guest stars, on and off the air.
- Even if you're cancelled, thank the network for the run and past support.
- There will always be another show on another day. or a changing audience with different creative focus.

Chapter 20

TRAINING AND PROFESSIONAL EDUCATION

You've Got to Be Taught

Training is the most important ingredient in corporate development. Today's workforce will need three times the amount of training that it now gets, if the organization intends to stay in business, remain competitive and tackle the future successfully.

Each year, one-third of the Gross National Product goes toward cleaning up problems, damages and the high costs of doing either nothing or the wrong things. Half of that amount goes toward some form of persuasion, instruction, spin-doctoring or educating.

More often that not, "training" is a vehicle to tout one's viewpoint, tinker with old problems or blame someone else for the course of events. If training is viewed as band aid surgery to fix problems, then it will fail. Managers who have this "fix those people" mindset are, in fact, the ones who need substantive training the most.

Training is rarely allowed to be extensive. It is usually technical or sales in nature. Employees and executives are rarely mentored on the people skills necessary to have a winning team. Thus, they fail to establish a company vision and miss their business mark.

Outside of "think tanks" for company executive committees, full-scope education does not occur. This is primarily because niche trainers recommend what they have to sell, rather than what the company needs. Niche trainers impart their own perspectives out of context to the whole of the organization.

Team building must be part of the corporate Vision first, not as a series of exercises delegated to trainers. I conduct Executive Think Tanks for corporate management. The success of this enables trainers with the "rank and file employees" to be optimally successful. Organizations of all sizes must have the Think Tank, which delineates future operations, including education and training.

Training is unfairly blamed and scapegoated for pieces of the organizational mosaic that Strategic Planning and cohesive corporate Vision should have addressed early-on. Trainers cannot reconstruct organizational structure, nor can other niche consultants.

Companies owe it to themselves to think and plan…before launching piecemeal training programs. After carefully articulating and understanding direction, then training needs (including team building and empowerment) will stand a chance of being successful.

7 Steps Toward Professional Development

1. Teaching-Training. Conveying information, insights and intelligence from various sources. Categorized by subject, grade level and methods of delivery. Expert teachers (fountains of learning material) are the building block in the educational process, and the student must be an active participant (rather than a non-involved or combative roadblock).

2. Studying. One cannot learn just by listening to a teacher. Review of material, taking notes, seeking supplementary materials and questing to learn additionally must occur.

3. Learning. The teacher instructs, informs and attempts to enlighten. The student accepts, interprets and catalogs the material taught. Periodically, the material is reviewed.

4. Information. As one amasses years of learning, one builds a repository of information, augmented by experiences of putting this learning into practice.

5. Analysis. One sorts through all that has been learned, matched with applicability to daily life. One determines what additional learning is necessary and desired. From this point forward, education is an ongoing process beyond that of formal schooling. If committed, the person turns the quest for knowledge into a life priority.

6. Knowledge. A Body of Knowledge is derived from years of living, learning, working, caring, sharing, failing and succeeding.

7. Wisdom. This requires many years of commitment to learning, compounded by the continuous development of knowledge. Few people attempt to get this far in the educational process. Those who do so have encompassed profound wisdom.

7 Levels of Training

1. Basic Education. There are certain things that every member of the workforce needs in order to do their jobs well. These include people skills, operational duties and requirements for each job description.

2. Mandated. Circumstances (usually regulators) insist that such training be conducted as the basis for getting or retaining funding. Progressively, mandated training tends to be utilized in these stages:
   - Fix Those People.
   - Stay Where You Are…and Don't Lose Further Ground.
   - This Is the Way It Is…Things We Have to Live With.
   - Accept Somebody's Pet Project.
   - Things "They" Are Making Us Do.
   - What We Want to Teach You.
   - You'll Do It, and You'll Like It.

3. Informational. This category enlightens workers on new ways to accomplish old tasks. It introduces new policies, procedures, concepts and directions in which the organization will pursue. In this category, workers are encouraged to offer suggestions for improvement and become part of the quality process.

4. Technical, Niche Skills. There are hundreds of categories of "technology," and each requires training and experience in order to maximize the job tasks. Providers of such training come from a plethora of niche specialties, both inside and outside the company.

5. Procedural. Every organization must create, fine-tune and benchmarks the processes by which it produces products-services. Process administration and procedural adherence assure consistencies.

6. Optional. Not every facet of running a successful company can be reduced to a process or technology. People need attention, enrichment, accountability, rewards and room to grow. It is at this level that Professional Development (a higher order than training) must take over. Every worker's quest to spread their wings must be developed. Most executives were never taught how to be real executives, and this arena for Executive Mentoring must become a company priority. Alas, these areas are not really "optional."

7. Insightful-Deep-Rich-Meaningful. Learning and growing professionally pre-empts burnout. Develop a Strategic Plan for your company and yourself. Participate in CEO think tanks. Mentor others, and reconnect with those whom you admire. Invest in the right consultants. Commit to a quality improvement program. View your company as part of a career Body of Work, not just a present job. Levels of Training That Are Rare But Truly Needed:
   a. Pride in Workmanship.
   b. Learning, Growing, Mentoring.
   c. Fully Actualized Professionalism.
   d. Amassing People Skills.
   e. Pursuing Excellence.
   f. Adding Value to the Organization.
   g. Developing a Body of Work-Knowledge.

Categories of Training, Which Programs Should Encompass

There is a difference between how one is basically educated and the ingredients needed to succeed in the long-term. Many people never amass those ingredients because they stop learning or don't see the need to go any further. Many people think they are "going further" but otherwise spin their wheels.

There is a large disconnect between indoctrinating people to tools of the trade and the myriad of elements they will need to assimilate for their own futures. Neither teachers nor students have all the necessary ingredients. It is up to both to obtain skills, inspiration, mentoring, processes, accountability, creativity and other components from niche experts.

Therein lies the problem. Training vendors sell what they have to provide… not what the constituencies or workforces need. Emphasis must be placed upon properly diagnosing the organization as a whole and then prescribing treatments for the whole, as well as the parts.

Training should be conducted within a formal, planned program that addresses the majority of organizational aspects, per categories on The Business Tree™:

1. The business you're in
   Core industry
   Subject experts
   Emerging trends
   Product design
2. Running the business
   Making products-services in an efficient manner
   Technical instruction
   Technological innovation
   Telephone etiquette
   Time management
   Physical plant operations instruction
   Computer operations, training, programming, repairs
   Telecommunications operations and maintenance
   In-service exercises, per organizational task
   Re-engineering of processes
   Administrative practices, procedures, operations, structure, review
   Equipment, supplies, systems
   Relationships with suppliers, vendors
   Distribution
3. Financial
   Accounting practices
   Banking practices

Payables and receivables administration

Insurance and benefits program administration

Purchasing

Forecasting, budgeting

Investor relations

Taking companies public

Mergers, acquisitions, expansion opportunities

4. People

Learning organization

Empowerment

Team building

Human relations skills

Recruiting, hiring and supervision of employees

Stress management

Negotiating skills

Leadership development

Professional development

Executive development

Re-engineering of policies and procedures

Re-engineering of the workforce

5. Business development

Business and marketplace development

Developing sales programs and strategies

Sales training

Marketing

Advertising

Public relations

Research

Corporate communications

Working with graphic artists-providers, audio-visual companies, printers

Special events planning-implementation

Specialty advertising

Direct marketing-research-telemarketing

Collaborating to build new business opportunities

6. Body of Knowledge

   Company performance reviews

   Big Picture views of company structure…the inter-relationship of Branches 1-5

   Professional development as a whole for the organization

   External influences and information

   Company general meetings, functions and overall events plan

   Government, regulators, marketplace limitors

   Community standards, opposition, support, constituencies

   Entering new industries, product lines, creating additional products-services

   Collaborations, joint venturing

7. The Big Picture

   Building a shared vision

   Strategic planning

   Outside-the-box thinking

   Executive Think Tanks

   Crisis management, preparedness

   The quality process

   Ethics

   Creative business practices, collaborations, innovations

   Changing markets, opportunities, barriers

   Walking the talk

7 Biggest Misconceptions About Training

1. One Size Fits All. If it's not customized, it's not going to be effective.
2. Trainers Are Business Experts. Generally, they are vendors who sell "off the shelf" products that target small niches within the organization. Few are schooled in full-scope business culture and have not been previously engaged to advise organizations at the top.
3. Human Resources Oversees Training. By their nature, HR departments are designed to uphold processes and systems. Training is about change, which contradicts the basic construction of HR. Not all HR people are versed in

the subtle nuances of people skills and are, thus, not the best to supervise training. It really should not be under the thumb of HR.

4. Trainers Write the Training Plans. All major departmental plans should be written objectively and in concert with the Strategic Plan…by qualified advisors. Training companies often give free assessments in order to sell their programs. Free surveys do not constitute a cohesive plan. Let trainers do what they do best: training. Let experienced planners design the training plan, with input from trainers included. Don't let the plan evolve from a training company's sales pitch.

5. Only Industry Experts Can Train in Your Company. What companies need most is objective business savvy and sophisticated overviews. Core industry "experts" only know core industry issues from their own experiences. Quality training must focus on dynamics outside the core business, yet should have relativity to the organization.

6. One Course Will Fix the Problem. Training is not a punishment for having done something "wrong." It's a privilege, a major benefit of employment. It unlocks doors to greater success, growth and profitability for those trained and for the sponsoring organization. In order to be competitive in the future, today's workers will need three times the training that they are now getting.

7. That It's Supposed to Be Popular. The biggest mistake that meeting planners make is determining the effectiveness of training and training professionals via audience survey. Most conference evaluation forms are lightweight and ask for surface rankings…rather than for nuggets of knowledge learned. Speakers and training budgets are therefore judged upon whimsical comments of individual audience participants…which get harsher when the training is for topics they need, rather than things they would "prefer" to hear. Voices of reality are always criticized by people who really are not qualified to assess them.

Evaluating Training Providers

These pointers are suggested in the selection of training providers: Ask a senior business advisor to help determine which consultants are needed, write the training program, evaluate credentials and recommend contracting options. Understand what your company really needs and why. Don't pit one consultant against another, just to get free ideas. Don't base the training decisions on "apples to oranges" comparisons.

These pointers are suggested in budgeting for and pricing services: Budget for training at the start of the fiscal year, averaging 10% of gross sales. See training as an investment (short-term and long-term), not to be short-changed. Every size of business needs training. The company which makes the small investment on the front end (training) saves higher costs later.

The ideal training provider:

- Clearly differentiates what he/she does and will not presume to "do it all."
- Is a tenured full-time consultant, not a recently down-sized corporate employee or somebody seeking your work to "tide themselves over."
- Has actually run a business.
- Has consulted companies of comparable size and complexity as yours.
- Has current references and case histories.
- Gives "value-added" insight, in contrast to simply performing tasks.
- Sees the scope of work as a professional achievement, rather than just billable hours.
- Pursues client relationship building, as opposed to just rendering a contract service.

Your Company Needs More Than Just Training

I would like to see these additional topics added to the Professional Development and Company Visioning programs, extending the concept of executive training:

- Marketplace factors outside your company, how they can hurt or help your business.
- Generational work ethics and why young people need executive mentoring to "go the distance" in their careers, offering value to the company and profession.
- Understanding the value of conducting independent company assessments, other than the "bean counter" approach.

- Workplace literacy. Much of the work force does not have basic skills, nor reasoning abilities. They embrace technology, rather than ideas and concepts.
- Understand and celebrate diversity. This is a blessing, not a mandate.
- Accept and embrace change. Research shows change is 90% beneficial. So why do people fight what is best for them?
- What business the company is really in, where they are headed, with what resources on what timeline and how (the process known as Visioning).
- Learning how to control change, rather than fear it.
- Steps to create company vision…and get buy-in from employees.
- What makes good companies go bad.
- How to take planning and quality management from the esoteric and into daily practice.

7 Biggest Benefits of Training

1. Measurements. Test scores, grades, class rankings, GPA, SAT, professional certifications, licensing examinations, juried awards. Whether in school or business, we are all measured. Knowledge helps to make and predict society's measurements which are expected.
2. Thinking-Reasoning Skills. What we learn is important. Further, what we do with lessons, how facts are interpreted, how we approach problems and the faculties of common sense are vital to economic, social and self-betterment success.
3. Socialization-People Skills. Through trial-and-error, success-and-failure and the observation of other people's strengths-and-weaknesses, we learn how to live and work with others. Mastering people skills makes for win-win propositions.
4. Professional Development. Education does not stop after the highest degree completed…it merely begins. Training, professional enrichment, membership in associations and constructive business interaction are vital for career longevity and economic independence.
5. Mentorship. Learning from others takes a higher plateau when under the wings of experts. Mentorship (which has seven levels) is a stair-step process of bettering all participants. Meaningful lessons, paying dues and

developing relationships empower those who make the effort "go the distance." Learning from different, unusual and informed sources is the art of mentorship.

6. Earning Power. Education (formal schooling, professional development and enhanced-relationship study) has a direct relationship to financial rewards. It begins with school but bears fruit in the willingness to learn, change and grow professionally.

7. Future Life. A truly successful person commits to mentoring others, giving back, mastering change and never failing to learn. Education is more than confirming one's held beliefs. It plants knowledge roots, which sprout in ideas and lifelong insights.

I recommend that team building training be conducted as part of a company Strategic Plan, with top management participating. Companies must plan… predicting (rather than reacting to) strengths, weaknesses, opportunities and threats.

Professional development must be offered to every employee, including mentoring for top executives and up-and-coming young people. Education should show decision makers all phases of the organization and what it takes to succeed and grow, personally and as a team.

Quotes on Education, Professional Development and Training

"Soon learned, soon forgotten."
— Proverb

"Knowledge itself is power. Studies serve for delight, ornament, and ability."
— **Sir Francis Bacon**

"Education is the best provision for old age."
— **Aristotle**

"They know enough who know how to learn. A teacher affects eternity and can never tell where his influence stops."
— **Henry Brooks Adams**, 19th Century U.S. historian

"The direction in which education starts a man will determine his future life."
— **Plato**

"Education is simply the soul of a society as it passes from one generation to another."
— **G.K. Chesterton** (1924)

"I have learned since to be a better student, and to be ready to say to my fellow students, 'I do not know.'"
— **William Osler**

"He who can does. He who cannot, teaches."
— **George Bernard Shaw**

"Training is everything. The peach was once a bitter almond. Cauliflower is nothing but a cabbage with a college education. Soap and education are not as sudden as a massacre, but they are more deadly in the long run."
— **Mark Twain**

"Human history becomes more and more a race between education and catastrophe."
— **H.G. Wells**

"Wisdom is oftentimes nearer when we stoop than when we soar."
— **William Wordsworth**

"What we have to learn to do, we learn by doing."
— **Aristotle**

"I am always ready to learn although I do not always like being taught."
— **Sir Winston Churchill**

Chapter 21

DEEP ROOTS THAT TAKE:
LEADERSHIP FOR GROWTH COMPANIES

Developing the right talent to reach the next level

This chapter is a primer for executives and the heirs apparent to company leadership. Critical topics include leadership development of executives, mindset changes in the evolution from manager to executive to leader, executive mentoring, insights into how top professionals evolve, plateaus of professional accomplishment, developing a winning work ethic, lifelong learning and the accrual of business wisdom.

Many books have been written on the subject of leadership. They came from training, team building and similar Branch 4 perspectives. This book sees the leader from the big picture perspective and how he-she paints career panoramas by interconnecting the pieces.

My own philosophy of leadership starts with the premise that every dynamic of a successful organization must be in some way aimed towards its stakeholders.

While all good leaders must keep the company's internal operations moving forward, the very best ones must also be looking outside the company towards the customers, clients, financiers, volunteers and the organization's entire affected constituencies.

If management is complacent or is not outward looking, then the same attitude and resulting behaviors will be held by employees who render the services. Failure to keep a clear focus upon the product, its marketplace, its customers and people who influence the company's ultimate success will eventually do great harm to the company.

I believe that a good leader is also a community leader. I once advised a U.S. President in fostering the Thousand Points of Light program, a national effort to spur volunteerism, hope and good works throughout the country, and will draw upon lessons learned from that program.

Most companies want and need to give back to the communities in which they do business. The most successful ones realize that everyone wins by such activities. They also know that executives who serve on community boards will improve their leadership skills through the process, thus making them more valuable to the company.

By recognizing and praising corporate organizations, entrepreneurs, and company rising stars, they will try even harder to do better. Community stewardship programs are opportunities for involvement, achievement and commitment to the wider scope of business.

The Management Tree, how and why leadership styles sprout

Branch 1. The business you're in. You are not just in the widget business (as a symbol for core business). You're in the business of making, processing, financing, empowering, selling, researching, marketing, benchmarking, administering and facilitating widgets to your customer base. Without thinking and acting beyond branch 1, you have no business in which to make your widgets.

Branch 2. Running the business. In assessing company operations, three rights offset a wrong. There is much more right about your organization that you might think. Recognize and salute strengths as such, rather than categorize them as weaknesses.

Branch 3. Financial. Just as widget creation (core business niche) constitutes 10%, please keep financial aspects in comparable perspective.

Branch 4. People. There's a big difference between experience and expertise. Training bridges the differences. Without empowering your people, you will not recognize full organizational potential. They must work with you, not for-or-against you. The more that people see what's in it for them (other than a paycheck), they will support and embody company goals, knowing that other people care.

Branch 5. Business development. Unless you're selling something, you're not in business. Growing a business isn't just a factor of selling more.

Category 6 (trunk). Body of Knowledge. When the organization stops learning, it is on the road to failure. Niche specialists look through their perspective, not through the full organizational lens. Leadership must view the business as a whole.

Category 7 (roots). The Big Picture. The best leaders bring out the sense of visionary in the management team and develop the next generation of leaders with the widest possible perspective.

Grounds and Turf, leadership realities for your tree

Not all executives are leaders. Not all managers are executives. Not all career people are professional.

Top company management usually comes from the ranks of those who sell the core business product-service, not from those on the firing line who deliver it. That's why in media, programming and news people rarely become management. Since advertising sales is the primary product of media, the sales people become the managers.

In education, good teachers stay in the classroom. In the energy industry, engineers dominate. Engineers steadfastly believe that they're in the energy exploration and production business. The companies themselves are in the energy marketing business. Restaurants are in the business of marketing atmosphere and service. Yet, they put food preparers (representing 20% of the pie) in charge. Decisions are always food driven, explaining in part the high failure rate of restaurants. Other reasons include poor planning, substandard customer service, low capitalization and inappropriate marketing.

A major problem with companies stems from the fact that management and company leadership come from one small piece of the organizational pie. Filling all management slots with financial people, for example, serves to limit the organizational strategy and focus. They all hire like-minded people and frame every business decision from their micro perspective.

The ideal executive has strong leadership skills first. He or she develops organizational vision and sets strategies. Leaders should reflect a diversity of focus, guaranteeing that a balance is achieved. The best management team looks at the macro, rather than just the niche micro.

None of us was born with sophisticated, finely tuned senses and highly enlightened viewpoints for life. We muddle through, try our best and get hit in the gut several times. Thus, we learn, amass knowledge and turn most experiences into strategies. Such a perspective is what makes seasoned executives valuable in the business marketplace.

Life has a way of forcing the human condition to change. Events which may inspire this to happen could include a recognition that the old methods are not working, financial failures or the monetary incentive to rapidly create or change plans of action. At most crossroads, there is no choice but to change the modus operandi. This may include the loss of substantial numbers of opportunities, customers, employees and market share or a "wake up call" of any type.

The most effective leaders accept that change is 90% positive and find reasons and rationale to embrace change. Leadership skills are learned and synthesized daily. Knowledge is usually amassed through unexpected sources.

Leadership for the New Order

Within every corporate and structure, there exists a stair-step ladder. One enters the ladder at some professional level and is considered valuable for the category of services for which he or she has expertise. This ladder holds true for managers and employees within the organization, as well as outside consultants brought in.

Each professional rung on the ladder is important. At whatever level one enters the ladder, he-she should be trained, measured for performance and fit into the organization's overall scope. This is the stair-step, paralleling The Business Tree:

1. **Resource.** One has experience with equipment, tools, materials and schedules.
2. **Skills and Tasks.** One is concerned with activities, procedures and project fulfillment.

3. **Role and Job.** The position is defined according to assignments, responsibilities, functions, relationships, follow-through and accountability.

4. **Systems and Processes.** These are managers, concerned with structure, hiring, control, work design, supervision and the effects of management decisions.

5. **Strategy.** These executives spend much of their energies on planning, tactics, organizational development and business development.

6. **Culture and Mission**. Upper management is most effective when it frames business decisions toward values, customs, beliefs, goals, objectives and the benchmarking of tactics.

7. **Philosophy.** These are the visionaries who advise management in refining the organizational purpose, vision, quality of life, ethics and contributions toward the company's long-term growth.

One rarely advances more than one rung on the ladder during the course of service to the organization unless he-she embodies that wider scope. The professional who succeeds the most is the one who sees himself-herself in the bigger picture and contextualizes what they do accordingly.

Value-added leadership is a healthy way of professional life that puts collaborations first. When all succeed, then profitability is much higher and more sustained than under the Hard Nose management style.

Value-added leadership requires a senior team commitment. Managers and employees begin seeing themselves as leaders and grow steadily into those roles. It is not acceptable to be a clone of what you perceive someone else to be. Those organizations and managers who use terms like "world class" are usually wanna-be's who won't ever quite make the measuring stick.

Leadership means being consistently excellent and upholding standards to remain so. There is no such thing as perfection. Yet, excellence is a definitive process of achievement, dedication and expeditious use of resources. Exponential improvement each year is the objective.

Good professionals must be role models. Leadership comes from inner quests, ethical pursuits and professional diligence. Often, we teach others what we were never taught or what we learned the hard way. That's how this book came into being...there was no executive encyclopedia for those to make it long-term. Those who take that knowledge into practice will lead their business and industry.

If every executive devoted at least 10% of his-her time to these activities, then corporate scandals would not occur. Thinking and reasoning skills are not taught in school, and they are amassed through a wealth of professional experiences. Planning is the thread woven through this book, and it is the key to the future. One can never review progress enough, with benchmarking being the key to implementing plans.

Many organizations fall into the trap of calling what they are doing a "tradition." That is an excuse used by many to avoid change and accountability. Just because something has been done one or two times, realize that it will get old and stale. Traditions are philosophies that are regularly fine-tuned, with elements added. Traditions are not stuck in ruts, though failing companies are.

If I could determine curriculum, every business school would require public speaking and writing courses. I'd have every professional development program devote more to leadership and thinking skills than they do to computer training. I'd also have courses with such titles as "The Business Executive as Community Leader," "Mentoring Your Own Staff" and "Role Model 101."

Management Leads in Strategically Planned Companies

Companies that are planned and have developed strategies to meet the future now subscribe to results based management, with the goal to improve program effectiveness, accountability and achieve results. This means that company leadership is committed to:

- Establishing clear organizational vision, mission and priorities, which are translated into a four-year framework of goals, outputs, indicators, strategies and resources.
- Encouraging an organizational and management culture that promotes innovation, learning, accountability, and transparency.
- Delegating authority, empowering managers and holding them accountable for results.
- Focusing on achieving results, through strategic planning, regular monitoring of progress, evaluation of performance, and reporting on performance.

- Creating supportive mechanisms, policies and procedures, building and improving on what is already in place.
- Sharing information, knowledge, learning lessons and feeding these back into improving decision-making and performance.
- Optimizing human resources and building capacity among staff to manage for results.
- Making the best use of financial resources in an efficient manner to achieve results.
- Strengthening and diversifying partnerships at all levels.
- Responding to external situations and needs within the organizational mandate.

We are the products of those who believe in us. Find role models and set out to be one yourself. To get, you must give. Career and life are not a short stint. Do what it takes to run the decathlon. Set personal and professional goals, standards and accountability.

Stand for something. Making money is not enough. You must do something worth leaving behind, mentoring to others and of recognizable substance. Your views of professionalism must be known and shown.

Mentoring and Lifelong Learning

Professionals who succeed the most are the products of mentoring. I heartily endorse that find a great mentor. I have had many excellent ones in my long career and have in turn mentored hundreds of others.

The mentor is a resource for business trends, societal issues and opportunities. The mentor becomes a role model, offering insights about their own life-career. This reflection shows the mentee levels of thinking and perception which were not previously available. The mentor is an advocate for progress and change. Such work empowers the mentee to hear, accept, believe and get results. The sharing of trust and ideas leads to developing business philosophies.

The mentor endorses the mentee, messages ways to approach issues, helps draw distinctions and paints pictures of success. The mentor opens doors for the mentee. The mentor requests pro-active changes of mentee, evaluates realism of goals and offers truths about path to success and shortcomings of mentee's approaches. This is a bonded collaboration toward each other's success. The mentor stands for mentees throughout their careers and celebrates their successes. This is a lifelong dedication toward mentorship…in all aspects of one's life.

The most significant lessons that I learned in my business life from mentors, verified with experience, are shared here:

1. You cannot go through life as a carbon copy of someone else.
2. You must establish your own identity, which is a long, exacting process.
3. As you establish a unique identity, others will criticize. Being different, you become a moving target.
4. People criticize you because of what you represent, not who you are. It is rarely personal against you. Your success may bring out insecurities within others. You might be what they cannot or are not willing to become.
5. If you cannot take the dirtiest job in any company and do it yourself, then you will never become "management."
6. Approach your career as a body of work. This requires planning, purpose and commitment. It's a career, not just a series of jobs.
7. The person who is only identified with one career accomplishment or by the identity of one company for whom he-she formerly worked is a one-hit wonder and, thus, has no body of work.
8. The management that takes steps to "fix themselves" rather than always projecting problems upon other people will have a successful organization.
9. It's not when you learn. It's that you learn.
10. Many people do without the substantive insights into business because they have not really developed critical thinking skills.
11. Analytical and reasoning skills are extensions of critical thinking skills.
12. You perform your best work for free. How you fulfill commitments and pro-bono work speaks to the kind of professional that you are.
13. People worry so much what others think about them. If they knew how little others thought, they wouldn't worry so much. This too is your challenge to frame how they see you and your company.
14. Fame is fleeting and artificial. The public is fickle and quick to jump on the newest flavor, without showing loyalty to the old ones, especially those

who are truly original. Working in radio, I was taught, "They only care about you when you're behind the microphone."

15. The pioneer and "one of a kind" professional has a tough lot in life. It is tough to be first or so far ahead of the curve that others cannot see it. Few will understand you. Others will attain success with portions of what you did. None will do it as well.

16. Consumers are under-educated and don't know the substance of a pioneer. Our society takes more to the copycats and latest fads. Only the pioneer knows and appreciates what he-she really accomplished. That reassurance will have to be enough.

17. Life and careers include peaks and valleys. It's how one copes during the "down times" that is the true measure of success.

18. Long-term success must be earned. It is not automatic and is worthless if ill-gotten. The more dues one pays, the more you must continue paying.

19. The next best achievement is the one you're working on now, inspired by your body of knowledge to date.

20. The person who never has aggressively pursued a dream or mounted a series of achievements cannot understand the quest of one with a deeply committed dream.

21. A great percentage of the population does not achieve huge goals but still admires and learns from those who do persevere and succeed. The achiever thus becomes a lifelong mentor to others.

22. Achievement is a continuum, but it must be benchmarked and enjoyed along the way.

These are my concluding pieces of leadership advice. Know where you are going. Develop, update and maintain a career growth document. Keep a diary of lessons learned but not soon forgotten. Learn the reasons for success and, more importantly, from failure.

Good bosses were good employees. They have keen understanding for both roles. Bad bosses likely were not ideal employees. They too are consistent in career history.

Being your own boss is yet another lesson. People who were downsized from a corporate environment suddenly enter the entrepreneurial world and find the transition to be tough.

Poor people skills cloud any job performance and overshadow good technical skills. The worst bosses do not sustain long careers at the top. Their track record catches up with them, whether they choose to acknowledge it or not.

Good workers don't automatically become good bosses. Just because someone is technically proficient or is an exemplary producer does not mean that he-she will transition to being a boss. The best school teachers do not want to become principals, for that reason. Good job performers are better left doing what they do best. Administrators, at all levels, need to be properly trained as such, not bumped up from the field to do something for which they have no inclination.

Truth and ethics must be woven into how you conduct business. If you do not "walk the talk," who will? Realize that very little of what happens to you in business is personal. Find common meeting grounds with colleagues. The only workable solution is a win-win.

Leadership and executive development skills are steadily learned and continually sharpened. One course or a quick-read book will not instill them. The best leaders are prepared to go the distance. Professional enrichment must be life-long. Early formal education is but a starting point. Study trends in business, in your industry and in the industries of your customers.

People skills mastery applies to every profession. There is no organization that does not have to communicate to others about what it does. The process of open company dialogs must be developed to address conflicts, facilitate win-win solutions and further organizational goals.

Quotes on Leadership

"A leader is a dealer in hope."
— **Napoleon Bonaparte**

"A president's hardest task is not to do
what is right but to know what is right."
— **President Lyndon B. Johnson** (1965)

"When you're leading, don't talk."
— **Thomas E. Dewey**

*"A leader who doesn't hesitate before he sends
his nation into battle is not fit to be a leader."*
— **Golda Meir**

"Leadership and learning are indispensable to each other."
— **President John F. Kennedy**, speech prepared for delivery
in Dallas the day of his assassination, Nov. 22, 1963

*"An empowered organization is one in which individuals have
the knowledge, skill, desire, and opportunity to personally
succeed in a way that leads to collective organizational success."*
— **Stephen R. Covey**

*"Men make history, and not the other way around. In periods where
there is no leadership, society stands still. Progress occurs when courageous,
skillful leaders seize the opportunity to change things for the better."*
— **President Harry S Truman** (1884-1972)

*"Leadership should be born out of the understanding
of the needs of those who would be affected by it."*
— **Marian Anderson**

*"Leadership has a harder job to do than
just choose sides. It must bring sides together."*
— **Reverend Jesse Jackson**

*"Jingshen is the Mandarin word for spirit and vivacity. It is an important
word for those who would lead, because above all things, spirit and vivacity
set effective organizations apart from those that will decline and die."*
— **James L. Hayes,** Memos for Management: Leadership, 1983

"The only real training for leadership is leadership."
— **Anthony Jay**

*"I start with the premise that the function of
leadership is to produce more leaders, not more followers."*
— **Ralph Nader**

*"Whether a man is burdened by power or enjoys power; whether he is trapped
by responsibility or made free by it; whether he is moved by other people and
outer forces or moves them—this is of the essence of leadership."*
— **Theodore H. White,** The Making of the President, 1960

*"You do not lead by hitting people over
the head. That's assault, not leadership."*
— **President Dwight D. Eisenhower**

"Leadership is practiced not so much in words as in attitude and in actions."
— **Harold Geneen**

*"Good leadership consists in showing average
people how to do the work of superior people."*
— **John D. Rockefeller**

"There are no office hours for leaders."
— **Cardinal James Gibbons**

"A leader never sets himself above followers except in carrying responsibilities."
— **Jules Ormont**

Chapter 22

PROCESS IMPROVEMENT AND QUALITY

Poise Organizations for Success

Q uality is not something that managers assign others to achieve. It is a mind-set that permeates organizations from top-down as well as bottom-up.

Rather than assume all is wrong or right with an organization and take a defensive posture, management must view quality as essential to their economic survival or growth. Quality entails four concepts:

- Success is determined by conformity to requirements.
- It is achieved through prevention, not appraisal. The quality audit by objective outside communications counsel is merely the beginning of a process.
- The quality performance standard is zero defects. That means doing things correctly the first time, without wasting counter-productive time in cleaning up mistakes.
- Nonconformance is costly. Make-good efforts cost more on the back end than doing things right on the front end.

Organizations measure quality by overall involvement. It is not enough for management to endorse quality programs; they must actively participate.

Quality should be viewed as a journey, rather than a destination. It applies to service industries and manufacturing operations. Even non-profit and public sector organizations must utilize quality approaches for staff and volunteer councils/boards.

Employees must buy into the process by offering constructive input. All ideas are worthy of consideration. Life-threatening experiences (loss of business or market share, economic recession) signal the urgency for the team to collaborate.

Empowerment of employees means they accept the challenges and consequences. They must view the company as a consumer would…being as discerning about buying their own services as they are about fine dining, premium clothing, gifts for friends, a car or a home.

What if we were all paid based upon customer perceptions of our service? That would make each of us more attentive to what we offer and whether our value is correctly perceived.

Each member of an organization must view himself/herself as having customers. Each must be seen as a profit center and as having something valuable to contribute to the overall group. Each is a link that lets down the whole chain by failing to uphold their part.

What is missing in most organizations is the willingness to move forward, not the availability of information or desire for improvement. Willingness requires complete and never-ending commitment by management. The first time the organization tolerates anything less than 100%, it is on the road back to mediocrity.

The most common pitfalls toward success include:

- Taking a piecemeal approach to quality.
- Thinking that quality needs apply to some other department, company or industry, not your own.
- Thinking that you are already doing things "the quality way."
- Failing to address structural flaws that fuel the problems.
- Focusing upon esoteric techniques, rather than true reasons for instilling quality.
- Saying that something is being done when it is not.
- Failing to engage customers and suppliers into the process.

- Failing to emphasize training.
- Setting goals that are too low.
- Communicating poorly with the organization and its publics. Without employee communications, suggestion boxes, publications, training videos, speeches and other professionally prepared instruments, the company is fooling itself and its customers about the commitment to quality. Without good communication from the outset, the program will never be understood and accepted.

Quality improvement is the only action that can simultaneously win the support of customers, employees, investors, media and the public. Productivity translates to profitability in an advantageous climate in which to function.

Investment Toward Economic Survival and Growth

Research shows the by-product costs of poor quality are high for any business, up to 40 percent. Lack of attentiveness to quality has cost the United States its global marketplace dominance. Other nations preceded the U.S. in adopting the quality process and overtook our nation in many areas.

In 1981, more than 70 percent of U.S. automobiles realized defects within six months of purchase. That figure has now dropped below 40%, compared with just under 30% in Japanese cars. Had quality been a focus in Detroit years earlier, then the obvious would not have transpired.

The Japanese have always viewed quality as a national issue…not just an individual company matter. The real victim of America's late entry into the quality process was every employee whose livelihood was endangered. Consumers did not worry; they simply bought goods and services elsewhere.

- Success via competitiveness has many dimensions:
- Production efficiency became America's focus by the 1950s.
- Marketing's importance was fully embraced in the 1960s. Marketing departments deal most often and immediately with the side effects of poor quality.
- The 1970s brought the first wave of strategic planning. Without mapping a course, how can any organization reach a destination?

- The 1980s brought us the quality process, which is the bow that wraps a package containing the other three elements. At the start of the decade, many executives viewed the quality process with indifference or fear. By decade's end, virtually all (92%) agreed that quality is the main prescription for survival.

Though quality is one element of competitiveness, it cannot cover defects in the other areas. The quality audit by objective outside communications counsel can also examine the production, marketing and strategic planning functions.

Companies must place demands upon their own organizations to embrace customer service tenets. Satisfied customers talk to others…encouraging them to buy based upon quality of the company. Dissatisfied customers will aggressively discourage higher numbers of prospects from buying.

The mark of any professional is the manner in which he/she corrects mistakes. Most often, this means correcting misperceptions about company attitude, rather than the condition of goods. The faster the correction, the better the level of satisfaction. Quality is the sum of impressions made on the customer.

Payroll is the biggest overhead item. Improvement can be quantified by increased productivity, reduced turnover and heightened employee morale.

The empowered team is trusted to seek quality on their own. Bad managers will fall by the wayside. Employees who do not pull their share will stick out like sore thumbs. The team will not be judged by the superstars but, instead, by the average. The whole is greater than the sum of its parts.

In order to complete the chain, organizations must insist that suppliers, professional services counselors and vendors show demonstrated quality programs, as well as ethics statements. Educational and incentive programs should be implemented.

During tough economic times, investment in a quality program is not costly. Anyone who is unwilling to spend for quality is hastening company decline.

Strategy Steers the Quality Process

Quality is one of the most vital ingredients of competitive success. Total Quality Management (TQM) is recognized as a prerequisite for survival. One fourth of all corporations now administer quality programs.

The focus on quality has gone beyond the finished product and addresses all processes throughout the organization. Evaluating quality is not just a question of meeting customers' expectations…but rather exceeding them.

Paying attention to quality can realize:

- Lower operating costs. Research shows they can be cut in half.
- Premium pricing for preferred goods/services.
- Customer retention.
- Enhanced reputation.
- Access to global markets.
- Faster innovation.
- Higher sales.
- Higher return on investments. TQM has increased profitability in some corporations up to six times.

Total Quality Management is customer-focused and strategy-directed. It is a top management activity, steered by public relations counselors. The human relations component is strong, but quality programs are substantially communications-driven.

Communications impacts value creation in every aspect of a business. PR counselors give feedback, data and project implementation to each department involved or impacted. Management and communicators must work and think as a team. The elements include employee relations (from suggestion boxes to volunteer activities), video training, management enrichment programs, newsletters, speeches, brochures and front-line participation by top management.

Communications is not just the passing of information. It is the catalyst that makes things happen. Talking and listening will enable the company to achieve more.

The successful quality program empowers employees, who will achieve quality on their own. The more positive results are shown, the more universal will be participation.

The quality process must have substance—not just rhetoric—in order to build momentum. There are no magic shortcuts. If the process is given proper attention and support by top management, it is a money-maker.

How to Institute a Quality Program

Change is painful for most people but is necessary. Conducting "business as usual" means standing still, which means losing ground while other companies move forward.

Quality does not mean that true perfection will exist. It is simply a commitment to keep the wheels of progress at top-of-mind motion.

To change and improve requires methodically and systematically undertaking actions that will make your company "world class." These actions include:

- Education.
- Communication.
- Reward and recognition.
- Employee suggestion systems.
- Involvement teams.
- Benchmark measurements of accomplishments.
- Statistical management methods.

Most companies implement quality programs as a reaction to a perceived negative image. Data is gathered in scattered areas, usually to produce flashy charts for customers. Because upper management does not know which programs to implement, the quality process stagnates.

Doing things for the wrong reasons or to temporarily pacify someone else spells failure. There are no quick fixes. Applying band aids will just reopen the wounds at a later date. Quality can never be identified too broadly enough.

In order to put a quality program into place, the following steps must be taken:

- Study the activities of admired companies. Interview them to provide insight. Set meetings to review what works for them. Read case studies of Malcolm Baldridge Award winners. Companies can and should be role models for each other.
- Retain outside experts. Quality programs are communications driven and should be captained by public relations counsel who possess this expertise. They will conduct communications audits and strategic planning. This is

not something that can be conducted alone by internal human resources departments. Good experts will tell you the hard facts and what needs to be done.

- Research drives most communications programs. Commission customer and employee surveys. It will provide comparisons between the realities and perceptions that are held.
- Ask counsel to write a plan of action for putting the quality program into place.
- Assemble an internal quality team…making sure that all major departments are represented. Together with outside counsel, this committee will pursue its objectives, per the written agenda.
- Set realistic timelines for putting recommendations into place.
- Set schedules for routine review of the process. This includes repeating surveys to assure that you are making adequate progress.

By successfully combining employee involvement, process improvement, customer focus and demonstrated management endorsement, any company can succeed at quality. Even on a limited investment, quality can be attained.

The challenge is to discover what mix of price and quality the customer wants and to deliver it. Slogans only create adversarial relationships. Once the system owns up to its shortcomings and responsibilities, then a true quality process will occur.

Failure to read the "handwriting on the wall" will thwart company growth and, thus, the overall economy.

Quotes on Process Improvement, Quality and Greatness

"A great man is always willing to be little. To be great is to be misunderstood. The essence of greatness is the perception that virtue is enough."
— **Ralph Waldo Emerson**

"Some are born great. Some achieve greatness, and some have greatness thrust upon them. He is not great who is not greatly good."
— **William Shakespeare**

*"Keep away from people who try to belittle your
ambitions. Small people always do that, but the really
great make you feel that you, too, can become great."*
— **Mark Twain**

"A truly great man never puts away the simplicity of a child."
— Chinese proverb

*"To be alone is the fate of all great minds...a fate deplored
at times, but still always chosen as the less grievous of two evils."*
— **Arthur Schopenhauer,** 19th Century German philosopher

*"Great men are true men, the men in whom nature has succeeded.
They are not extraordinary—they are in the true order. It is the
other species of men who are not what they ought to be."*
— **Henri-Frederic Amiel**

*"All great men are gifted with intuition. They know
without reasoning or analysis, what they need to know."*
— **Alexis Carrel**

*"The reason why great men meet with so little pity or
attachment in adversity, would seem to be this: the friends of a
great man were made by his fortune, his enemies by himself, and
revenge is a much more punctual paymaster than gratitude."*
— **C. C. Colton**

"The superior man is modest in his speech but exceeds in his actions."
— **Confucius**

*"No pain, no palm; no thorns, no throne;
no gall, no glory; no cross, no crown."*
— **William Penn**

Chapter 23

LEARNING BUSINESS LESSONS FROM THE ENTERTAINMENT INDUSTRY

T his chapter was a source of enjoyment and completion for me. Back in 1969, I started going to Hollywood.

I visited the studios and the sets of current television shows, the same ones that are now being called "classics." Some of the shows that I visited were hits, and others were up-and-coming ones that the networks wanted to promote and find public attention for them.

35 years later, classic television is a hobby with me. It's fun, and you can share the shows, the memories and the messages contained therein with friends and family.

I wrote this book because pop culture affects all of our lives, always has and always will. By refocusing upon the industry that brought us our pop culture, we find new applicability to a changed and troubled world. Understanding how and why TV blossomed and came of age in the 1950s and 1960s helps us understand how organizations in general progress or stagnate in a changing world.

Thus, I took the bold move to take a nostalgic walk down memory lane and make the bold move to inject business book material into it. This book should empower audiences to reach within themselves for basic answers, to become their best and to realize that excellence is attainable thorough wider scope and focus.

My emphasis today is upon studying and advising organizations and businesses that really want to do the things necessary to grow steadily and be successful. I see too many businesses that think they can take shortcuts or believe that the recent corporate scandals do not apply to them. I've written other books about these business phenomena and the strategies necessary to turn the tide and create successful operations.

I see many analogies from classic television series to modern business strategies. Reflecting upon the glory days of television and how the industry came of age, I see the following basic business thematic concepts that emerged in this book:

1. **Entrepreneurism.** In the 1950s, the entrepreneurs of Hollywood sought to produce filmed programs for the infant medium of television. The New York network establishment was tied to having programming originate on the East Coast.

The innovative TV entrepreneurs proved to the networks that they could produce filmed programs on limited budgets. Many overshot their original budgets, betting on long-term residual benefits to accrue from reruns.

When the major studios saw the inroads that the entrepreneurs made into television programming, they wanted to join the action. They retooled their studios in order to meet economical production schedules and budgets. Like the entrepreneurs, the studios learned that quality popular programs could emerge, in spite of limited budgets and other factors previously seen as constraints.

Individuals and organizations amass values based upon a series of experiences. Often, values depend upon the context and reflect the facets of professional achievement:

- Core Industry…The Business You're In.
- Rendering the Service…Administering Your Work.
- Accountability…Qualities with Which You Work.

- Your Relationships-Contributions to Other People…Colleagues, Stakeholders.
- Professional-Leadership Development…Your Path to the Future.
- Your Contributions to the Organization's Overall Goals…Your Place in its Big Picture.
- Body of Work…Your Accomplishments to Date and Anticipated Future Output.

2. **Collaborations.** The best tends to attract the best. When entrepreneurs Lucille Ball and Desi Arnaz founded Desilu Productions, they attracted the best talent from the film community. The results were superior productions that have stood the best of time.

Many great talents joined forces with Desilu, sometimes working with them and other times working in collaborative productions. This set the tone for the multiple production company situations that are the rule in contemporary Hollywood, rather than the exception.

The biggest source of growth and increased opportunities in today's business climate lie in the way that individuals and companies work together.

It is becoming increasingly rare to find an individual or organization that has not yet been required to team with others. Lone rangers and sole-source providers simply cannot succeed in competitive environments and global economies. Those who benefit from collaborations, rather than become the victim of them, will log the biggest successes in business years ahead.

Here are my definitions of three terms of teamwork, intended to help by differentiating their intended objectives:

Collaborations—Parties willingly cooperating together. Working jointly with others, especially in an intellectual pursuit. Cooperation with an instrumentality with which one is not immediately connected.

Partnering—A formal relationship between two or more associates. Involves close cooperation among parties, with each having specified and joint rights and responsibilities.

Joint-Venturing—Partners come together for specific purposes or projects that may be beyond the scope of individual members. Each retains individual identity.

The joint-venture itself has its own identity…reflecting favorably upon work to be done and upon the partners.

3. **Value-Added, Customer Service.** Television has its own Customer Service Index. The ratings system, though often criticized, is a fair way of measuring audiences. Public tastes are catered to, as well as measured. Usually, programming is designed to address public tastes. The most innovative programs predict public appetites and deliver hit shows that beat the competition into the marketplace.

In today's highly competitive business environment, every dynamic of a successful organization must be toward ultimate customers. Customer focused management goes beyond service and quality. There is no business that cannot improve its customer orientation. Every organization has customers, clients, stakeholders, financiers, volunteers, supporters or other categories of "affected constituencies."

Customer focused management is a concept that goes far beyond just smiling, answering queries and communicating with buyers. It transcends customer service training. In today's highly competitive business environment, every dynamic of a successful organization must be toward ultimate customers.

Companies must change their focus from products and processes toward the values which they share with customers. Customer focused management goes beyond just the dynamics of service and quality.

Everyone with whom you conduct business is a customer or referral source of someone else. The service that we get from some people, we pass along to others. Customer service is a continuum of human behaviors…shared with those whom we meet.

Customers are the lifeblood of every business. Employees depend upon customers for their paychecks. Yet, you wouldn't know the correlation when poor customer service is rendered. Employees of companies behave as though customers are a bother, do not heed their concerns and do not take suggestions for improvement.

There is no business that cannot undergo some improvement in its customer orientation. Every organization has customers, clients, stakeholders, financiers, volunteers, supporters or other categories of "affected constituency."

4. **Corporate Culture.** The television industry took upon a different corporate culture, once it reconciled the differences of its New York establishment and the influence that the Hollywood film community added.

Corporate cultures, if allowed to occur unchecked, will develop the negative qualities of those organizations from which its key players previously came. In forming a new corporate culture, which filmed television was in the 1950s, it is necessary to plan and build a hybrid of the best transferable qualities.

How organizations start out and what they become are different concepts. Mistakes, niche orientation and lack of planning lead businesses to failure. Processes, trends, fads, perceived stresses and "the system" force managers to make compromises in order to proceed. Often, a fresh look at previous knowledge gives renewed insight.

The purpose of re-examining and refining an organization's corporate culture is to:

- Think Big Picture.
- Conceptualize and communicate your company's own goals.
- Understand conflicting societal goals.
- Fit your dreams into the necessities and realities of the real world.
- Find your own niche…do your thing.
- Get satisfactions from doing something well and committing to long-term excellence.
- Seek truths in unusual and unexpected sources.
- Share your knowledge, and learn further by virtue of mentoring others.

In many industries and professions, business development has occurred primarily by accident or through market demand. Because of economic realities and the increased numbers of firms providing comparable services, the notion of business development is now a necessity, rather than a luxury. Competition for customers-clients is sharpening. The professions are no longer held on a pedestal…a condition which mandates them to portray or enhance their core values.

I would encourage business leaders to fill out a Core Values Worksheet These are the key criteria for basing your professional vision:

- Core Industry, The Business You're In.
- Rendering the Service and Administering Your Work.
- Accountability and Qualities with Which You Work.
- Your Relationships-Contributions to Other People., Colleagues and Stakeholders.
- Professional-Leadership Development, Your Path to the Future.
- Your Contributions to the Organization's Overall Goals, Your Place in its Big Picture.
- Body of Work, Your Accomplishments to Date and Anticipated Future Output.

5. **Innovation, Strategic Priorities.** Television is predicated upon the newest thing being supplanted by the next new thing. Innovations of one season become the watermarks for others.

Organizations must periodically assess and review their value systems as part of Strategic Planning and corporate Visioning processes. Every business leader should likewise develop and commit to nurturing their own personal value statement.

Here are some examples of Core Values which could be included:

- To be truthful, forceful and forthright in personal relationships.
- To treat others as I would like to be treated.
- To expect that I deserve and will receive the best out of life.
- To be the kind of person that others can count upon, like, love and admire.
- To be true to my word and consistent in my actions.
- To show loyalty and commitment to those causes and projects which I undertake.
- To show loyalty and commitment to family and friends who are important to me.
- To never stop growing emotionally and continuing my journey.

Here are some examples of Strategic Priorities which could be included:

- To be the best that I can be.
- To be the best in my chosen field.

- To create new applications and set new standards for my chosen field.
- To successfully mentor others.
- To creatively approach projects in ways that others did not or could not do.
- To achieve results that are realistically attained and honestly reached.
- To continue building respect for myself and the self-assuredness to stay focused.
- To know that I am doing the right things and taking the best possible courses of action.
- To never stop growing professionally and continuing to evolve to the next tiers.

6. **Expanding to New Marketplaces.** In the late 1940s, there were only a few television stations. As their numbers grew in the early 1950s, network affiliates began dotting each major U.S. city. As more channels were added, independent stations experienced a demand for programming.

Since there was not yet a body of reruns in the early years of television, a radio syndication company headed by Frederick Ziv moved to television. They shot filmed shows that could be shown anytime and anywhere, with local sponsorship opportunities. The first shows were Cisco Kid and Boston Blackie, reviving the old movie serial format.

An early original Ziv series was "I Led Three Lives," the story of a government counter agent working as an undercover Communist Party member. In the city in which I grew up, the local furniture company sponsored the show. Its owner sat on a stool in the local TV studio, delivering the commercials and some occasional civic commentaries. Due in part to the fame created by his TV show sponsorship, Louis Shanks was subsequently elected to our city council. That was the power of early TV at the local level. Organizations put disproportionate attention behind image…if the sake of business is only to become rich and famous.

In analyzing the promotional hype that one hears, some companies claim that purchasing their product is the "be all, end all" panacea for life's dilemmas. If only you will buy their version of "The Answer," then you can surely fast-forward your way to instant riches, success and an easy life.

This is not written to take swipes at responsible branding, marketing and advertising. More than 80% of what one sees and hears is clever, informative, research-based, sensibly executed and intended to orient target audiences toward marketplaces. This is written to address the bigger issue that some companies believe the hype that they are issuing.

Some companies are downright parsimonious about themselves. Some either skillfully lie to get what they think they want…or may really believe themselves to be what they hype to publics who don't know any better.

Many consumers are gullible, "name" crazy and susceptible to grandiose claims. They take what is said at face value because they have not or don't care to develop abilities to discern what is hyped by others. They believe distortions faster than they believe facts, logic and reason.

This negatively impacts our society, which continually seeks button-pushing answers for life's complex problems without paying enough dues toward a truly successful life. Consumers naively believe mis-representations…to the exclusion of organizations which are more conservative, yet substantive, in their informational offerings.

Here are some of the worst "red flag" expressions. When you hear them, beware of false claims:

- Our Mission.
- Family Tradition.
- Fastest Growing.
- In One Easy Lesson.
- Better.
- #1 in Sales.
- World Class.
- The Best.
- For All Your Needs.

Many of the hucksterish promotions represent "copywriting" by people who don't know anything about corporate vision. Their words overstate, get into the media and are accepted by audiences as fact. By default, companies have the appearance of credibility based upon mis-representations.

Companies put too much of their public persona in the hands of marketers and should examine more closely the distorted messages and partial images which they put into the cyberspace. Our culture hears and believes the hype, without looking beyond the obvious. People come to expect easy answers for questions they haven't yet taken the time to formulate.

7. **Investing in the future.** In television, trends come and go. One must expect that the current crest of success will not last forever. One must predict, plan and constantly re-examine what will work. Futurism means creatively planning for alternate eventualities.

In 1960, Warner Brothers was at the top of its television game, or so they thought. Its programs occupied 30% of ABC-TV's schedule. As stars left or sued the studio, they were interchangeably replaced by other actors. Scripts were retread from one series to another, often giving the writing credit to "W. Hermanos" (Warner Brothers in Spanish).

The studio's accountants and lawyers called many of the shots. They insisted that each episode make a profit, little realizing the investment in better productions toward longer-term residual rights.

The episodes began to all look alike. The quality dipped. There was too much sameness to the productions. Alas, the shows began getting cancelled. WB had not diversified its productions to other networks, syndication and changing public tastes. Soon, they were without any TV productions. The surviving studio became a home for independent production companies, rather than try to captain all the productions.

Futurism is one of the most misunderstood concepts in business and organizational life. It is not about gazing into crystal balls or reading tea leaves. It is not about vendor "solutions" that quickly apply band aid surgery toward organizational symptoms. Futurism is not an academic exercise that borders on the esoteric or gets stuck in the realm of hypothesis.

Futurism is an all-encompassing concept that must look at all aspects of the organization…first at the Big Picture and then at the pieces as they relate to the whole.

Futurism is a connected series of strategies, methodologies and actions which will poise any organization to weather the forces of change. It is an ongoing process of evaluation, planning, tactical actions and benchmarking accomplishments. Futurism is a continuum of thinking and reasoning skills, judicious activities, shared leadership and an accent upon ethics and quality.

I offer nine of my own definitions for the process of capturing and building a shared Vision for organizations to chart their next 10+ years. Each one gets progressively more sophisticated:

- Futurism: what you will do and become…rather than what it is to be. What you can and are committed to accomplishing…rather than what mysteriously lies ahead.

- Futurism: leaders and organizations taking personal responsibility and accountability for what happens. Abdicating to someone or something else does not constitute Futurism and, in fact, sets the organization backward.

- Futurism: learns from and benefits from the past…a powerful teaching tool. Yesterdayism means giving new definitions to old ideas…giving new meanings to familiar premises. One must understand events, cycles, trends and subtle nuances because they will recur.

- Futurism: seeing clearly your perspectives and those of others. Capitalizing upon change, rather than becoming a by-product of it. Recognizing what change is and what it can do for your organization.

- Futurism: an ongoing quest toward wisdom. Commitments to learning, which creates knowledge, which inspire insights, which culminate in wisdom. It is more than just being taught or informed.

- Futurism: ideas that inspire, manage and benchmark change. The ingredients may include such sophisticated business concepts as change management, crisis management and preparedness, streamlining operations, empowerment of people, marketplace development, organizational evolution and vision.

- Futurism: developing thinking and reasoning skills, rather than dwelling just upon techniques and processes. The following concepts do not constitute Futurism by themselves: sales, technology, re-engineering, marketing, research, training, operations, administration. They are pieces of a much larger mosaic and should be seen as such. Futurism embodies thought processes that create and energize the mosaic.

- Futurism: watching other people changing and capitalizing upon it. Understanding from where we came, in order to posture where we are headed. Creating organizational vision, which sets the stage for all activities, processes, accomplishments and goals. Efforts must be realistic, and all must be held accountable.

- Futurism: the foresight to develop hindsight that creates insight into the future.

8. **Technology.** In 1951, Desi Arnaz got the call from CBS-TV. His "I Love Lucy" series had sold, and when were he and Lucy coming to New York to perform the show live?

Desi stated that he and Lucy would stay in California and film their show. He went out and recruited one of Hollywood's top cinematographers and devised a three-camera technique, so that Lucy could work her best in front of a live studio audience. Desi saw the added expense of filming the shows as creating a permanent record and an after-market, thereafter known as "TV reruns."

As a result, American TV shows could fly on film anywhere in the world. Filmed programs opened up new opportunities for local independent channels, foreign film sales and, alas, cable television.

Technology is important but not the most important part of running an organization. We must learn how to use it, in order to put it into perspective.

Often, technology is a "bells and whistles" project that companies readily put money behind, rather than first addressing total-organizational issues, problems and opportunities. It does not solve all problems, nor should it be blamed for creating all problems.

People need more than technology to be productive. Yet, without adequate technology, they are handicapped. We must not give a disproportionate amount of attention to technology and leave people (any organization's best resource) the short end of the stick.

Each year, companies spend billions of dollars on the latest technology but do not reward their people for creative thinking. People are trained in the use of technology but are not trained adequately in other aspects of business operation...

notably in the powers of reason, communications and the people skills necessary to work optimally with each other.

The bigger priority is to apply creative thinking to all aspects of company operation. Use technology as a tool. Utilize people as the masters of that tool. Encompass planning and bigger-picture thinking into all business operations. Therefore, those who use technology do so with a bigger understanding of its place in the Big Picture.

When technology is thought of as a component in the "macro," rather than a "micro" world unto itself, it will have mature utilization. Otherwise, it will be viewed as a bunch of high-priced toys which are played out of context to the main game.

9. **Creative processes.** The three-camera technique was adopted as the industry standard for TV situation comedies, both those produced live on tape and those produced on film.

Videotape was first introduced into the industry in 1954. By the late 1960s, it was dominantly used by the networks and by local TV stations. By the late 1970s, videotape was utilized for the home market. Many of us recorded programs off the air and began stockpiling libraries. For others, an innovative marketplace and creative marketing process brought us retails stores that rented videos for home exhibition.

Along with knowledge of the industry in which one works, there is a creative art to being effective at every aspect of running and sustaining each facet of a successful business. These are details per each of the seven categories on my trademarked Business Tree:

Branch 1: The business you're in. There are skills attached to rendering the service or manufacturing the products. People get into businesses because they have expertise in an area, such as widget making. It is for this that they have received education, training, professional development, mentoring and much more. Business founders and leaders are good at making widgets and are exceedingly comfortable with Branch 1.

The art comes in amassing professional abilities, specialties and skills in working with industry consultants, technical specialists, sub-contractors, vendors and core business suppliers.

Branch 2: Running the business. This involves administrative practices, procedures, operations, structure, the physical plant, technologies, equipment, supplies and distribution. Once people get onto Branch 2, the problems begin and start to multiply. Few widget experts are taught how to manufacture widgets and deliver them to market. Nor, are widget makers really taught the multi-dynamics of actually operating a business. Hence, all decisions are made from a Branch 1 perspective, mentality and orientation.

The art comes in working with lawyers, engineers, technology experts, non-core business suppliers, communications providers and repair-maintenance companies

Branch 3: Financial Components include cash flow forecasting, budgeting, equity and debt financing, accounting, record keeping, banking and investing.

No company stays in business without money…incoming and, to a hopefully lesser degree, outgoing. Making money is not the only reason for being in business. Usually, it's to make the best possible widgets and, then, to be very successful at it. Financial expertise helps Branch 1 founders stay focused upon fiduciary responsibilities.

Branch 4: People. Leadership tasks include recruiting, hiring and supervision. Companies are successful by possessing an attained art to human resources management, empowerment, team building, training, incentives and professional executive development.

This is the largest and most under-nourished branch on the tree. Organizations cannot operate with people. However, many organizations tend to misuse, ignore, ill-advise, misguide, neglect and mistreat the people working for and with them. Employees are most often hired for Branch 1 expertise and put to work. Like the company founders, most widget experts are not well versed in the other branches of the tree. Even in their Branch 4 interface with other employees, they function from a Branch 1 vantage.

There is an art to motivating people and optimizing their performance. Research studies show that money is rarely the primary motivation for people in careers and their professional lives. All people in the organization need lots of professional attention, mentoring, training and administrative support. Few ever get their needs satisfied, and thus, companies realize reduced work output and a less-than-zealous attitude.

Management cries, "Fix those people," without realizing that they are a large part of the problem. All of us can stand having our people skills refined. That's why widget makers, administrative staff, bean counters and all other leaves on the tree must embrace empowerment, team building, open communication and other concepts to relate better to human beings.

Branch 5: Business development. The components include corporate imaging, marketplace perceptions and realities, sales, marketing, public relations, advertising and research.

One cannot stay in business unless they market and sell something. Branch 1 creators think incorrectly that they are in the "widget" business. Actually, they are in the "widget manufacturing and marketing" business. Many companies are principally in the "widget marketing" business. Having a better widget is but a small part of that equation.

Branch 1 experts in management tend to fight marketing and sales, branding those two different professional specialties as necessary evils that someone else must deal with. The astute upper management will integrate all five branches and participates personally in Branch 5…taking their widget to market.

Using another analogy, a person who gives birth and does nothing more toward their child is not a good parent. That person is successful after shepherding the offspring through the various stages of growth and facets of life.

Categories 6 and 7 are the nurturing-strength (basis of business), which enable Branches 1, 2, 3, 4 and 5 to interrelate and function most successfully.

Category 6 (trunk): Body of Knowledge. The components include professional development, product-service development, external influences and information, collaborations, partnering, joint venturing, government, regulating factors, marketplace limitations, community standards and niche constituencies.

No company can stay in business without understanding the relationship of each branch (business function) to the other, each limb (department) to the other, each twig (niche consultant) to the other, each leaf (employee) to the other and each part of the Business Tree has its proper responsibility and should learn to interface with the others.

This sophisticated and vital category includes research and consultation with management on external forces affecting company growth…mostly outside their control but which can limit business opportunities. There is an art to fine-tuning the processes by which management gains new insight about the future of business, viabilities for change management, emerging issues and the next necessary steps. This category also includes crisis management and preparedness programs and the building of strategic business alliances.

Category 7 (roots). The Big Picture. The components include building a shared vision, corporate responsibility, creative business practices, strategic planning, innovations, outside-the-box thinking, the quality process, ethics, changing markets and walking the talk.

The successful company takes the time and appropriates the resources to develop a Big Picture. This costs one-sixth that of continually applying "band aid surgery" to problems as they arise. Business is approached as a Body of Work…a lifetime track record of accomplishments.

10. Leadership.

The biggest problem with business stems from the fact that management and company leadership come from one small piece of the organizational pie. Filling all management slots with financial people, for example, serves to limit the organizational strategy and focus. They all hire like-minded people and frame every business decision from their micro perspective.

The ideal business or organizational executive has strong leadership skills first. He or she develops organizational vision and sets strategies. Leaders should reflect a diversity of niche focus, guaranteeing that an overall balance is achieved. Those with ideologies, strategies, process upholding and detail focus are all reflected. The best management team looks at the macro, rather than just the niche micro.

None of us was born with sophisticated, finely tuned senses and highly enlightened viewpoints for life. We muddle through, try our best and get hit in the gut several times. Thus, we learn, amass knowledge and turn most experiences into an enlightened life-like perspective that moves us "to the next tier." Such a perspective is what makes seasoned executives valuable in the business marketplace.

Many people, however, stay in the "muddling through" mode and don't acquire seasoning. They "get by" with limited scope and remain complacent in some kind of security. As their clueless increases, they sink through the following seven numbers, like they would fall into a well.

Life has a way of forcing the human condition to change. Due to circumstances, people start "cluing in." By that point, substantial career potential has been lost. Much damage cannot be recovered. Therefore, many people likely will stay on safe tracks…which will rarely ride the engine to glory.

The most effective leaders accept that change is 90% positive and find reasons and rationale to embrace change. They see how change relates to themselves, realizing that the process of mastering change and turning transactions into a series of win-win propositions constitutes the real meaning of life.

Leadership is learned and synthesized daily. Knowledge is usually amassed through unexpected sources. Any person's commitment toward leadership development and continuing education must include honest examination of his-her life skills. Training, reading and pro-activity are prescribed.

Chapter 24

THE FINE ART OF FAILURE

Leadership Primer on Benefiting from
Mistakes We Make, in Order to Assure Success

uccess and failure…it's a matter of perspectives. Out of every 10 transactions in our lives, five will be unqualified successes. One will be a failure. Two will depend upon the circumstances. If approached responsibly, they will become successful. If approached irresponsibly, they will turn into failures. Two will either be successful or will fail, based strictly upon the person's attitude.

A 90% success rate for a person with a good attitude and responsible behavior is an unbeatable percentage. There is no such thing as perfection. Continuous quality improvement means that we benchmark accomplishments and set the next reach a little further.

Throughout our lives, we search for activities, people and meaning. We venture down roads where we find success. Other activities bring us failure…from which we learn even more what to do to achieve success the next time.

We learn three times more from failure than from success. The longer that success takes to attain has a direct relationship to how long we will hold onto it.

Success is easily attainable. So, why do people psyche themselves into failing more often they have to…especially when they succeed much more often than they give themselves credit for.

Let a mistake occur, and then the stream of remarks starts flowing: "We failed. They'll blame it on me. It's not my fault. There must be a traitor someplace. Once again, I screwed up. I can't seem to do anything right. Just my luck to get saddled with a bunch of idiots who don't know what they're doing. Does anyone know how to do this the right way? Hasn't anybody ever taught them?"

Sadly, there are elements of truth in explosive remarks. The bigger question is how people's mindsets toward mistakes and failures got that way.

7 Degrees of Failure, Plateaus in the Learning Curve

1. **Education-Growth**—Didn't know any better. Made some dumb mistakes, based upon incorrect assumptions, insufficient information or lack of sophistication to "see beyond the obvious." Beginning to learn better approaches by analyzing the wrong ways of doing things.

2. **Evolution**—Tried some things that worked and some that didn't work. Beginning to understand that things do not fail without a reason or cause. Learns constructively from trial and error. Visualizing patterns of failure as barriers to success.

3. **Experience Gathering**—Circumstances within and outside your control caused the projects to fail. Learns which external factors to trust and which cannot be controlled. The importance of research, due-diligence and marketplace understanding surface.

4. **Grooming**—The team let you down…understand why. Learns what you are capable of doing. Learns who to work with and in which capacities. Success-failure is a function of seizing-creating your own opportunities. No individual or organization can have success without experiencing and learning from failures.

5. **Seasoning**—Understand outcomes before they transpire…and the myriad of failure-producing factors. Most people and organizations fail due to never having control over certain ingredients, improper planning and the inability to change.

6. **Meaningful Contributions**—Attitude is everything…affecting the approach to problems. People say they fear failure the most, when they, in fact, sabotage their own opportunities for success. Develops sophisticated understanding of attitudes, behaviors and interpersonal skills as the motivator to convert failures into bigger successes.

7. **Body of Knowledge**—With time, seasoning, leadership development and a career track record, one experiences repeated successes and failures. Develops better understanding of cause-effect ratios. Develops profound insights and lifelong perspectives into the teachings of success and failure (learning three times more from failures than success).

Understanding and Comprehending Failures

Failing to meet objectives and believing that you have failed in life and work are two different perspectives. I reviewed a 20-year segment of my career, working with professionals who helped me to formally analyze. From a "time and motion" perspective, we found that considerable time was wasted on the wrong projects, non-supportive work environments, the wrong mix of clients and conditions for providing advise-counsel.

Through the review, I learned that my "failures" at time-intensive projects shined light on what I was better suited to do: generate wisdom and foster the enthusiasm for top executives to see things differently. A seeming failure to manage time and motion was ultimately a success in the many revelations that occurred.

My frustrations with menial "busy work" projects (just to produce billings and pay the salaries of other people) crystallized into insightful recollections, such as the one you are now reading. From a value perspective, among the wasted hours (due-diligence administrative work) were gems of wisdom that I later abstracted and polished into a series of books. The light bulb would not have shined if I hadn't learned the lessons through experience.

We learn from the failures of all people and organizations around us. Looking in the third person enables self-reflection. How would we handle things if they happened to us? Playing "what if" helps us think through situations and be better prepared to handle when they arise.

Why We Must Fail in Order to Succeed

Learning the stumbling blocks of failure prepares one to attain true success. Fear is the biggest contributor to failure, and it can be a motivator for success. You cannot make problems go away, simply by ignoring that they exist.

Everybody fails at things for which they are not suited. The process of learning what one is best suited to do is not a failure…it is a great success. Learn from the best and the worst. People who make the biggest bungling mistakes are showing you pitfalls to avoid.

Many of us make the same mistakes over and over again. That is to be expected and teaches us volumes, preparing us for success. There is no plan that is fool-proof. One plans, learns, reviews and plans further.

One learns three times more from failure than success. One learns three times more clearly when witnessing and analyzing the failures of others they know or have followed. History teaches us about cycles, trends, misapplications of resources, wrong approaches and vacuums of thought. People must apply history to their own lives-situations. If we document our own successes, then these case studies will make us more successful in the future.

Things we do that set us up for failure include:

- Remembering things like they once were, trying to recreate as we believe they were.
- Doing things purely for creative fulfillment…without comprehending the realities.
- Thinking that business acquaintances really care about us as human beings.
- Expecting that others will treat us as fairly as we treat them.
- Hoping that volunteer contributions to the community will be repaid in business referrals.

Fear is the biggest contributor to failure, and it can be a motivator for success. I use FEAR as an acronym for Find Excellence After Reflection. We are just as afraid of the things we don't know as the things in front of us. Most unknown fears turn out to not be as we had imagined.

Opportunists trade and capitalize upon fear. Several professions exist to help people get a grip on their fears. Those trying to sell will tell people what they want to hear or portray the product as being in their best interest. Some people and organizations turn others' fears into propaganda weapons for their own agendas (open or hidden). Some people and organizations take great delight in capitalizing upon the fears of others.

People are most afraid of what they don't understand. If a person scares easily, so will his neighbor. Both can know it, but they're more scared that each other will see it. After awhile, fearful people feel manipulated by others and don't know who to trust.

It is difficult to figure how people will behave when the chips are down. The definition of bravery is a person who is scared but still does what he-she has to.

Learning from Mistakes Which I Have Made in Business

Personal Abilities, Talents
- Making the same mistakes more than twice, without studying the mitigating factors.
- Taking incidents out of context and mis-diagnosing situations.
- Rationalizing occurrences, after the fact.
- Appearing self-contained, therefore precluding others from wanting to help me.
- Inability to cultivate other people's support of me at the times that I needed it most.

Resources
- Attempting projects without the proper resources to do the job well.
- Not knowing people with sufficient pull and power. Thinking that friends would help introduce me or help network to key influential persons.
- Failure to effective networking techniques early enough in my career path.
- Inability to finely develop the powers of people participating in the networking process.

Other People

- Accepting people at their words without questioning.
- Showing proper respect to other people and assuming that they would show or were capable of showing comparable respect to others.
- Doing favors for others without asking anything in return...if I expected quid pro quo at a later time. Not telling people what I wanted and then being disappointed that they did not read minds or deliver favors of their own volition.
- Befriending people who were too needy, always taking without offering to reciprocate. Continuing to feed their needs, making it.a one-way relationship.
- Picking the wrong causes to champion at the wrong times and with insufficient resources.
- Working with the false assumption that people want and need comparable things. Incorrectly assuming that all would pursue their agendas fairly. A better understanding of personality types, human motivations and behavioral factors would have provided insight to handle situations on a customized basis.
- Offering highly creative ideas and brain power to those who could not grasp their brilliance, especially to those who were fishing for free ideas they could then market as their own.

Circumstances Beyond My Control

- Working with equipment, resources and people from a source without my standards of quality control...trying to make the best of bad situations.
- Changing trends, upon which I could not capitalize but which others could.

Mis-Calculations

- Incorrectly estimating the time and resources necessary to do something well.
- Getting blindsided because I did not do enough research.

- Failure to plan sufficiently ahead, at the right times.
- Setting sights too low. Not thinking big enough.

Timing
- Offering advice before it was solicited.
- Feeling pressured to offer solutions before diagnosing situations properly.
- Not thinking of enough angles and possibilities sooner.

Marketplace-External Factors
- Not reading the opportunities soon enough.
- Not being able to spot, create or capitalize upon emerging trends at their beginnings.

Stages of Mistakes:
1. Discovering errors (sensory-motor, sounds-language and logical selection).
2. Recognizing mistakes.
3. Separating successful elements from failures we do not need to duplicate.
4. Learning from mistakes.
5. Learning from success.
6. Mentoring yourself and others toward a higher stream of knowledge.
7. The wisdom that comes from making mistakes, comprehending their outcomes, and developing a knowledge base to achieve success.

Gradations of Failing:
- Not seeing the warning signs.
- Distinguishing among friends, enemies and the majority group, those who could care less about you but who will tap whatever resources available to get their needs met.
- Never seeing victories as quite enough.
- Feeling that someone else wins when you fail.
- Repeating self-defeating behaviors.
- Holding unrealistic views.

- Thinking that you never fail…that failing is for other people and organizations.

Gradations of Learning from Mistakes:

- Distance one's self from one's actions.
- Become self-critical.
- Recognize that actions have consequences.
- Begin accepting responsibility for the consequences.
- Learn how to eliminate errors.
- Learn how to learn from mistakes.
- Accept fallibility, become open to critical feedback and modify actions accordingly.

Gradations of Success (learning from failures)

1. **How "Success" is Overrated.** Ask various people their definitions of success, and you get many definitions: wealth, power, creativity, leadership, perks, respect, insight, etc. Holding realistic views of success will make you more successful. Unrealistic dreamers set themselves up for failure.
2. **Never Stop Paying Dues.** Realize that success is earned and is a progression.
3. **The In-Between Zone.** Getting the most from the ordinary. Learning from every step in between.
4. **Put Accurate Labels on Human Transactions.** Learn what makes other people tick. Frame situations in a win-win mode. Study behavioral styles.
5. **Deal with Fear and Turn it to Your Advantage.** Studying the subtleties and sophistications of learning, perceiving and feeling is the mark of maturity. "I failed. Therefore, I learned." Knowledge and perspective equate to success.
6. **Continually Shifting and Updating Your Perspectives.** How Quickly Things Change. Relish change. Understand how you turn things around.
7. **Critical Factors of Success.** Study the dynamics of (1) People who just want to get by. (2) Organizations which don't really know why they exist. (3) People who think they're taking short cuts to get riches the fast way. (4) Situations which demand failure before success can be realized. (5) Situations which prevent true success from ever being attained.

Quotes About Failure and Success

"To do a great right, do a little wrong."
— **William Shakespeare**

"The only one who makes no mistakes is one who never does anything."
— **Theodore Roosevelt**

"A life spent in making mistakes is not more honorable
but more useful than a life spent doing nothing."
— **George Bernard Shaw**

"Tis better to have loved and lost than never to have lost at all."
— **Samuel Butler**

"A miss is as good as a mile."
— Proverb

"There's no success like failure."
— **Bob Dylan**

"That's life. That's what the people say. You're flying high in
April…shot down in May. Each time I find myself flat on my
face, I pick myself up and get back in the race. That's life. I can't
deny it. I thought of quitting, but my heart ain't gonna buy it."
— **Frank Sinatra** (lyrics to the song,
"That's Life," authors **D. Kay-K. Gordon**) (1966)

"Well, back to the old drawing board."
— **Peter Arno**, 20th Century cartoonist

"The crime is not to avoid failure. The crime is not to give triumph a chance."
— **Huw Wheldon**, 20th Century British broadcaster

*"There's a little bit of success in every failure
and a little bit of failure in every success."*
— **O. Henry**, short story writer

"The only thing we have to fear is fear itself."
— **Franklin D. Roosevelt** (1933)

*"You may take the most gallant sailor, the most intrepid
airman, or the most audacious soldier. Put them at a table
together. What do you get? The sum of their fears."*
— **Winston Churchill**

*"To fight a bull when you are not scared is nothing. To
not fight a bull when you are scared is nothing. But, to
fight a bull when you are scared, that is something."*
— **Manolete**, bullfighter

*"The reasonable man adapts himself to the world. The
unreasonable man persists in trying to adapt the world to himself.
Therefore, all progress depends on the unreasonable man."*
— **George Bernard Shaw**

"Fear has many eyes and can see things underground."
— **Cervantes, Don Quixote**

*"We are like dwarves upon the shoulders of giants,
and so able to see more and farther than the ancients."*
— **Bernard of Chartres**

"People only see what they are prepared to see."
— **Ralph Waldo Emerson** (1863)

"A moment's insight is worth a life's experience."
— **Oliver Wendell Holmes**

"A danger foreseen is half avoided."
— **Thomas Fuller**

"Two men look out through the same bars.
One sees the mud, and one the stars."
— **Frederick Langbridge**

7 Benefits Stemming from Failure

1. **Immediate Feedback.** It is far better to succeed or fail…being stuck in that great middle on uncertainty doesn't give much feedback. Not knowing where we're going or how we're doing causes us to make many more mistakes.

2. **Starting Over.** When you get the chance to try new things or do things new ways, it serves to re-level the playing field. Without being bogged down by systems and processes that haven't worked, you can create as you go. Starting over is difficult for most people to do. After they've done it, they feel richer for the experience, though knowing of riches on the front end doesn't make starting over any easier.

3. **Learn What Not to Do Next Time.** Gives you a clear frame of reference, assuming that you clearly understand factors behind the failure, rather than blaming them on someone else.

4. **How the Pendulum Swings.** One succeeds much more than one fails. By studying swings of the pendulum (likelihoods of failures), one better understands their progress.

5. **Failures Make the Best Case Studies.** When the facts and fallacies are studied, they are less likely to be replicated in the future. Case studies of success and failure form the basis for training, Strategic Planning, Continuous Quality Improvement, Visioning, Futurism and other sophisticated business practices.

6. **Lessons Learned But Not Soon Forgotten.** One learns three times more from failures than success. One succeeds 5-9 times more often than one fails (depending upon the individual's attitude, resources and abilities to develop insights).

7. **Qualities of Achievements.** The more sophisticated the understanding of failures and their factors, the more successful in business and life the person-organization will be.

Chapter 25

ETHICS, GOVERNANCE AND CORPORATE SUSTAINABILITY

T he term Corporate Responsibility is being bandied about in many out-of-context terms. It is important to look at the whole of business, rather than at the micro-niche parts. Depending upon whose definition of Corporate Responsibility we hear, it could currently symbolize:

- Political agendas for both parties in upcoming elections.
- Committee hearings by Congress.
- Brief moments of glory for whistle-blowers and watchdog groups.
- A total obsession with accounting (which only occupies 2% of a company's Big Picture).
- Media circuses, focusing upon selective business issues but not the Big Picture.
- Opportunities for non-business experts to opine and mandate behaviors.

In reality, Ethics has long been with us., though some companies did not observe, designate or prioritize it Discussions about ethics in business come from the shadows when crises of magnitude present themselves. Also in reality, companies will continue to make catastrophic blurs in public confidence unless their eyes are widely opened.

In order to succeed and thrive in modern society, all private and public sector entities must live by codes of ethics. In an era that encompasses mistrust of business, uncertainties about the economy and growing disillusionment within society's structure, it is vital for every organization to determine, analyze, fine-tune and communicate their value systems.

In my opinion, Ethics is more than just a statement that a committee whips together. It is more than a slogan or rehash of a Mission Statement. It is an ongoing dialog that companies have with themselves. It is important to teach business domestically and internationally that:

1. We must understand how to use power and influence for positive change.
2. How we meet corporate objectives is as important as the objectives themselves.
3. Ethics and profits are not conflicting goals.
4. Unethical dealings for short-term gain do not pay off ultimately.
5. Good judgment comes from experience, which, in turn comes from bad judgment.
6. Business must be receptive—not combative—to differing opinions.
7. Change is 90% beneficial. We must learn to benefit from change management, not to become victims of it.

Ethics relates to every stage in the evolution of a business, leadership development, mentoring and creative ways of doing business. It is an understanding how and why any organization remains standing and growing, instead of continuing to look at micro-niche parts.

Diplomacy and Pro-Active Measures

Integrity is personal and professional. It is about more than the contents of a financial report. It bespeaks to every aspect of the way in which we do business. Integrity requires consistency and the enlightened self-interest of doing a better job.

Financial statements by themselves cannot nor ever were intended to determine company value. The enlightened company must be structured, plan and benchmark according to all seven categories on my trademarked Business Tree™: core business, running the business, financial, people, business development, Body of Knowledge (interaction of each part to the other and to the whole) and The Big Picture (who the organization really is, where it is going and how it will successfully get there).

One need not fear business nor think ill of it because of the recent corporate scandals. One need not fear globalization and expansion of business because of economic recessions. It is during the downturns that strong, committed and ethical businesses renew their energies to move forward. The good apples polish their luster in such ways as to distance from the few bad apples.

Mandated reforms cannot take the place of personal responsibility, company ethics programs and industry standards that uphold values. No piece of legislation cannot cause sweeping actions overnight.

Taking the Ethical High Road, Reading the Signs

Ethics means operating a business in ways that meet or exceed the ethical, legal, commercial and public expectations that society has of business. This is a comprehensive set of strategies, methodologies, policies, practices and programs that are integrated throughout business operations, supported and rewarded by top management.

The growth of corporate responsibility as an issue and a mandate stems from several events and trends:

- Changing expectations of stakeholders regarding business.
- Government's reduced role in a deregulated era.
- Increased customer interest and pressure.
- Supply chain responsibility in the age of collaborations, outsourcing and partnering.
- Growing investor insistence upon accountability.
- Intensively competitive labor markets.
- Voiced concerns by activist organizations.
- Demands for increased communication and disclosure.
- Emerging issues that widen the scope of business.
- Identification of new pockets of stakeholders.

The value of corporate responsibility can be measured in quantitative and qualitative ways. Companies have experienced bottom-line benefits, including improved financial performance, reduced operating costs, access to capital, increased sales and customer loyalty, positive reactions to brand image and reputation, heightened productivity, employee commitments to quality, empowered loyal workforces and reduced regulatory oversight.

Corporate Social Responsibility is concerned with treating stakeholders of the company ethically or in a socially responsible manner. Consequently, behaving socially responsibly will increase the human development of stakeholders both within and outside the corporation.

Corporate Sustainability aligns an organization's products and services with stakeholder expectations, thereby adding economic, environmental and social value. This looks at how good companies become better.

Corporate Governance constitutes a balance between economic and social goals and between individual and community goals. The corporate governance framework is there to encourage the efficient use of resources and equally to require accountability for community stewardship of those resources.

Ethical priorities for your company in the New Order of Business may likely be addressed in the event that you:

- Create a corporate code of ethics.
- Create the role of Corporate Ethics Officer.
- Learn to identify issues involved in making corporate ethical decisions.
- Recognize the considerations in the analysis and resolution of ethical dilemmas.
- Apply ethical rules and guidelines toward corporate workplace situations.
- Refine your company's complaint process and investigation procedures.
- Adjudicate employee conduct arising under the corporate Code of Ethics.
- Widen the sensitivity toward issues which may lead toward legal liabilities.
- Embrace standard ethical reporting and compliance procedures.
- Increase the frequency of corporate and personal ethical judgments and decisions.

Burst Bubbles, Being Refilled

Perception is reality. It is no longer sufficient to pay lip service to ethical issues, such as investor protection, consumer accountability, issues management, protecting the environment and diversity. Concern must be demonstrated. The public needs to see action on every company's part. The same holds true for public sector institutions.

Credibility is formed by the ability to impact all other issues. Total quality means that we must communicate cross-culturally. Find out what people need to know, when they need it and then deliver it.

Organizations who fail to address ethical issues of the day are endangered species. Whatever the public expects of companies, then those companies should expect the same of themselves. My concerns revolve around these areas:

1. **Society that Produced the Business Scandals.** If we decry the scandals and wrong doing, then modern society must accept our roles in letting them happen.

Too many artificial measurements abound and are based upon flash, sizzle and hucksterism. Having the weekend movie box office grosses for movies on TV and in newspapers every Monday is bogus. Momentary box office grosses are not accurate measures of a film's worth. So much coverage of sales volumes leads media pundits to use ludicrous terms like "X knocked off Y this weekend." When the public hears that misleading statements, they start talking that way too. The public consciousness needs to get away from teasers and slogans.

Anybody who hangs their hats on changeable, temporary rankings is headed for a fall. Top rankings as the ultimate measure of worth and value lead to cottage industries that manipulate the numbers. Bogus research gets purchased. Inflated production reports, unrealistic market shares and improvement quotes receive the spin of those vested in perpetuating the myths. Projecting futures by past momentary successes will escalate the sweepstakes mentality. As long as the media keeps posting movie box office receipts as the only measure of films' standing, then films will be made to match those criteria.

Business has turned into a smoke and mirrors aura. When perceptions matter more than realities and hype more than substance, then the stakes keep escalating to a frenzy. They parlayed the hype to the media, who conveyed to the public, who re-conveyed to each other via idol chatter. The buzz created an unrealistic stock marketed, populated by get-rich-quick day traders.

The frenzy for slogans and clever quips has anointed the word "solutions" into the business lexicon. Solutions are vendor commodities that appeal to purchasers who don't know any better. We keep investing in technology, rather than developing "human intelligence." We buy "solutions" from providers rather than address real, systemic and long-term challenges and opportunities for the company.

The computer consulting industry gave us the Y2K event in 1999, a fever frenzy that was designed to generate billings for consulting, training and sales of technology. American business spent more than $600 billion on Y2K consulting, paying for it by cutting such more important activities as strategic planning, training, employee compensation and marketing. Research shows that 91-99% of those problems never would have occurred. The vendors perpetuated the spin that their work kept the problems from occurring, with unsuspecting buyers believing and perpetuating the justifications.

2. **Accounting.** Too much emphasis and control of business has been placed in the hands of accountants. Their focus is micro-niche (only about 2% of the Big Picture of business), and to turn over all framing of business issues to accountants is shortsighted. Large accounting firms have influenced the system in their favor. Public companies must be audited by one of them, thus creating as monopoly situation that cuts qualified mid-sized and local accounting firms out of public company work.

Accountants see business through the financial dimension. To pick most the top management from the financial ranks tends to perpetuate the myopic viewpoint. Accounting firms are notorious at not wanting to collaborate with other consultants and professional disciplines. By not allowing other perspectives on their radars and controlling the business model in their favor, a continuum of sameness has occurred. It will continue to occur until business widens its scope and perspective.

3. **CEOs.** Too much romanticism has been placed upon the term CEO by others who want to be rewarded by them. No Chief Executive Officer by

himself or herself can make or break a company. They need codependents in order to do damage. The company that lays down all the gold to one CEO in hopes of magical results is inviting being ripped off.

Conversely, as a reaction to corporate scandals the term CEO is currently in disfavor. The public decries CEOs for the same reasons that we canonize them. People envy the power, status and wealth and cannot fathom the endless behind-the-scenes work conducted by reputable CEOs and management teams.

Most CEOs are not adequately groomed for their roles as company role model and leader. They come from the ranks of core business or financial, without proper exposure to other facets that make a winning company. Thus, they surround themselves with like minds or yes-men. Many CEOs do not take counsel of qualified experts, thus remaining isolated, partially-focused and lonely at the top.

A CEO is only as good as the team that he-she leads. A top CEO fulfills roles and responsibilities across every business unit. The CEO must amass people skills, marketing savvy, planning expertise, quality orientation, leadership tenets, marketplace championing and much more. The days of the internal, bottom-line-only-focused CEO are long obsolete.

4. **Boards of Directors.** Companies must hold boards of directors, management teams, mid-manager ranks and line directors more accountable. These folks expect financial rewards and must be more accountable. They must work in collaboration with the CEO, not as pawns of his-her ideology. Chapter 10 covered the dynamics of board service and the myriad of responsibilities that good directors undertake.

Widening the Frame of Business Reference

Ethics is the science of morals, rightness and obligations in human affairs. Institutions must conduct many activities that impact their general welfare. Ethical issues go beyond nice rhetoric and must encompass duties, principles, values, processes, responsibilities and governing methodologies.

Organizations who fail to address ethical issues of the day are endangered species. Whatever the public expects of companies, then those companies should expect the same of themselves.

The Ethics Statement must be more than a terse branding slogan. Like the Mission Statement in the Strategic Plan, it is the amalgamation of careful thought, weighed insights and tests for fairness and durability. The Ethics Statement must be a part of the Strategic Plan, as are such other fundamental statements covering customer-focused management, diversity, valuing stakeholders, quality management and an empowered workforce.

Every organization differs in how it will implement Corporate Responsibility and Ethics programs. The differences are factored by the company's size, sector, culture and the commitment of its leadership. Some companies focus on a single area of operation. The Code of Ethics may include Fundamental Canons, Rules of Practice and Professional Obligations.

Business ethics encompass much more than accounting fraud and the publicly stated values of stocks. Ethics should be attached to many other important areas of business. Elements in the Ethics internal company review, which could subsequently be addressed in the full ethics plan, may include:

- Accountability by all top managers.
- Accountability by all mid-managers.
- Accountability by all board members.
- Fair practices regarding collaborators, suppliers and vendors.
- Codes of conduct, standards and guidelines.
- Security issues.
- Financial reporting, accounting and disclosures.
- Statement of assets.
- Professional development, training and education goals.
- Performance reviews.
- Workplace issues.
- Diversity.
- Benchmarks of progress.
- Marketplace activities, competition and intelligence.
- Community investment.
- The environment.
- Strategic management.
- Corporate welfare.

- Corporate governance.
- Strategic planning.
- Corporate citizenship.
- Accounting principles.
- Auditing standards.
- Compilation and review standards.
- Technical standards.
- Reputation assurance.
- Social accountability.
- Compliance with all applicable laws (to the letter and spirit).
- Meet and exceed guidelines of regulators.
- Protection of purchasers of equipment and systems.
- Reliable treatment of vendors, suppliers and partners.
- Treat as confidential all information learned about the business of a customer.
- Full disclosures.
- Responsible advertising, promotions and public statements about the company.
- Reliable representations about products and services.
- Accurate representation of experience and capabilities of employees and agents.
- Voluntary code of ethics.
- Commitment to integrity.
- Value of empowered employees.
- Respect for the environment.
- Corporate leadership style.
- Reliability.
- Quality.
- Flexibility.
- Consistency.
- Integrity, objectivity and independence.
- Confidentiality.
- Professional competence.
- Position within the company's own industry.
- The company's Visioning efforts for the future.

The corporate ethics program may include a code of ethics, training for employees for ethical behaviors, a means for communicating with employees, reporting mechanism, audit system, investigation system, compliance strategy, prevention strategy and integrity strategy. The program seeks to create conditions that support the right actions. It communicates the values and vision of the organization. It aligns the standards of employees with those of the organization The program relies upon the entire management team, not just the legal and compliance personnel.

A formal and well documented corporate ethics program will prevent ethical misconduct, monetary losses and losses to reputation. If communicated well, it may breed customer trust. In fact, I highly recommend using executive summaries of the ethics program as a corporate communications tool. The sending of the Ethics Statement to customers, suppliers, regulators and other stakeholders demonstrates the extra length to which the company goes to become a model. It becomes a good marketing mailing, and it's the right thing to do.

As part of strategic planning, corporate ethics helps the organization to adapt to rapid change, regulatory changes, mergers and global competition. It helps to manage relations with stakeholders. It enlightens partners and suppliers about a company's own standards. It reassures other stakeholders as to the company's intent.

Quotes on Ethics

"The end must justify the means."
— **Matthew Prior**

"If I am not what I say I am, then you are not what you think you are."
— Novelist **James Baldwin**

"What is moral is what you feel good after.
What is immoral is what you feel bad after."
— **Ernest Hemingway**

*"Virtue is not always amiable. The happiness
of man, as well as his dignity, consists in virtue."*
— **President John Adams** (1779)

"Very often, our virtues are only vices in disguise."
— **La Rochefougauld**

"Always do right. This will gratify some people and astonish the rest."
— **Mark Twain** (1901)

"The laugh is always on the loser."
— German proverb

"The function of wisdom is discriminating between good and evil."
— **Cicero**

*"Ethical axioms are found and tested not very differently from
the axioms of science. Truth is what stands the test of experience."*
— **Albert Einstein**

*"The humblest citizen in all of the land, when clad in the armor
of a righteous cause, is stronger than all the hosts of error."*
— **William Jennings Bryan**

*"We can act as if there were a God; feel as if we were free;
consider nature as if she were full of special designs; lay
plans as if we were to be immortal; and we find then that
these words do make a genuine difference in our moral life."*
— **William James**

"We must learn to distinguish morality from moralizing."
— **Henry Kissinger**

Chapter 26

AMERICA'S CITIES IN TRANSITION

Case Studies on the Travel and Tourism Industries

I have conducted management assessments for many industries and companies. This is a representative growth strategies assessment, conducted on behalf of travel and tourism industries. It is indicative of the way in which overviews and strategies are developed with a Big Picture of Business approach.

100 years ago, less than 5% of the American population lived and worked in large cities. Most people were still rural and agriculturalists. The city was still an oasis in the rural universe. The rural population was still the majority in the industrialized countries of Europe.

At the end of World War II, one-fourth of the American population and 60% of the Japanese population were still rural. Today, in both countries, that has shrunk to less than five percent and still shrinking.

The key to development of cities is the sense of community. In rural areas, there is a strong sense of community. Rural areas are thought of as idyllic. Yet, the reality is somewhat different. The rural community is often coercive and intrusive.

For centuries, the dream of rural people was to escape into the city. An old German proverb from the 11th Century said "Stadtluft Macht Frei" ("city air sets you free"). The serf who escaped to the city became a free man and a citizen. China and India are still dominantly rural, and the people cannot wait to move to the cities, where the jobs are.

What made the city also created its seamier aspects. Anonymity, centers of culture, urban sprawl, stress and diversity all flourished and conflicted. Human beings need a sense of community, for constructive activities and positive outcomes. Otherwise, there will be chaos, crime and other dangers.

No business can give security to all human beings. The "lifetime employment" of the Japanese is proving to be delusional. The tenets of American unions are not applicable to the modern age of information and entrepreneurial societies. The private sector has become more a way to make a living than a way to make a life. The social sector must create and sustain what we now need. Non-profit organizations fulfill the need for community stewardship.

Even in the digital era of global business, geography still matters. What has changed are the rules governing geography and what constitutes successful locations in which to do business.

America uses its space very unevenly. 80% of the population lives on 2% of the land. The vast majority now live and work in high-density areas. There are more than 50 cities whose Metropolitan Areas contain populations in excess of one million. They account for one-half of the nation's total population. In a dozen of those cases, the cities have sprawled so much that they blended into each other as "megalopolises." Yet, the word "urban" has become a code word for poverty, crime, violence, unemployment and decay. These same cities also have factors of culture, community involvement and hope for the future.

Characteristics of cities in stagnation and decline include:

- The harmony trap.
- Competing use of urban space among professionals.
- Growing social polarization in society, creating hyper-ghettos.
- Fiefdoms and feuding factions.
- Refusal to change.

- Constantly trying to maintain past accomplishments and replace with components that resemble the past.
- The working poor condition.
- Workplace illiteracy.
- Poverty and socio-economic exclusion.
- Growth of racism, violence and crime.

Most large urban areas have these characteristics:

- Increasingly becoming more chaotic.
- In chaos, there are patterns.
- Economic barriers.
- Racial barriers.
- Walls separating lifestyles, classes or ideologies.
- The homeless and unemployed.

The growth of specific regions depends upon the decisions of entrepreneurs and workers to locate there. These individuals are known as "consumers of place." The more that technology frees us of past affiliations, the greater is the need for alternative places to make themselves enviable. Firms are looking for communities that have good quality of life, low taxes and the room for growth.

Small compact cities such as Denver, San Francisco, Boston and Seattle exemplify a modern resurgence in urban life. They enjoy low vacancy rates, high education levels for workers and the highest degree of Internet penetration.

Some sections of New York, Chicago and Los Angeles are enjoying growth spurts, while other sectors of the same cities are dying. East Los Angeles has enjoyed a resurgence in a district known as Toytown, where a myriad of Asian dialects are spoken. Of the five boroughs of New York City, Manhattan accounts for 80% of the collective payrolls,

The Economic City can be divided into these parts:

- The controlling city as the site of big decisions.
- The city of advanced services.
- The city of direct production.

- The sections with luxury housing.
- The gentrified city, occupied by professional groups.
- Hospitality industries.
- The suburban city.
- The abandoned city.
- The city of unskilled work and informal production.
- Service industries.

Other cities which were once the paragons of the industrial age are now marginalized and decaying in the New Order of business. These include Detroit, Newark, Pittsburgh, Baltimore and St. Louis. Some cities have suffered the decimation of major industries, such as auto manufacturing in Detroit, tobacco industries in Virginia, shipbuilding in Baltimore and textiles around Boston.

Decline in older U.S. cities has been exacerbated by the migration of corporate business and contracts out of the country. This has succeeded in leaving legacies of abandoned shopping districts, vacant buildings, reduced tax bases, ravaged neighborhoods and broken people across the country.

While the large cities are still growing, there has been a trend toward urban flight over the past 60 years in America. Over the last 40 years, 15 of the top 25 cities have lost four million people, while the total population has risen by 60 million.

While vertical cities have been losing population, mid-sized horizontal cities with high levels of educated workers have emerged as production centers in the technology age. These include Irvine, California; Austin, Texas; Chandler, Arizona; Boise, Idaho; Salt Lake City, Utah, and Raleigh-Durham, North Carolina.

Companies prefer these regions for a variety of reasons, including skilled labor, lack of distractions, low crime rates, advantageous taxation situations and the promise of lifestyle for company executives. This author grew up in Austin, Texas, and can remember when the population was 50,000. Today, the Austin population nears one million. Tiny Fort Collins, Colorado, mushroomed from 30,000 to more than 200,000, over a five-year growth spurt.

Suburbs have changed their face since they were built in the1950s and 1960s. Inner city redevelopments have attracted cultural, affluent and young skilled workers.

Even the hinterlands are attracting business, commerce, wealth and prominence. These communities include Boulder, Colorado; Santa Clara, California; Park City, Utah; Jackson Hole, Wyoming; Silicon Valley, California; and Fort Collins, Colorado.

Other cities represent grounds for rebirths because they have large immigration populations, many of whom are knowledge workers. These include Houston, Los Angeles, Dallas, San Jose, Miami, Phoenix, Philadelphia, Atlanta and San Diego. The economies of these regions display powerful opportunities to communicate, network, do business and enjoy community life. The energy and work ethics of immigrants tend to inject further vitality into these communities. These formerly unattached new urbanities constitute the critical new blood for the post-industrial urban economy.

The Market for Travel and Tourism

Travel & Tourism is one of the world's largest industries, accounting for more than 200 million jobs worldwide and 10% of the world's Gross Domestic Product. It is a $3 trillion industry, accounting for 7.5% of capital investment in the world.

Travel & Tourism is a great source of economics to developing nations. Last year, Germans took 65 million trips abroad. Americans took 47 million trips abroad. Brits took 34 million trips abroad.

The tourist is a moving target, seeking distractions from the familiar. Tourism is divided into well-defined circuits, locales and attractions. Mass tourism involves movement of people, and there is an increase in demand. Possessing many offerings by suppliers, travel and commerce are inextricably linked.

Cities are sold to potential customers. If the infrastructure that nourishes tourists does not exist, it must be constructed. In resort cities (Cancun, Las Vegas), infrastructure is woven anew. Some cities have no past and owe it all to the attractions.

Cities must do more than shape the images. They must adapt the product. They must transform themselves into tourism business. Tourism operators must distinguish among types of tourists and their motivations for coming. We will continue to see standardization of the tourism industry globally.

In conducting community planning for future survival and growth, we submit the following questions:

- What are special components of the tourist community?
- How much variation is there?
- How do we evaluate the effects of tourism on the local population?
- How does tourism fit into economic and development and your city's quality of life?
- In what ways do citizens benefit from tourism amenities?
- How equitable is the access to those amenities?
- Does tourism maintain or undermine the local culture?
- How open is the tourism industry to new participants?
- Does the tourism industry collaborate with other businesses?
- Is it a more of a closed fortress than it used to be?
- How respectful is the relationship between tourism and other businesses?

Port and industrial cities that have declined now try to weave tourism into a fabricated past. Cities that have survived see waterfronts and attractions complimenting the city itself. Some cities absorb tourists seamlessly: New York, San Francisco, Boston. Other cities have evolved into Festival marketplaces:

Boston, Harbortown
Milwaukee, Grand Avenue
Philadelphia, Market Street East
Salt Lake City, Trolley Square
San Diego, Horton Plaza
St. Louis, Union Station
New York, South Street Seaport
Baltimore, Harborplace
Upper Michigan, Bavarian Village
Ontario, African Safari Lion Park

Some cities are known as convention meccas: Kansas City, San Diego, Phoenix. Others have fallen short of projections. Here is a ranking of the top convention cities:

1. New York
2. Chicago

3. Atlanta
4. Las Vegas
5. Dallas
6. Los Angeles
7. Anaheim
8. San Francisco
9. New Orleans
10. Boston
11. Detroit
12. Kansas City
13. Philadelphia
14. Indianapolis
15. Houston
16. St. Louis
17. Atlantic City
18. Columbus
19. Minneapolis
20. San Antonio

In tandem with promoting tourism, cities have funded arts districts, sports complexes and historical districts. This is complimented by real estate developments, such as Renaissance Center in downtown Detroit. In the 1970s, Flint, Michigan, tried to build a tourism industry. Rather than project a positive image, it came across as sad and pathetic. Its future was tied to the industrial image and fortune losses of General Motors.

Few venues had gambling facilities until the early 1980s. In 1978, Atlantic City broke the stronghold by Las Vegas, which itself had risen from the ashes of a 1940s gambling industry in Galveston.

In Las Vegas, the Flamingo was opened by gangster Bugsy Siegel in December, 1946. Individuals owned casinos in the first two decades. With Howard Hughes in 1967, corporations began taking control of hotel resorts and casinos. Many corporations built other casinos around the world. There was a family-friendly era in Vegas in the 1990s but was deemed as unprofitable. The convention trade drives modern Las Vegas. Modern hotels are thematic cities. 45% of the Nevada employment is in the service industry, compared with 27% nationally.

The social costs of tourism include traffic, pollution, poverty, crime and other inequities. Las Vegas experiences low living standards for most employees. Little of the wealth is distributed back into the community, save jobs. The city is vulnerable to competition from numerous gambling venues throughout the U.S.

Other cities to have embraced gaming include Kansas City, St. Louis, Chicago and selected locations in Colorado. The first casino in New Orleans (1992) went into bankruptcy.

World Tourism is expanding rapidly. Canada and Mexico have large industries. Other nations which are aggressively developing World Tourism include Prague, Jerusalem, Singapore, Southeast Asia, Dubai, Barbados, Indonesia and Third World Tourism. The Middle East is poised to develop travel.

Variables in the classification of tourism include context, types of facilities, location, developers/ownership and planning processes. Also, how a tourism industry is developed, markets and marketing, reinvestment, quality controls, impact, spin-off community benefits and coalitions/collaborations.

These are the different types of tourism:

- Pleasure vacations.
- Business tourism.
- Industrial tourism.
- Educational tourism.
- Sensual pleasure tourism.
- Activity tourism.
- Special interest group tourism.
- Cultural tourism.
- Health tourism.
- Family tourism.
- Community tourism.
- Gifts and incentive tourism.
- Civic promotional tourism.

Visioning for Communities

These are characteristics of cities on the threshold of a new era:

- Common goals.
- Ethics, governance and value systems.
- Strategic Planning and Visioning.
- The whole and the parts establish distinguished identities.
- Identification with local urban areas (regional, nationally, internationally).
- Achieving balance, rather than replacing something else.
- Institutional learning process.
- Support systems for promoting communities and citizens' organizations.
- Community stewardship and contributions toward the more global good.
- Competition.
- Risk.
- Interdependence.

And then, there are the hospitality venues of Nashville, Tennessee; Orlando, Florida; Branson, Missouri, and Las Vegas, Nevada. All put formerly small towns on the international map by taking planned community status and marketing to much wider audiences.

As commerce becomes more dependent upon non-material products, the characteristics on intellectualism, independence and the ability to construct economic relationships makes the cities of the future more attractive. Where urban culture meets the frontiers of commerce, then the opportunities will build the communities.

Increasingly, cities are pursuing aggressive Economic Development programs. They are trying to attract enterprises. Our society is presently undergoing social restructuring of labor markets. This is marked by these developments:

- Growth of high-skilled occupations.
- Growth of semi-skilled occupations.
- Precarious and flexible employment conditions.
- Formal and informal economies.
- Growing job migration.

Changes in labor markets prompted by globalization are producing new career models, recruitment patterns, job environments and a new set of values. The new class of service providers requires career-oriented, well-educated people who are obliged to perform well and to keep growing as professionals.

The metropolis of the future will be a geographical intersection for production, finance and control in an increasingly trans-national economic organization. This metropolis must adopt the World City hypothesis. In it, the way in which this city integrates into the global economic system will determine its economic, social, spatial and structural developments.

Core values of thriving communities include:

- Community as a place or turf.
- Community as shared ideals and expectations.
- Community as a network of social allegiances and ties.
- Community as a collective framework.
- Community as reflecting diversity.
- Community as pursuing the common good.

Characteristics of successful planned communities include:

- A place to come together.
- Character of the city.
- Health of the city.
- Economic development.
- Interaction with other cities…functionality in the Global Village.

Challenges, Trends and Opportunities for Cities

Challenges in visioning and strategizing municipal planned growth include:

- Spaces and circulation.
- Functions and activities.
- Corporate identity, realities and perceptions.
- Growth strategies program.
- Stakeholder relations.

- Spirit of place, corporate culture.
- Governing organization.

Trends which cities must address include:

- There is a growing demand for locations of production, out of congested urban settings.
- The new-time organization of the city of the future is based upon flexible working and production times. It will be a 24-hour society.
- There will be an elimination of low value, low-yield space. It will be replaced by a high-value and highly profitable headquarters economy.
- Of all the potential groups of external cooperation partners, the one that innovative companies cooperate with most is that of research establishments within their own region.
- Establishing the community's prominence based upon the innovative companies and institutions which move here and do business here.
- The most successful focused communities host Think Tanks, which are sources of wisdom, planning, strategy and leadership. Think tanks set the tone, encourage the community's knowledge and supply professional development.

Challenges in promoting local identity include:

- Local citizens and those economically active must identify with this changing status.
- A feeling of belonging and a common pioneering effort must be nurtured among players, actors and stakeholders.
- Local communications networks must be maintained.
- The external image and the internal realities must match.
- A formal Visioning process must ensue. Innovative ideas for infrastructure must be generated. Ideas for growth cannot be abstract, but must be practical, planned and accountable.
- Public sector services must be comprehensive.
- Forums for citizen input and participation should be highlighted.

- Contractors should agree upon models for community construction.
- A formal Supply Chain Management program will assure that specialty contractors, vendors and other suppliers adhere to the highest standards.
- A Continuous Quality Improvement program will assure consistency and accountability.
- Associations should involve tenants, residents and stakeholders in the decision processes.
- The promotion of community is vital, including clubs, non-profit organizations and professional associations.
- Entertainment and hospitality industries must be developed. If people feel useless and bored, they will lose interest in joint action and social ties.

Tackling the Future

Charting the course of an organization is a lofty responsibility, with so many factors riding on the outcome. It's lonely at the top, and most corporate executives are hard pressed to know where to turn for informed opinion. Effectively utilize outside advisors.

Long-term planning facilitates a total and cohesive business approach. It signals the future and new, creative ways of doing things. Think to the future, and analyze where your company wishes to be. With strategic planning and implementation, success is attainable.

Recognize and benefit from changing marketplaces. The old ways of doing business will not cut it in the future. Every organization must look forward in order to survive and succeed. The skill with which one adapts, changes and makes the difference between a company simply existing and moving forward in a growth mode. You can evolve to the next tier in your professional quest.

Important stages in visioning the future of cities include:

1. Applying the Cosmetics.
2. Picking the Movers and Shakers.
3. Creating a Sense of Urgency.
4. Choosing Themes and Vehicles.
5. Preparing People.

6. Getting the Facts Straight and Making Compelling Presentations.
7. Structuring the Organization.
8. Fine Tuning the Organization.
9. Collaborations with Partners.
10. Development of Further Stakeholders.
11. Undertaking New Initiatives.
12. Growing the Concept in Further Directions.
13. Periodic Rethinking of the Agenda.
14. Fine Tuning for Quality.
15. Commitment to Further Excellence and Accomplishment.

Create and sustain the 7 most important business mindsets:

1. Steady, Managed Growth. Look to craft innovative strategies.
2. Product & Process Realignment. Collaborations build sustainable communities.
3. Human Intelligence. You are in the credibility business.
4. Professional Development, Performance Reviews, Ethics, Values, Accountabilities and the Court of Public Opinion all matter.
5. Body of Knowledge. Representing the heartland of America is honorable, laudable and market-savvy.
6. The Big Picture. Careful nurturing of your Business Tree yields results.
7. Think, Plan, Dream and Team.

Chapter 27

HOW INVESTOR RELATIONS AND COMMUNICATIONS AFFECT AND POSITION THE FINANCIAL PICTURE

F inancial markets constantly change. With new ownerships, forecasts, indexes and societal actions, every business needs the ability to succeed and thrive. Now, every perception of the company—as a potential investment— matters. Communicating the benefits of financial management and shareholder benefits means survival in recessionary times.

Because of the information explosion and available technology, every corporation attempts to communicate, not necessarily well, nor effectively. Within that vacuum stands the potential for the well-poised companies to break away from the pack.

The availability of instant, convincing information usually impacts securities trading. This is accomplished through a cohesive financial communications program, which includes:

- The annual report.
- Quarterly earnings statements.

- Video presentations to the financial and investment communities.
- The annual meeting and regional stockholder meetings.
- News and feature media coverage of the company and its market successes.
- Financial and corporate image advertising.
- Announcements of joint ventures and other cooperative marketing with colleagues.
- Speeches by key company executives at business forums and the distribution of speech reprints to key constituencies.
- Folders interpreting company policies, proposed changes and external factors affecting company profitability.
- Routine sending of shareholder surveys…and publishing the results.
- Stockholder correspondence, including reprints of stories on the company.
- Informational tours of company locations for financial analysts, the financial press and others who may talk positively about the company (road shows).
- Services to stockholders, including locating dealers, distributing samples of products, arranging visits to factories/branches and assisting the sale of large blocks of stock.

Every corporation should reappraise its financial communications program every three years. Outside management business counsel should be retained to work with the Chief Financial Officer. Professional communicators bring objective perspective and interface with company resources in auditing financial relations efforts to date. Together, they craft and sustain an image that offers utmost bottom-line results.

Counsel will build organizational profiles, assess management resources that are most often overlooked and inventory company achievements. Conversations with analysts and the financial press will validate opinions held (or not held) regarding the company.

Maintaining a good relationship with shareholders is sound investor relations practice. It is also sound management. A solid base of loyal stockholders is advantageous for any company.

Shareholder positioning takes a more direct approach than other business communications. Creativity has a relationship to the messages being received and understood. About 90$ of audiences are not moved to take substantive actions unless unequivocal reasons to do so are perceived. The job of communicators is to move the inactive prospects toward action.

Annual Report

Each company's annual report is its primary mirror of momentum and vision. The document's look and content must effectively portray the company. Thus, the following must be considered and observed:

- The process of creating each annual report is a yearly reappraisal of the company...what distinguishes it from competitors.
- Messages must convey company credibility.
- Graphics and writing must focus upon company character, not the "artistic" view that designers or photographers might give.
- Have one person be responsible for overseeing writing and production. Reports that are written by committee lose their focus.
- Be sure that SEC guidelines and procedures are observed.

When the annual report is humanized to the point where it can be understood by the smallest investor, then copies should be mailed to other key constituencies. This document also has marketing, community relations, government relations and media relations applicability.

Other publications carry forward the theme and serve multiple purposes during the year. These opportunities to affect behavior—through informing— include newsletters, dividend stuffers and a corporate fact book. These say things in ways that quarterly earnings statements cannot.

Annual Meeting

Stockholders are owners of the company and have the right to review activities. The annual meeting represents an opportunity to build bases of support...including financial backing for company expansion.

Management must see that shareholders receive equal, courteous treatment but not allow a vocal few to disrupt the proceedings. Presentations via video and other graphics tend to answer most questions, dispel criticism and interest audiences. That is why visionary companies employ strategic planning counsel to produce these illustrative visuals, as well as publications.

Annual meetings should be followed with a recap report. Inclusion in the next newsletter or magazine will accomplish this obligation for those who were unable to attend. It clarifies what transpired for those who were in the audience. It represents another way to sell management's perspective to its financial base.

Financial Publicity

Articles in newspapers and magazines reach present investors, prospective investors, customers of the company, those who impact stock buying decisions, employees of the company and other publics. No company can sell stock without a public persona.

The five outlets for financial publicity include:

1. News releases, accompanied by copies of such documents as the annual report, quarterly reports and other mailings to stockholders.
2. Releases on dividend declarations, mergers and acquisitions, financing, expansion of facilities, labor relations, shareholder meetings, management changes, litigation, security redemptions, research data, statements on industry trends and statements on the company's outlook.
3. Handling of inquiries from the media.
4. Speeches for company officials before business, government and securities audiences.
5. Interviews with financial publications, business writer and broadcast media.

Security Analyst Relations

Opinion leaders in the financial community include security analysts in brokerage houses, banks, institutions, insurance companies, investment advisory services and mutual funds. They are specialists in acquiring and evaluating company information and then making appropriate recommendations.

Financial community positioning helps companies to communicate with analysts by:

- Scheduled visitations by key executives, backed with compelling literature.
- Special reports containing detailed information on exciting new plans.
- Tours of facilities…particularly new and unique projects that establish and market the company's "point of difference."
- Dissemination of news to analysts at the same time as to the financial press.
- Fulfilling specific requests for information where securities rules permit.
- Visitations by company officials to analyst meetings.
- Appearances before business groups which may impact the analysts.
- Regularly scheduled presentations for analysts at company headquarters.

Crisis Program

Because of incidents covered in the news, corporations now know the importance of planning for emergencies, such as oil spills, plant explosions and other disasters. Those who are forthright with the information will appear to be in command and are respected by their constituencies.

Proactive activities are necessary during such financial transaction phases as takeover efforts, proxy fights and tender offers. Every corporation should have a crisis communications program in place.

This is not the time to "clam up." Companies with fundamentally strong characteristics must intensify efforts to tell their strengths to the financial community. The objectives are to regain confidence of present shareholders and attract the interest of potential investors.

Recommendations

Stock prices are based upon perceptions of reality, as is overall company image. Perceived profit is based upon impressions of performance. Many companies grossly overspend for investor relations activities because they try anything. In the long-run, a cohesive, written communications program is more cost effective.

To maximize financial communications efforts, the following tips are recommended:

- Develop, maintain and update a list of institutional investors and security analysts who follow the company. Keep them serviced with ample information on company developments, especially expansions. Maintaining lists is more important than a clerical function.
- After releasing information, routinely call selected prospects to make sure they are aware of the news. Banks refer to this as an "officer call program."
- Develop a crisis communications program, with all likely contingencies. Test the program and be sure that employees know how to optimize it. The military calls this "war games."
- Don't cover up bad news. Let investors quickly know how the company is dealing with the situation. You will be respected for taking this posture.
- Be sure that the annual report offers a balanced picture of the company's situation. If there have been setbacks, discuss steps being taken to overcome them. Incorporate a clear overview of corporate strategy. Communicate in terms that every investor can comprehend.
- Expand information presentations. Use graphics and video. Utilize all distribution aids, both electronic and paper. Apply marketing approaches to make the information enticing.
- Step up the company's presence in the business and trade press. Be sure that company spokespersons are media-trained by PR counsel. Give more than the basic information.
- Tighten the response time. Answer routine shareholder questions immediately. Hold meetings and teleconferences once every quarter. Be as forthright in communicating as possible.

There are more companies vying for investor attention today than ever before. There is a shrinking number of investors. Institutional decision makers handle investments in a programmed way. Within that scenario, ask what more your company can do to position itself.

Each company can strengthen its financial image program. Public relations counselors maintain rules of credibility and conduct. They advise chief financial officers, controllers and other financial management on ways to affect behavior via communications (within SEC guidelines).

Investor relations programs help people reach decisions to buy or hold the company's stock. Success is best reflected in a realistic appraisal of the company and its securities.

Building a reputation for integrity in transactions is accomplished through thoughtful public relations. Quality financial relations will position the company for the long-term as a consistent and innovative performer.

Chapter 28

STAKEHOLDERS

Fostering Business Growth

E veryone needs friend to support their initiatives. Especially when things get tough, it's nice to have constituencies to count upon.

Companies must bank support. Times to call for endorsements inevitably arise. The time to build bridges is today, not when a crisis strikes.

In selling goods and services, third party support may include past and present clients, suppliers and industries affected by your customers.

In affecting policies and disposition toward your doing business, liaisons must be established with elected officials, the judiciary, regulatory agencies, the public sector, advocate groups and private sector opinion makers.

Most companies realize the impact of special-publics support, including various socio-economic and ethnic groups. Cause-related marketing, environmental sensitivity and meaningful "giving back to the community" are essential for the coming years.

Stakeholder Management is an important discipline that successful people use to win support from others. It helps them ensure that their projects succeed where others fail.

Stakeholder Analysis is the technique used to identify the key people who have to be won over. You then use Stakeholder Planning to build the support that helps you succeed.

The benefits of using a stakeholder-based approach are that:

- Use opinions of the most powerful stakeholders to shape your projects at an early stage. Not only does this make it more likely that they will support you, their input can also improve the quality of your project
  - o Gains support from powerful stakeholders can help you to win more resources. This makes it more likely that your projects will be successful
  - o By communicating with stakeholders early and frequently, you can assure that they fully understand what you are doing and understand the benefits of your project. This means they can support you actively when necessary
- Anticipate what people's reaction to your project may be.
- Build into your plan the actions that will win people's support.

Third Party Building Affects Business Climate

These recommendations are offered in a Stakeholder Program for gaining and maintaining third party support of business initiatives:

- Make lists of your company's current friends and enemies. Update them regularly.
- Determine why friends support you…and what would happen if their backing was lost.
- Understand why some people and groups oppose you. Ascertain what would have prevented their objections and what it would take to turn them around.
- List whom you want to win as friends and with whom you are most afraid of becoming enemies.
- Analyze what your competitors are doing to win friends and build coalitions.
- Foresee what would happen if you sat still and did nothing.

- Project the financial and other benefits of pro-active building of credible third party endorsements.
- Make this initiative a primary responsibility for top management.
- Retain outside counsel with demonstrated expertise in issues management, business forecasting, community relations, cause-related marketing, minority relations, government relations and grassroots constituency building.

Third party support can move mountains when you need it the most…or it can wreak havoc on your bottom line and the future in which you do business. Be honest about your current status. Take stock of opportunities. Make decisive actions, and reap future rewards.

Identifying Stakeholders

Stakeholders are people who:

- Will be impacted by the company and its Strategic Plan
- Have information, experience, or insight that will be helpful in developing the company.
- May be in a position to either support or block your progress.
- Have a vested in interest in the work of the organization.
- Are final decision makers or people who must approve the Strategic Plan.
- Will implement any aspect of the plan.
- Need to be informed of changes in company direction.
- Have been champions or critics of your work in the past.
- Are visionary thinkers interested in exploring new business opportunities.

1. **Identifying Your Stakeholders.** The first step is to ascertain who your stakeholders are. Think of all the people who are affected by your work, who have influence or power over it, or have an interest in its successful or unsuccessful conclusion.

Some of the people who might be stakeholders in your job or in your projects include:

- Shareholders.
- Company management.
- Employees.
- Alliance partners.
- Trade and professional associations.
- Customers: impact on supply of product or service.
- Supply chain members, including subcontractors and suppliers: impact on supply costs and deliverability.
- Opinion leaders in industries affected by our services.
- Regulators.
- Insurance companies.
- Government agencies: regional development agencies; agencies providing other grants; employment training agencies.
- Financial institutions.
- Analysts.
- Communities in which we do business.
- Advocate groups.
- Special interest groups
- The media.
- Employee families.
- Global communities.
- Prospective customers.
- Future recruits.
- Communities in which we would like to expand the business.

Remember that although stakeholders may be both organizations and people, ultimately you must communicate with people. Make sure that you identify the correct individual stakeholders within a stakeholder organization.

2. **Prioritize Your Stakeholders.** You may now have a long list of people and organizations that are affected by your work. Some of these may have the power either to block or advance initiatives. Some may be interested in what you are doing.

Map out your stakeholders on a Power/Interest Grid and classify them by their power over your work and by their interest in your work. Someone's position on the grid shows you the actions you have to take with them:

- High power, interested people. These are the people you must fully engage and make the greatest efforts to satisfy.
- High power, less interested people. Put enough work in with these people to keep them satisfied, but not so much that they become bored with your message.
- Low power, interested people. Keep these people adequately informed, and talk to them to assure that no major issues are arising. These people can often be very helpful with the detail of your project.
- Low power, less interested people. Monitor these people, but do not bore them with excessive communication.

3. **Understanding Key Stakeholders.** You now need to know more about your key stakeholders. You need to know how they are likely to feel about and react to your project. You also need to know how best to engage them in your project and how best to communicate with them.

Key questions that can help you understand your stakeholders are:

- What financial or emotional interest do they have in the outcome of your work? Is it positive or negative?
- What motivates them most of all?
- What information do they want or need from you? How do they want to receive information from you? What is the best way of communicating your message to them?
- What is their current opinion of your work? Is it based on good information?
- Who influences their opinions generally, and who influences their opinion of you?
  - o Do some of these influencers therefore become important stakeholders in their own right?

- If they are not likely to be positive, what will win them around to support your project?
- If you don't think you will be able to win them around, how will you manage their opposition?
- Who else might be influenced by their opinions? Do these people become stakeholders in their own right?

A very good way to answer these questions is to talk to your stakeholders directly. People are often quite open about their views, and asking people's opinions is often the first step in building a successful relationship with them.

Stakeholders, as used here, refers to our primary reference groups, those who contribute regularly to our "vocabulary of meaning." Summarize the understanding you have gained, so that you can easily see which stakeholders are expected to be blockers or critics, and which stakeholders are likely to be advocates and supporters or your project.

4. **Stages of Stakeholder Involvement include:**

- Stakeholder identification
- Stakeholder communication
- Stakeholder development
- Stakeholder monitoring
- Stakeholder influencing
- Stakeholder involvement

In recent years, a wider variety of goals have been suggested for a business. These include the traditional objective of profit maximization. They also include goals relating to earnings per share, total sales, numbers employed, measures of employee welfare, manager satisfaction, environmental protection and many others.

A major reason for increasing adoption of a Stakeholder Concept in setting business objectives is the recognition that businesses are affected by the "environment" in which they operate. Businesses come into regular contact with customers, suppliers, government agencies, families of employees, special interest groups. Decisions made by a business are likely to affect one or more of these stakeholder groups.

The stakeholder concept suggests that the managers of a business should take into account their responsibilities to other groups and not just the shareholder group, when making decisions. The concept suggests that businesses can benefit significantly from cooperating with stakeholder groups, incorporating their needs in the decision-making process.

Stakeholder programs have the potential to transform the quality of business life. Their main strength is in combination with an appropriate business philosophy, which does not yet exist. Widely respected business values can be identified, but they need to be founded on basic principles, which is a requirement for any discipline to move from ideology to maturity.

Businesses are decision making units made up of a variety of decision makers. Most classifications of types of decisions are based on the predictability of decisions. It is possible to contrast decision making according to the time available to make the decision:

- Short term operational decisions have to be frequently made and relate to the management and supervision of activities.
- Periodic control decisions are made less frequently. They involve making decisions to keep the organization on track. The include decisions about taking actions when there are budget variances, or falling behind production schedules.
- Strategic decisions are the long term plans of the organization. These decisions are taken by top management, with some consultation of lower levels within the organization.

5. **Roles for Stakeholders.**

Serve as a Design Team Member: A diverse group of people who are highly invested in this work and who provide a critical perspective by engaging throughout the entire planning process. Their time commitment is the largest. They are the key collaborators on what will be included in the plan drafts. Design teams are often composed of 5-10 people, representing different stakeholder groups. They also are asked to consider perspectives other than their own or those of the stakeholder group(s) of which they are a part.

Provide Input: Which stakeholder groups should be asked for their input at various points in the process? Who could have critical insight, experience, or information that can be incorporated into the process? Who will be most impacted by the strategic plan?

One strategy for gathering input is to utilize existing meetings (e.g. community partner forums, faculty curriculum committees, staff meetings, student organization meetings) to gather input on their visions for community engagement, or what they perceive to be the greatest barriers or opportunities for strengthening community engagement in higher education.

Provide Feedback: Who should read drafts of the full plan or portions of it, and provide feedback?

Approve the Plan: Who needs to formally approve the plan? Who needs to informally approve of the plan because their support is critical?

Disseminate the Plan: Who should receive a copy of the final plan?

Other: Are there other processes in which stakeholders should be involved?

What a Stakeholder Program Seeks to Accomplish

- Prestige or favorable image…and its benefits.
- Promotions of products and sales.
- Good will of the employees.
- Prevention and solution of labor problems.
- Fostering the good will of communities in which the company has units.
- Good will of the stockholders, board of directors, and owners.
- Overcoming misconceptions and prejudices.
- Good will of suppliers.
- Good will of government.
- Good will of the rest of your industry.
- Attraction of others into the industry.
- Ability to attract the best personnel.
- Education of the public to the purposes and scope of the product.
- Education of the public to a point of view.
- Good will of customers (and their friends and colleagues).

- Seeing that the industry is properly represented in the curricula of schools and colleges. Assisting educators in teaching about the industry.
- Creating public support for legislative proposals that the industry favors or public opposition to legislation that it opposes.
- Obtaining public recognition for the social and economic contributions that the industry makes to the nation.
- Combating government interference or competition with the industry.
- Public understanding of the regulation of the industry by the government, in order to assure equitable regulation.
- Consumer understanding of how to use the product.

Community Relations, Thoughtfulness Pays Dividends

For those doing business on a long-term basis, a respect for and understanding of the company will improve its chances. No matter the size of the organization, goodwill must be banked. Every company must make deposits…for those inevitable times in which withdrawals will be made.

To say that business and its communities do not affect each other, is short-sighted…and will make business the loser every time.

Communities surround business but are not subject to its policies and operations. While business usually caters to its own agenda, the community is flexible, unpredictable and emotional.

Business marries the community that it settles with. The community has to be given a reason to care for the business. Business owes its well-being and livelihood to its communities.

When business practices and performance pose potential harm to the community, an expected backlash will occur. Communities used to be passive because company presence meant jobs and economic incentive. The mobility of business has forced communities to compete for other businesses, which makes them very leery of companies that defy the public's best interests.

Since one cannot market a problem-ridden culture, the communities are addressing the troubles…in order to attract more responsible organizations. In this era, the community has spoken out. Business is on fair notice to get its act together.

Communities are clusters of individuals, each with its own agenda. In order to be minimally successful, business must know the components of its community intimately.

No company can cure community problems by itself, unless it is the problem. But each company has a business stake for doing its part. Community relations is a function of self-interest, rather than just being a good citizen.

No company can deal with all components of a community or take on all the problems. The art is to identify those constituencies who serve or can harm the company's strongest needs.

To prioritize which spheres or causes to serve, business should list and examine all of the community's problems. Relate business responses to real and perceived wants/needs of the community. Set priorities.

The only constraints upon community relations are regulatory standards and the amount of resources that can be allocated. There can never be a restraint upon creativity.

Every community relations program has five steps:

1. Learn what each community thinks about the company…and, therefore, what information needs to be communicated to each public. Conduct focus groups. Maintain community files. Organize an ongoing feedback system.

2. Plan how to best reach each public…which avenues will be the most expedient. Professional strategic planning counsel performs an independent audit and guides the company through the process. Get as many ideas from qualified sources as possible. Find compatible causes to champion. Maintain contingency plans.

3. Develop systems to execute the program, communicating at every step to publics. All employees should have access to the plan, with a mechanism that allows them to contribute. If others understand what the company is doing, they will want to be part of it.

4. Evaluate how well each program and its messages were received. Continue fact-finding efforts, which will yield more good ideas for future projects. Document the findings. Build into all community relations programs some realistic mechanisms by which results can be shown. When planning, reach for feasible evaluation yardsticks.

5. Interpret the results to management in terms that are easy to understand and support. Community relations is difficult to evaluate, unless a

procedure for doing so is set. Provide management with information that justifies their confidence. Squarely address goals and concerns.

Companies should support off-duty involvement of employees in pro bono capacities...but not take unfair credit. Volunteers are essential to community relations. Companies must show tangible evidence of supporting the community... by assigning key executives to high-profile community assignments. Create a formal volunteer guild, and allow employees the latitude and creativity to contribute to the common good. Celebrate and reward their efforts.

Community relations is action-oriented and should include one or more of these forms:

1. Creating something necessary that did not exist before.
2. Eliminating something that poses a problem.
3. Developing the means for self-determination.
4. Including citizens who are in need.
5. Sharing professional and technical expertise.
6. Tutoring, counseling and training.
7. Repairing, upgrading or restoring.
8. Promotion of the community to outside constituencies.
9. Moving others toward action.

Many people see problems before they occur. The companies that overcome imagined fears are better positioned than those who wait to do damage control.

Publicity and promotions should support effective community relations...not be the substitute or smokescreen for the process. Recognition is as desirable for the community as for the business. Good news shows progress and encourages others to participate.

It is important to involve public relations specialists (within the company and credible outside consultants) in programming community relations, as well as for effective publicity.

Timing of communications, seeking all likely media and tailoring the message are vital. Community relations becomes most successful when third parties say good things about the business. That creates more news, which creates recognition, which leads in the direction of goodwill, which challenges the business to work even harder to sustain.

The well-rounded community relations program embodies all elements: accessibility of company officials to citizens, participation by the company in business and civic activities, public service promotions, special events, plant communications materials and open houses, grassroots constituency building and good citizenry.

Never stop evaluating. Facts, values, circumstances and community composition are forever changing. The same community relations posture will not last forever. Use research and follow-up techniques to reassess the position, assure continuity and move in a forward motion.

Companies need community relations at all times:

- Prior to coming into locales.
- Every year in which they do business there, in good and bad economic times.
- When they are leaving an area.
- Even after they have ceased operation in certain communities.

In today's economy, no business can operate without affecting or being affected by its communities. Business must behave like a guest in its communities...never failing to show or return courtesies.

Community acceptance for one project does not mean than the job of community relations has completed. Programs always shift into other gears... breaking new ground.

Community relations is not "insurance" that can be bought overnight. It is tied to the bottom line and must be treated accordingly...with resources and expertise to do it effectively. It is a bond of trust that, if violated, will haunt the business. If steadily built, the trust can be exponentially parlayed into successful long-term business relationships.

Anticipated Results of Ongoing Stakeholder Activity

- Your company's product-service is efficient and excellent, by your standards and by the public's.

- The organization is sensitive to the public's needs and behaves flexibly and humane in meeting them.
- Company management and staff are professional and competent. They demonstrate initiative and utilize their best judgment, with the authority to make the decisions they should make.
- Your company has a good reputation and is awake to community obligations. It contributes much to the economy and provides leadership for progress, rather than following along.
- The company always gives customers their money's worth. Charges are fair and reasonable.
- The organization employs state-of-the-art technology and is in the vanguard of its industry and marketplace.
- Management is quality oriented and provides a good place to work. Your company offers a promising career and future for people with ideas and initiative. Your people render quality work, are highly creative and are results-oriented.
- The size of your organization is necessary to do the job. Your integrity and dependability make the public confident that the company will use its size and influence rightly.

Chapter 29

PERFORMANCE BASED BUDGETING

L egislatures created a Performance Based Budgeting program (PB2) process that links funding to the agency products or services and results. Under this system, agency budget requests not only include the funding that agencies would like to receive, but also the outputs and outcomes they expect to produce as a result of that funding. The Legislature then establishes performance targets for outcomes and outputs in the implementing act to the appropriations act.

Agencies then report their actual performance in their long range program plans and budget requests for the following fiscal year. Agencies may be given incentives for performance that exceeds standards or disincentives for performance that falls below standards. These incentives and disincentives can be monetary or non-monetary. An example of a monetary incentive would be performance bonuses for employees and managers. An example of a non-monetary incentive would be an increase in budget flexibility.

Key Players in the PB2 Process: State Agencies, The Executive Office of the Governor, The State Legislature. The Legislature and The Comptroller's Office.

Other key states initiating performance-based budgeting efforts include Florida and Minnesota. These states are at various stages of the budget reform process and are experiencing varying degrees of success.

The Performance Based Budget parallels most recent Strategic Planning pre-work and shapes perimeters for the finished plan. Factors in priorities come from the Strategic Plan.

Unit costs are the costs of producing an output or outcome. These costs can be calculated in a number of ways, the most common of which are the direct costs of producing one unit of output and allocated costs, using a methodology that assigns indirect or overhead costs to each unit.

Direct, indirect, and allocated costs provide important information for managers and policy makers, and the type of cost data used depends on the purpose of the analysis. Direct costs that are separated from indirect costs are most useful for budgeting purposes and privatization decisions. However, cost comparisons are best done with allocated costs.

The categories that departments are using to report costs are useful for budgetary purposes. However, the precision of agency cost estimates will vary. The estimates of agencies that structure their organizations around business practices will be more accurate than the cost estimates of agencies that structure their organizations in other ways.

Priorities Report Card

The budget can encompass such factors as:

- Core Business, Programs and Services.
- Driver: Growth.
- Driver: Rate Improvement.
- Running the Business, Organizational Stewardship.
- Financial Stewardship.
- People, Staff, Administration, Board and Stakeholders.
- Community Building.
- System-wide Operations.
- Institutional Visioning, Growth and Future.

The budget is broken down by program, per line items and organizational units. It addresses changing markets, opportunities, barriers. Hopefully, it reflects Big Picture issues, building a shared vision and institutional values.

These are the types of measurements that the budget can ask to be made:

- Administrative costs as a percentage of overall operating budget.
- Number of customers served.
- Number of business development calls, events, activities.
- Percentage of projects that make, as an indicator with continuing to offer them.
- Number of training courses offered.
- Percentage of time spent on each activity.
- Implementation of programs by deadlines.
- Recruitment of the best and brightest new talent.
- Improved access.
- Streamlining in operations by criteria.
- Savings.
- Opportunities for collaboration with business partners.
- Management skills applied and perfected.
- Results attached to each indicator.
- Figures and dates attached.
- Indicators of growth.
- Change, rather than stagnation.
- Ways of better utilizing existing resources.
- Customer focus attached to each program area.
- Applying flexible and accountable management.
- Institutional focus and system advancement reflected in individual programs.
- Justify levels of funding. Show what could be done with more.
- Increase some programs. Reduce others. Expand the scope of some programs.
- Reviews institutional criteria.

Criteria for Performance Based Budgeting to Be Successful

These are questions to follow in adopting Performance Based Budgeting as part of the Strategic Planning and Visioning processes:

- Does this process increase your accountability to funding sources and to the public?
- Are measures from the General Appropriations Act used to manage performance?
- Is the performance management system focused upon outcomes?
- Do the key measures the best representation of progress of the institution?
- Can the information be accessed regularly?
- How useful are the findings to management?
- How well can management interpret and apply the findings to the decision process?
- Does your strategic plan adequately describe what your organization does?
- Does the strategic plan provide necessary guidance to the activities that you will measure?
- How diverse is the planning committee?
- Has a Visioning process occurred?
- Do performance measures provide an early warning system for problems and opportunities to correct?
- How do you handle crisis management and preparedness?
- Have you prioritized and fully defined key measures?
- Have you done scenario planning of measures beyond your immediate control? What are the external factors which will profoundly impact your livelihood?
- Do the measures address both internal management and external perceptions and accountabilities?

Systems of rewards and penalties should be tied to the system. Performance measures should be included in contracts with all resources, such as adjuncts, vendors and suppliers. Supply chain management should be implemented. Quality management should be implemented. Adjustments must be periodically made to target markets, definition of terms and modification of strategies.

Performance Based Budgeting, Compared to the Current Budgeting Process

Current features that are continued under Performance Based Budgeting include:

- The Revenue Stabilization Law.
- The Personnel Classification and Compensation Law.
- Specification of the authorized positions in the Budget Request and Appropriation Bill.
- Specification of the Budget Request by line items of expenditures.
- A Biennial budget process.
- Legislative budget hearings preceding an upcoming State Legislature.
- Annual Operations Plans as currently required.
- Miscellaneous Federal Grant process.
- Miscellaneous Cash Fund Appropriation process.

Changes Under Performance Based Budgeting:

- Strategic Plans would be required of all agencies and institutions.
- The budget entity would be a "Program" as defined by the State Legislature.
- Performance Measures and Performance Targets by programs would be incorporated into the Appropriation Bill for each agency.
- Each Program would receive a Lump Sum appropriation amount instead of various line items of appropriation.
- Anticipated funding sources for each program would be set out in the Appropriation Act.
- Procedures would be defined for limited transfers of appropriation and funding between Programs.
- Interim Progress Reports would be required.
- Performance would be reviewed in connection with the subsequent biennial budget process.
- An explicit system of Incentives and Disincentives would be deferred until additional experience is gained in Performance Based Budgeting.

Because budgets are built from the ground up, every department manager should participate in the process. The typical steps include:

- Learn the principles of PBB
- Learn how to define activities and workload in your department
- Perform an activity analysis interview
- Learn how to calculate activity cost
- Use the activity cost data to define a cost improvement plan
- Learn how to define activity cost
- Learn the steps necessary in order to prepare a Performance Based Budget
- Present PBB to pre-selected government leaders
- Define the next steps

Results Based Management

The practice of Results Based Management is a comprehensive, life cycle, approach to management that integrates business strategy, people, processes and measurements to improve decision-making and to drive change. The approach focuses on getting the right design early in a process, implementing performance measurement, learning and changing, and reporting performance.

Organizations are adopting Results Based Management with the aim to improve program and management effectiveness, accountability and achieve results.

Results Based Management means:

- Establishing clear organizational vision, mission and priorities, which are translated into a four-year framework of goals, outputs, indicators, strategies and resources.
- Encouraging an organizational and management culture that promotes innovation, learning, accountability, and transparency.
- Delegating authority, empowering managers and holding them accountable for results.
- Focusing on achieving results, through strategic planning, regular monitoring of progress, evaluation of performance, and reporting on performance.
- Creating supportive mechanisms, policies and procedures, building and improving on what is already in place.

- Sharing information and knowledge, learning lessons, and feeding these back into improving decision-making and performance.
- Optimizing human resources and building capacity among staff and national partners to manage for results.
- Making the best use of financial resources in an efficient manner to achieve results.
- Strengthening and diversifying partnerships at all levels towards achieving results.
- Responding to external situations and needs within the organizational mandate.

A shift from reporting on activities to results-based lines of business creates a balance between "rules and processes" and "values and results." It is focused upon citizens, clients and taxpayers.

Results Based Management provides basis for departmental accountability for results achieved with resources allocated. It relates the internal management accountability and business planning regimes of the department to information presented in government documents. It insures consistent bases of presentation to government.

This concept is reflected in:

- Auditing processes.
- Performance reviews.
- Ethics.
- The quality processes.
- Communications.
- Community relations.
- Policies and procedures.
- Strategic planning and long-term visioning.
- Outcome-based scrutiny.
- Changing the way in which the institution does business.
- Competitive sourcing.
- Informing the public.

What Results Based Management includes in its procedures:

- Clarifies who customers are.
- Specifies results and performance expectations,
- Factors customer satisfaction and the company's customer orientation.
- Performance Based Budgeting links budget allocation to output delivery of products and services.
- Requires performance reporting procedures.
- Promotes performance analysis and continuous quality improvement.
- Encourages new ways of optimizing human capital.
- Has capacity building.
- Encourages a system wide approach.
- Incentives are essential.
- Internal ownership and commitment are necessary.
- Is based upon performance data management and reporting.
- Builds high-performance teams.
- Embraces change management.
- Strengthened by coaching and counseling of company leaders.
- Institutes tenets of conflict management.
- Allows for creativity.
- Effective methods of managing stress and change
- Results-Based performance management.
- Workplace ethics and corporate sustainability.
- Evaluation and accountability planning
- Evaluation Studies
- Utilizes evaluation tools and training

Results, Benchmarking and Measurements

Fundamental to strategic planning is that the goals and objectives be tied to measurable activities. Gaining confidence is crucial, as business relationships are established to be long-term in duration. Each organization or should determine and craft its own character and personality, seeking to differentiate from others.

Effective benchmarks must be applied to all aspects of the business: Core Business, Running the Business, Financial, People and the interrelationship of these five major business functions to each other.

Benchmarking usually shows that customer service suffers during fast-growth periods. They have to back-pedal and recover customer confidence by doing surveys. Even with results of deteriorating customer service, growth-track companies pay lip service to really fixing their own problems.

Public perceptions are called "credence goods" by economists. Every organization must educate outside publics about what they do and how they do it. This premise also holds true for each corporate operating unit and department. The whole of the business and each sub-set must always educate corporate opinion makers on how it functions and the skill with which the company operates. Top management must endorse corporate communications, if your company is to grow and prosper.

Benchmarking for success is a factor of how diverse the company can and would like to be. Diversity is an enlightened mindset that affects workforce dynamics, plateaus of professionalism, work ethics, jobs and careers. Diversity embodies what it takes to succeed long-term, by diversifying the product mix, marketplace and customer focus. Every company is affected by external influences, and a diversity of ideas directly leads to pro-active approaches and measurements of achievements. Diversity is about the organization being all they can be, attaining levels of standards and questing for more. The wider scope that one takes with diversity, then it will be more embraced and coveted.

Business Model is a term that some people use to criticize the business failures of others. Few businesses are ever modeled. Business models relate to financial structures only, which represent less than 10 percent of the importance of each business. Less than two percent of businesses have strategic plans, which are umbrella frameworks for success. Business needs to strategize and plan first, with models for each sub-heading (core business, running the business, financial, people, business development, body of knowledge and the Big Picture) addressed.

To some, the Dot.Com Bust was a crashing blow to business. Actually, it was a much-needed market correction, with liberal doses of reality. Too many dot.com companies were predicated upon fluff, hype and over-exaggeration. Owners felt they were exempt from the corporate practices and protocols of older companies. Analysts and those in the media who publicized companies' spins without investigating their facts were partly to blame. So-called "new school" ideologies proved to be tech excuses for not planning and developing corporate visions. Worthwhile fledgling companies now have greater chances of success in the future because a brief time of worshipping companies with no products and processes was exposed. As business moves forward, companies of substance will prosper.

Today's workforce needs three times the amount of training they are now getting in order to remain competitive and optimally productive. There is a difference between how one is basically educated and the ingredients needed to succeed in the long-term. Many people never amass those ingredients because they stop learning or don't see the need to go any further. Many people think they are "going further" but otherwise spin their wheels. There is a large disconnect between indoctrinating people to tools of the trade and the myriad of elements they will need to assimilate for their own futures. Training vendors sell what they have to provide…not what the constituencies or workforces need. Emphasis must be placed upon properly diagnosing the organization as a whole and then prescribing treatments for the whole, as well as the parts. Training should be conducted within a formal, planned program that addresses the majority of organizational aspects.

People who rise in upper corporate ranks do so for reasons other than themselves. The art is to understand and work with those factors, rather than to become a pawn of them. Executive development is a finely tuned art. It is a tireless yet energizing process. The old ways of rising to the top have changed. The savvy executive masters the new ways. Don't become a "flavor of the month." Trends and fads in business and in people will subside. Posture yourself for the long-run. Develop and trust your gut instinct. It's right most of the time.

Quotes on Results, Benchmarking and Measurements

"Desperate cuts must have desperate cures."
— Proverb

*"You can do anything in this world if you
are prepared to take the consequences."*
— **W. Somerset Maugham**

"The reward of a thing well done is to have done it."
— **Ralph Waldo Emerson**

"In nature, there are neither rewards nor punishments. There are consequences."
— **Robert G. Ingersoll**, attorney

"War is a series of catastrophes that results in a victory."
— **Georges Clemenceau** (1841-1929)

"Don't tell people how to do things. Tell them what to do and let them surprise you with their results."
— **General George S. Patton** (1885-1945)

"Insanity is doing the same thing over and over again and expecting different results."
— **Albert Einstein** (1879-1955)

"Medicine is a collection of uncertain prescriptions the results of which, taken collectively, are more fatal than useful to mankind."
— **Napoleon Bonaparte** (1769-1821)

"Dreams surely are difficult, confusing, and not everything in them is brought to pass for mankind. For fleeting dreams have two gates: one is fashioned of horn and one of ivory. Those which pass through the one of sawn ivory are deceptive, bringing tidings which come to nought, but those which issue from the one of polished horn bring true results when a mortal sees them."
— **Homer** (800 BC-700 BC), "The Odyssey"

"For the truth of the conclusions of physical science, observation is the supreme Court of Appeal. It does not follow that every item which we confidently accept as physical knowledge has actually been certified by the Court. Our confidence is that it would be certified by the Court if it were submitted. But it does follow that every item of physical knowledge is of a form which might

be submitted to the Court. It must be such that we can specify (although it may be impracticable to carry out) an observational procedure which would decide whether it is true or not. Clearly a statement cannot be tested by observation unless it is an assertion about the results of observation. Every item of physical knowledge must therefore be an assertion of what has been or would be the result of carrying out a specified observational procedure."
— **Sir Arthur Eddington** (1882-1944), The Philosophy of Physical Science

"Advice is judged by results, not by intentions."
— **Cicero** (106 BC-43 BC)

"You ask me why I do not write something. I think one's feelings waste themselves in words. They ought all to be distilled into actions and into actions which bring results."
— **Florence Nightingale** (1820-1910)

"Results! Why, man, I have gotten a lot of results. I know several thousand things that won't work."
— **Inventor Thomas Edison** (1847-1931)

Chapter 30

IT'S ALMOST TOMORROW

Arriving at the New Address
Futurism and Organizational Transformation

What individuals and organizations start out to become and what we evolve into being are two decidedly different things. The future is a series of journeys along a twisting and turning course, affected by what we choose to do with our careers and the priorities we assign.

Along the way, there are warning signs that we either recognize or pay the price for overlooking. Our futures are determined by choices we make, talents that we do or don't develop and circumstances beyond our control.

Our present tense and, thus, our future is further influenced by time and resources we spend interacting with other people and the actions of other people, directly or indirectly affecting us. The perspective of future actions is based upon mistakes we make…and what we learn from them.

Companies and individuals undergo continual transformation. Recognizing it enables the successful ones to benefit from change, rather than become victims of it.

Society is filled with many strange and conflicting quirks. One must understand and deal with several odd dynamics. Some people are more comfortable with failure than success. Organizations do many things that set themselves up to fail (knowingly and by instinct).

The old ways of doing business will not cut it in the future. Every organization must look forward in order to survive and succeed. The skill with which one adapts and changes makes the difference between the company simply existing and moving forward in a growth mode.

These truths about change management set the tone by which one plans to succeed in the future, rather than being a victim of it:

- Nothing stays the same. Everything and everyone change but not at comparable paces.
- Tomorrow is not all that far away.
- Clinging to yesterday may lead to disaster.
- Today is the nostalgia of tomorrow, as well as the future of yesterday.
- They are fast, furious, painful, pleasurable, expected and unexpected.
- The pace of the future never stalls.
- History is a prelude to today and tomorrow.

Viewing Tomorrow, Where Each Company is Headed

This chapter is intended to take Futurism out of the esoteric and into the weekly practice of business. I offer nine of my own definitions for the process of capturing and building a shared Vision for organizations to chart their next 10+ years. Each one gets progressively more sophisticated:

1. Futurism: what you will do and become…rather than what it is to be. What you can and are committed to accomplishing…rather than what mysteriously lies ahead.
2. Futurism: leaders and organizations taking personal responsibility and accountability for what happens. Abdicating to someone or something else does not constitute Futurism and, in fact, sets the organization backward.
3. Futurism: learns from and benefits from the past…a powerful teaching tool. Yesterdayism means giving new definitions to old ideas…giving new

meanings to familiar premises. One must understand events, cycles, trends and subtle nuances…because they will recur.

4. Futurism: seeing clearly your perspectives and those of others. Capitalizing upon change, rather than becoming a by-product of it. Recognizing what change is and what it can do for your organization.

5. Futurism: an ongoing quest toward wisdom. Commitments to learning, which creates knowledge, which inspire insights, which culminate in wisdom. It is more than just being taught or informed.

6. Futurism: ideas that inspire, manage and benchmark change. The ingredients may include such sophisticated business concepts as Change Management, Crisis Preparedness, Streamlining Operations, Empowerment of People, Marketplace Development, Organizational Evolution, Vision.

7. Futurism: developing thinking and reasoning skills, rather than dwelling upon techniques and processes. The following concepts do not constitute Futurism by themselves: sales, technology, re-engineering, marketing, research, training, operations and administration. They constitute micro pieces of a large mosaic. Futurism embodies thought processes that create and energize the mosaic.

8. Futurism: watching other people changing and capitalizing upon it. Understanding from where we came, in order to posture where we are headed. Creating organizational vision, which sets the stage for all activities, processes, accomplishments and goals. Efforts must be realistic, and all must be held accountable.

9. Futurism: the foresight to develop hindsight creates insight into the future.

The Search for Truths in Your Business

We are temporary caretakers. We tend the earth and must give back to it. If we believe that we are just here to get all that we can, we are in for a rude awakening.

Each segment of society has an obligation to the other. Adults do things in the name of their children. Young people need to do things for their elders and must show proper respect. If the cycle is not reciprocal, then it is an empty life.

Companies driven only by money (making it and keeping it) see business as a game, not a philosophy of productivity.

Human beings and the organizations they inhabit are products of change. The manner in which they accept change has a direct relationship to their future success. The ability to adapt, learn and innovate is the basis of change management. Thriving upon change and mastering it is the basis for Futurism.

Yesterdayism, The Past as a Teaching Tool

People and organizations who do not learn from the past cannot see the future. People and organizations who do not study the mistakes of the past are doomed to repeat them.

Yesterdayism is a concept that I use in planning and visioning processes as sources of Insights. It does not mean living in the past. We study those before us… and our own past mistakes. Review the mistakes of those who haven't learned from them. Understand the scope of those who saw things happen. By reviewing the case histories, we teach our organizations, reapply the lessons to our own future growth and keep the creative juices to continue innovating.

Yesterdayism is filled with the lessons of past choices made (how you've evolved), good choices (why they worked) and bad choices. Lessons in Future planning may be learned by reviewing choices made against your will or for the good of the project, career or company.

People concerned only with processes and procedures cannot see The Big Picture of their business. They set up screens to keep truths from filtering in.

A piece does not constitute the whole. Computers only constitute 2% of technology, which only constitutes less than 1% of the importance-emphasis of the overall organization. Recycling only constitutes 2% of a total environmental protection-awareness-advocacy program. Affirmative action is only a small piece of the important mosaic toward racial equity, which in turn is a fraction of the broader concept of multicultural diversity.

Sets of circumstances are not provable evidence. Busy work should not be compared to professional work. Holding a job is not the same thing as a career Body of Work.

The costs of acting too hastily include band aid surgery to haphazard processes, make-goods for errors, material overruns, overtime wages and delays passed on to other scheduled work projects. The broader opportunity costs include damage to goodwill, reputation and customer relationships, as well as executive time to review-modify-correct (three times what it would have taken to plan on the front end).

The costs of acting too slowly include small priorities absorbing larger chunks of time and resources than they need, interrupted flow of work. Uneven schedules-processes create concerns, wastes and worker uneasiness. Being unsure of what is expected and company goals lead to quality management issues. Moving slowly or little at all becomes a habit. The company gets stuck in a rut.

The Big Picture of Futurism

If you ask the best of other people, then you must offer the best. It is difficult for a competitive company to see things changing. You don't always have to be better than other people. Be the best when it counts.

The only good opportunity is the one in front of you. To make the most of it, understand the ones in back of you. Also, it is knowing how and when you do your best work: John Lennon and Paul McCartney set deadlines of two hours in which to write each of their masterpiece songs.

The seven main ingredients of Futurism are:

1. Change Management
2. Crisis Preparedness
3. Streamlining Operations
4. Empowerment of People
5. Marketplace Development
6. Organizational Evolution
7. Long-term Vision.

Factors of Futurism which must be addressed include new kinds of products, a new company, economic necessities, changing competition and turning competitors into collaborators and sometime-suppliers.

By putting people above technology, keeping a customer focus and looking to impact your customer's customer. In today's era of information overhead, the planning process cuts through the clutter, changes definitions of productivity and concurrently re-engineers the organization.

The more creative forms of planning and Visioning are where new ideas come from, thus, creating new business concepts, philosophies, processes. Expanded levels of understanding and thinking ahead and developing insights-visions beyond the information starting point.

These are the actual steps in the Futurism Process:

1. Synthesize information, data.
2. Draw parallel analogies.
3. "What If" situational analysis.
4. Map strategies.
5. Create alternate visions.
6. Prioritizing visions.
7. Select the right vision.
8. Package the vision.
9. Communicate and articulate the vision.
10. Get buy-in.
11. Implement the vision.
12. Leadership development of executives.
13. Altering the organizational climate.
14. Organizational learning.
15. Organizational leadership.
16. Executive mentoring.
17. Vision scope adjustments.
18. Vision contexts (understanding, monitoring, updating).
19. Vision choices (contemplated, made, benchmarked).
20. Continuing Futurism.
21. Behavioral modification.
22. Commitments to do more, learn more, change more.
23. Reap realities of successes and failures.
24. Take vision to the next plateaus.

Why Futurism is Misunderstood

Hucksterism and Hype. People buy easy solutions and instant answers, such as those offered by technology peddlers. Futurism must embody ideas that inspire, manage and benchmark change.

Definitions of Change. Society is filled with many strange and conflicting quirks. Gossip sells. Media thrives on it. People believe what they see and hear to be fact. The system tends to disseminate opinion with instant analysis, so as to discourage individual examination, rationale and investigative activity. One must understand and put speculations and hypotheses of others into proper perspective.

Process vs. Vision. People focus upon micro details of jobs, rather than reasons for the organization being in existence. Each task, tool and technology must be related to the bigger purpose.

Realistic Degrees of Change. People are more comfortable with failure than success. Organizations do many things that set themselves up to fail (knowingly and by instinct), rationalizing that they are adhering to proven formulas. Research shows that change is 90% beneficial. So, why do organizations fear what is in their best interest?

Esoteric vs. Pragmatic. People are inclined to be armchair quarterbacks. Few dare to innovate. Many will criticize, nit-pick, copy or try to change what the few created. The art of survival is to find some kind of stake in new ideas and, at least, buy into pieces of them.

Predictions Without Follow-Through. Organizations say one thing and often do another. It takes rare courage to truly "walk the talk."

Futurism Is What Can Be…Not What People Are Selling. Futurism constitutes what you will do and become…rather than what it is to be. It is what you can and are committed to accomplishing…rather than what mysteriously lies ahead.

Recommendations for Futurism to be successful:

1. Refrain from using the words "technology" and "sales" as crutches or scapegoats.
2. Refrain from making third-hand references to other organizations' accomplishments.
3. Gossip about others does not constitute a marketplace study.
4. Say what we believe and feel, rather than recite procedural details.
5. Look at what the organization is, can become and will create, rather than what it does.

6. Look outside as much as inside. Inner-focus without the rest is self-defeating.
7. Learn from the past to plan for the future.
8. Refine your ability to analyze.
9. Maintain the urge to thrive, not just survive.
10. Sustain complete accountability for actions, consequences.
11. Caring for and nurture the people of the organization, a bonded family.
12. Keep the quest for possibilities, tempered with practicalities.
13. Stimulate your ability to dream.
14. Commit to "walking the talk," embodying excellence, developing insights-wisdom.

Through Futurism, as charted by the Strategic Planning and Visioning processes, you see how far you've come. By continuing to benchmark and recognize progress, you see what things that you could not do before this process began.

End goals are not the objective…making strides is most important. Recognize that no end goal may be reached and that goals are constantly changing. Create a "buddy system," a network of supporters for your pro-active process. Continue to change in realistic increments.

Quotations on Futurism, The Future

"The future ain't what it used to be."
— **Yogi Berra**

"Tomorrow is another day."
— **Margaret Mitchell**, *Gone With the Wind*

"You ain't heard nothin' yet, folks."
— **Al Jolson** in The Jazz Singer (1927)

"You cannot fight the future. Time is on our side."
— **William Gladstone** (1866)

"I like the dreams of the future better that the history of the past."
— **Thomas Jefferson** (1816)

"The fellow who can only see a week ahead is always the popular fellow, for he is looking with the crowd. But the one that can see years ahead, he has a telescope but he can't make anybody believe that he has it."
— **Will Rogers**

"Everything flows and nothing abides; everything gives way and nothing stays fixed. The way up and the way down are one and the same. From out of all the many particulars comes oneness, and out of oneness come all the many particulars. A dry soul is wisest and best."
— **Heraclitus**

"The future is neither ahead nor behind, on one side or another. Nor is it dark or light. It is contained within ourselves; its evil and good are perpetually within us."
— **Loren Eiseley**, The Chresmologue

"The best way to predict the future is to invent it."
— **Alan Kay**

"The best thing about the future is that it comes one day at a time."
— **Abraham Lincoln**

"I have but one lamp by which my feet are guided, and that is the lamp of experience. I know no way of judging the future but by the past. The future belongs to those who dare."
— **Anonymous**

"There is always one moment in childhood when the door opens and lets the future in."
— **Graham Greene**

"Run to meet the future or it's going to run you down."
— **Anthony J. D'Angelo**, College Blue Book

"Let him who would enjoy a good future waste none of his present."
— **Roger Babson**

"Conservation is humanity caring for the future."
— **Nancy Newhall**

"The empires of the future are the empires of the mind."
— **Winston Churchill**

"The future is not a result of choices among alternative paths offered by the present, but a place that is created—created first in the mind and will, created next in activity. The future is not some place we are going to, but one we are creating. The paths are not to be found, but made, and the activity of making them, changes both the maker and the destination."
— **John Schaar,** futurist

"A generation which ignores history has no past and no future."
— **Robert Heinlein,** The Notebooks of Lazurus Long

"As long as anyone believes that his ideal and purpose is outside him, that it is above the clouds, in the past or in the future, he will go outside himself and seek fulfillment where it cannot be found. He will look for solutions and answers at every point except where they can be found—in himself."
— **Erich Frohm**

"The future belongs to those who prepare for it today."
— **Malcolm X**

"The illiterate of the future will not be the person who cannot read. It will be the person who does not know how to learn."
— **Alvin Toffler**

"In a time of drastic change it is the learners who inherit the future. The learned usually find themselves equipped to live in a world that no longer exists."
— **Eric Hoffer**

"The only use of a knowledge of the past is to equip us for the present. The present contains all that there is. It is holy ground; for it is the past, and it is the future."
— **Alfred North Whitehead**

"The future is not something we enter. The future is something we create."
— **Leonard I. Sweet**

"The most decisive actions of our life—I mean those that are most likely to decide the whole course of our future—are, more often than not, unconsidered."
— **Andre Gide**

"My past is my wisdom to use today… my future is my wisdom yet to experience. Be in the present because that is where life resides."
— **Gene Oliver**

"It is because modern education is so seldom inspired by a great hope that it so seldom achieves great results. The wish to preserve the past rather that the hope of creating the future dominates the minds of those who control the teaching of the young."
— **Bertrand Russell**

"To make no mistakes is not in the power of man; but from their errors and mistakes the wise and good learn wisdom for the future."
— **Plutarch**

"Many people think that if they were only in some other place, or had some other job, they would be happy. Well, that is

doubtful. So get as much happiness out of what you are doing as you can and don't put off being happy until some future date."
— **Dale Carnegie**

"How small a portion of our life it is that we really enjoy! In youth we are looking forward to things that are to come; in old age we are looking backward to things that are gone past; in manhood, although we appear indeed to be more occupied in things that are present, yet even that is too often absorbed in vague determinations to be vastly happy on some future day when we have time."
— **C. C. Colton**

"Philosophy triumphs easily over past evils and future evils; but present evils triumph over it."
— **Fran‡ois, Duc De La Rochefoucauld**

"Poetry reveals to us the loveliness of nature, brings back the freshness of youthful feelings, reviews the relish of simple pleasures, keeps unquenched the enthusiasm which warmed the springtime of our being, refines youthful love, strengthens our interest in human mature, by vivid delineations of its tenderest and softest feelings, and through the brightness of its prophetic visions, helps faith to lay hold on the future life."
— **William E. Channing**

"Children have neither a past nor a future. Thus they enjoy the present…which seldom happens to us."
— **Jean De La Bruyere**

"We think very little of time present; we anticipate the future, as being too slow, and with a view to hasten it onward, we recall the past to stay it as too swiftly gone. We are so thoughtless, that we thus wander through the hours which are not here, regardless only of the moment that is actually our own."
— **Blaise Pascal**

"All science is concerned with the relationship of cause and effect. Each scientific discovery increases man's ability to predict the consequences of his actions and thus his ability to control future events."
— **Lawrence J. Peters**

"Look not mournfully into the Past. It comes not back again. Wisely improve the Present. In is thine. Go forth to meet the shadowy Future, without fear, and a manly heart."
— **Henry Wadsworth Longfellow**

"The greatest loss of time is delay and expectation, which depend upon the future. We let go the present, which we have in our power, and look forward to that which depends upon chance, and so relinquish a certainty for an uncertainty."
— **Seneca**

"At the bottom no one in life can help anyone else in life; this one experiences over and over in every conflict and every perplexity: that one is alone. That isn't as bad as it may first appear; and again it is the best thing in life that each should have everything in himself; his fate, his future, his whole expanse and world."
— **Rainer Maria Rilke**

"STRATEGY is a style of thinking, a conscious and deliberate process, an intensive implementation system, the science of insuring FUTURE SUCCESS."
— **Pete Johnson**

"Man has a limited biological capacity for change. When this capacity is overwhelmed, the capacity is in future shock."
— **Alvin Toffler**

Strategies in Creating Distinctive Value for Business

You have more strengths than the others.

Yours must be seen as a "demand" industry.

Opportunities far outweigh the threats.

Turn others' weaknesses into your threats.

Nothing can grow without proper nurturing, care and attention.

Everyone has to market and promote the cause.

Use experts from outside your industry.

Champion change.

Business and public stewardship are honorable public trusts.

Being a role model, you become a better executive and leader.

Success is more about building and sustaining relationships.

Most of life's great secrets are found through creativity of people.

SYNOPSIS OF THE
FIRST VOLUME IN THIS SERIES...

The Big Picture of Business
Book 1
Big Ideas and Strategies
7 Steps Toward Business Success
By Hank Moore

With change come opportunities for those who plan and strategize. The Big Picture of Business motivates companies to grow, envisioning the whole of business, the pieces as they relate to the whole, then the whole again. It offers an original business model, utilized in Hank Moore's work with thousands of clients over decades. It is an invaluable resource for the corporate and small business markets.

Hank Moore is the highest level of business overview expert and is in that rarified circle of visionaries such as Peter Drucker, Stephen Covey and W. Edwards Deming. The Business Tree™ is his trademarked approach to growing, strengthening and evolving business, while mastering change. He advises companies about growth strategies, visioning, planning, leadership, futurism and Big Picture issues. He has written a series of business books, plus his Legends series, paralleling pop culture, history and innovative strategies.

Digest of Excerpts from the Author's Other Books

Appendix

OTHER WRITINGS BY HANK MOORE

Classic Magazine Article by Hank Moore...

HemisFair '68, the San Antonio World's Fair, GO Magazine, April, 1968

HEMISFAIR

By Hank Moore

For months newspapers and magazines have been heralding it. Radio and television have talked about its unique attractions. A special six-cent stamp has been issued by the government commemorating Hemisfair '68.

Hemisfair, for years in the planning and building, is now a reality, opening in San Antonio April 6 and running through October 6.

The $156 million World's Fair is situated on 92.6 acres in downtown San Antonio—the first ever held in the southern half of the United States, the first World's Fair ever held in a downtown area.

All elements are combined: the frontier and the Space Age. The past is reflected, praising our existing accomplishments, and the future is heralded for its endless possibilities. Fittingly, the Hemisfair theme is "The Confluence of Civilizations in the Americas."

Theme structure is the 750-foot-high Tower of the Americas, dazzling spire of slip-form concrete which commands a view of a 100-mile radius from the top, a revolving restaurant. It is the tallest observation tower in the Western Hemisphere! Three elevators to the top will run on the outside of the structure.

Visitors will tour the Hemisfair grounds on elevated walkways. Strolling mariachis, trios, and choral groups will provide entertainment along the malls.

A lake runs through the grounds, encircling Fiesta Island, the amusement area which contains the finest in night life, sidewalk, cafes, water shows, midway rides, and games. A flowerboat will take tourists around the island.

More than 30 nations will be represented in a variety of exhibits in Las Plazas del Mundo, an international village. Every continent has some nation in representation.

Also in view will be a number of religious and cultural exhibits. Several of the world's top industrial corporations (Coca Cola, IBM, Ford, Kodak, etc.) maintain business and amusements attractions.

Your guides will be dressed in "op art" styles designed especially for Hemisfair. Hostesses will wear a three-piece suit with helmet hat, shoulder purse, A-line skirt, overblouse, and blazer coat. Hosts will be decked out in black and white striped blazers with duck pants, helmet hat, and tie made of the same material as hostess' ensembles. Eighty guides in all representing 15 nationalities, each speaks at least two languages fluently: English and usually Spanish. Each has been given extensive courses in grooming and on the geographic, economic,

and historical facts of San Antonio.

If you wish an overview of the fair grounds, travel the "Mini-Monorail," a simulated Swiss Skyride. It has been in operation since the first of March and has carried a 1,000-passenger-per-day load since completion. Ride from one point to another for 35 cents, or take the full excursion for $1. There will be 10 trains in all, each with a 60-passenger capacity.

Look for frequent TV coverage from Hemisfair after you return home. The Tower of the Americas, originally 622 feet is now 750 feet, extended by broadcasting transmitters. All major networks will have regular news features and occasional specials on the fair. Ed Sullivan will originate one of his Sunday night CBS variety shows from Hemisfair, and no doubt other TV entrepreneurs will follow.

There will be 100 eating places on the Hemisfair grounds, offering delacacies from every land. It has been figured that visitors may eat daily on the grounds for 3 months before they duplicate a meal.

a 1,200-seat theatre to show frequent films, with the interior walls lifting at the breaks to merge the audience (from separate sections) and create even larger screens. Exhibits will occupy the second edifice.

A $10 million Texas Pavilion has been built to stay after the fair is over. It occupies 13 acres of fair ground, literally titled the Institute of Texan Cultures, featuring historic relics of all kinds. Next year the Institute will begin producing educational films and other visual and audio aids on Texan heritage.

Expect to be entertained by the most lavish shows and biggest entertainment names in the world, appearing in that 2,800-seat theatre in San Antonio's civic complex. Appearing will be: the opera "Don Carlo." Apr. 6, 8, and 11; San Antonio Symphony, Apr. 7 with pianist Hilde Comer and Apr. 13 with guest conductor Arthur Fiedler; Ballet Folklorico de Mexico, Apr. 5-18; Texas Boys Choir, Apr. 19; Isaac Stern, Apr. 20; John Gary, Apr. 29-May 4; Grand Ole Opry, Apr. 30-May 13; Bob Hope, May 2-4; Jack Benny, June 3-8; Ferrante & Teicher, June 10-13; Don Adams, June 24-29; Phyllis Diller, July 15-20; Jimmy Dean, July 29-Aug. 3; Wayne Newton, Aug. 7-12; Bob Newhart, Aug. 19-24; and the Ice Capades, Sept. 12-29. See daily puppet and water shows on the fair grounds.

(Continued on Page 22)

The biggest permanent structure is San Antonio's new $10½ million civic center complex. Three buildings comprise it: a 3,000 seat banquet hall and meeting rooms in one; a 2,800-seat theatre in another; and a 93,000-square-foot circular arena, seating 10,000 persons.

The Federal Pavilion is the United States' two-building exhibit. There is

Texas Nuclear Corporation, Austin Magazine, December, 1968

DEC., 1968

THE RANGE OF
TEXAS NUCLEAR. . .

From The Tiny World
Of The Atom
To Outer Space

by Hank Moore

As a research leader, Austin-born Texas Nuclear Corporation is a nationally renowned scientific center. Their business is making simple the complex nature of atoms and the scarcity of knowledge about them.

Texas Nuclear was begun in 1956 by four graduates of the University of Texas Department of Physics. They had studied together and foreseen the need for commercial research to aid industry.

The company has grown, now employing more than 100 at its 50,000 - square - foot plant in northwest Austin (originally 4,000 feet in 1956). In 1961, Texas Nuclear became a wholly owned subsidiary of Nuclear-Chicago Corporation, world's largest manufacturer of atomic instruments. The G. D. Searle Pharmaceutical C o m p a n y bought Nuclear - Chicago in 1966.

Texas Nuclear serves two distinct markets: first as a laboratory for government-sponsored research, and secondly as a developer and manufacturer of radiation equipment.

Thirty people comprise the research staff, 20 of them with advanced degrees. Research contracts undertaken range from $10,000 to $130,000. Regular clients are the Atomic Energy Commission and the United States Department of Defense, who accept both reports and deliverable equipment. Texas Nuclear is most widely known nationally as a specialist in basic nuclear physics, including radio biology and atomic instrumentation.

An example of the company's continuing research includes these areas for the AEC: study of the interaction of neutrons with matter; gaining more information on the structure of matter; and publishing results in technical journals.

Texas Nuclear offers four major product lines: accelerators; industrial instruments; health physics and monitoring

equipment; and equipment for outside research and as instructional aids.

Examples of recently-filled contracts are:

A radiation detection system for the US Navy. The instruments were tested and developed to military specifications, taking one year, and costing the Navy $60,000.

A hand-held portable X-Ray fluorescent analyzer to market at $5,000. This replaces the conventional X-Ray generator marketed at $100,000. TN filled the contract in one year for $60,000. This machine is a scintillation detector (the geiger counter is a more common derivative) which gives out more and higher quality information on the presence and amount of minerals; then it further analyzes their content.

The bombardment of protons (positive electrical charges) from the Sun could endanger astronauts on future long space flights. Presently, the effect of the protons in space can only be assessed on earth. Texas Nuclear developed an instrument to assess protons in space which itself cannot be impaired by solar radiation. The $50,000 contract was completed in one year also.

TN generally fulfills 8 to 12 of these contracts yearly, all upwards of $50,000, and most requiring one year or more from research to production to testing to demonstration for clients. A four-man team, including a physicist, electronic engineer, and radioisotope specialist, steers the projects to finish, with the aid of another dozen researchers and producers.

Under its own company banner, TN manufactures accelerators for industry in the $20,000 product category, density guages in the $5,000 range. In the "several hundred dollar" range is

Hank's Original Manuscript for the Texas Nuclear Article, written on technology of the era, a Royal typewriter

TEXAS NUCLEAR   *original draft*

A leader in research and innovations for industry, Texas Nuclear Corporation is a nationally renowned scientific center based in Austin. Their business is making simple the complex nature of atoms and the scarcity of knowledge about them.

Texas Nuclear was begun in 1956 ~~on a few thousand dollars capital~~ by four graduates of the University of Texas Physics Department. They had studied together and foresaw the need for commercial research to aid industry.   *Nuclear chicago Corp*

The company has grown, now employing more than 100 at its ~~xxx~~ 50,000-square-foot plant in northwest Austin (originally 4,000 feet in 1956). In 1961, Texas Nuclear became a wholly owned subsidiary of Nuclear Corporation of Chicago, world's largest manufacturer of atomic instruments. The G. D. Searle Pharmaceutical Company bought Nuclear of Chicago in 1966.

Texas Nuclear serves two markets: first as a laboratory for government sponsored research, and secondly as a developer and manufacturer of radiation equipment.

Thirty people comprise the research staff, 20 of them with advanced degrees. Research contracts undertaken range from $10,000 to $130,000. Regular clients are the Atomic Energy Commission and the US Department of Defense, who accept both reports and deliverable equipment. Texas Nuclear is most widely known nationally as a specialist in basic nuclear physics, including radiobiology and atomic instrumentation.

An example of the company's continuing research includes these areas for the AEC: study the interaction of neutrons with matter; gain more information on the structure of matter; and publish results in technical journals.

Texas Nuclear offers four major product lines: accelerators; industrial instruments; health physics, and monitoring equipment; and equipment for outside research and as instructional aids.

Examples of recently-filled contracts are:

A radiation detection system for the US Navy. The instruments were tested and developed to military specifications, taking one year, and costing the Navy $60,000.   *about $60,000 — radiation*

A hand-held portable ~~x~~ X-Ray fluorescent analyzer to market at $5,000. This replaces the conventional X-Ray generator marketed at $100,000. TN filled the contract in one year for $100,000. A geiger counter ~~xxxxx~~ the presence *and amount* of minerals; this ~~xxxx~~ apparatus further analyzes the content of the minerals.

The ~~x~~ bombardment of protons (positive electrical charges) from the sun ~~(radiation of light)~~ could endanger astronauts on future long space flights. Presently the effect of the protons in space can only be assessed on Earth. Texas Nuclear developed an instrument to assess protons in space which itself cannot be impaired by solar radiation. The $50,000 contract was completed in one year also.

Texas Nuclear generally fulfills ~~xx~~ of these contracts yearly, all upwards   *8-12* of $50,000, and most requiring one year or more from research to production to testing to demonstration for clients. A four-man team, including a physicist, electronic engineer, and radioisotope specialist, steers the projects to finish, with the aid of another dozen researchers and producers.

Partying with the Rat Pack at a Hollywood Nightclub,
TV Digest Magazine, August, 1970

The Tube's Greatest Hits   191

Candy Store feature, by Hank Moore.
First published in August, 1970.

INSIDE THE
TUBE...

By Hank Moore

HOLLYWOOD - Saying you are going "to the Store" out here is not a grocery shopping errand. What you're saying is you are going to tinseltown's "in" spot, THE private club discotheque. I made the scene on various occasions, and it's something to behold, in the eyes if nothing else.

The Candy Store is the town's most posh house of GO-GO. No more memberships are available, though at last soliciting the joining fee was $1,000. In exclusive Beverly Hills on an unlikely-named Rodeo Street, you are met by a uniformed parking guy who kindly deposits your wheels at a nearby parking meter or loading zone (there is no lot). The building front is modest and sports (surprise!) a counter with candy jars filled with motley - colored canes.

I got met by a receptionist wearing a pair of dungarees reminiscent of my yard work and a yellow translucent blouse, sucking on a peppermint cane as she unlocks a door which appears to be signed by every patron who ever crossed the portal. First of the greeters was a spritely mod dressed Gene Shacore, a Beverly Hills hair stylist and boutique operator who also owns the Store. I'm told he makes three quarters of an annual million skins off this project alone.

Each time my party was the guest of an exciting young actor, Don Knight. He co-stars with Charlton Heston in "The Hawaiians" and with Chris George in ABC's new fall series "The Immortal." (An interview

with our multi-faceted friend is upcoming in TV Digest in September.)

The building is rectangle with a bar on the right as you enter and booths on the left. In the middle of the room is a dance floor, where I noticed Dean Martin whooping up and a table full of girls at a facing booth. Toward the back are more booths and a stairway leading to the "game room" (pool, etc.). All the top rock hits are blasting away from a 2-turntable console operated by an especially limber chick who dances to her own music. I hear she's not as involved as her departed predecessor, who insisted on doing her thing topless.

Joey Bishop enters with a couple of friends who are hardly ever away from him the rest of the evening. One looks like Marty Allen with short hair and the other like a television engineer I used to know. Joey and Dean exchange several quips, but Joey sits on the stairs watching the action for the most part with sad eyes. A member of our party said Joey's so. sad these days that he's getting a bald spot in his hair transplant!

I'm drinking my usual bloody mary, and it has an after taste of ammonia cleanser. The waitresses are dressed in various fashions from Shacore's boutique: one evening a floor length gown, another a white pant-suit creation with a 3-stage gold belt. The girls' tableside manner sounds like something out of the mind of a public relations agency

(Continued on Page 17)

192   Classic Television Reference

copywriter, which is good in that they are diplomatic at taking orders, enthusiastic about the business atmosphere, and socially ingratiating.

The customers were a sight to behold. Across the way was Don Mitchell of "Ironside" and Bill Bixby of "The Courtship Of Eddie's Father" with their girls. I think Dino is having the best time of anyone in the place. Most of the guys and gals appear to be secretary-actor types and are dressed in a colorful array of fashions.

A guy wanders by in a crocheted shirt I could have easily mistaken for Grandmother Hill's tablecloth. There's a guy in dungarees buttoned up by 2 rows of snaps (sort of a double-breasted zipper). A chick at a neighboring booth is in a backless frock with a mane of blonde hair draped over one shoulder. Dino is in a black turtleneck, and our Don is wearing a shirt right out of "The Hawaiians." We've got to heave sighs of interest as a steady parade of chicks pass in review, wearing everything as sightly as a bedroom sheet loosely draped, see-through fashions of all kinds, and an air 5 feet off the ground

More of Inside the Tube.......

A chick drifts by in a stoned daze. One of our party asks, "Janet?" She floats a-while and turns to me: "You can call me anything you want!" I give a "That's quite alright" nod and decline in favor of another swig of cleaning fluid.

As the crowd gets thicker, the manager is quickly jamming in other tables and stools for more customers. Next thing I know, a couple of guys ask if they may join us. I nod and surreptitiously whisper to a companion if the guy who's ordering a refill on the table's drinks isn't football star-actor Jim Brown. Dogged if it isn't, and the big guy is congenial company.

I notice Joey and Dean are speaking, and Dean and Frank are speaking. But Joey and Frank aren't. On comes Stevie Wonder's latest record, "Signed, Sealed, and Delivered," which moves Bishop to dance, right across from Sinatra's table. Next is Norman Greenbaum's "Spirit in the Sky," and Frankie has to dance too, 'cause his record company waxed disc.

The girl at the turntables is agonizingly good at programming the evening's music. I observed that she didn't miss a single record cue, and the "musical crests" that we refer to in radio were flowing right along. (12 years in radio, and I'm not that good!) The music prompts Jim Brown to dance, and darned if he didn't end up with that stoned chick; he could have done lots better.

Another evening I'm on vodka collinses, and an aside that they taste like Gatorade cracks up the waitress. Dean Martin is trying hard to get upstairs, but the action keeps him bugalooing away. Bishop's men are try-

We're in the half of the crowd which is really having a good time. The other half seems to be on parade and looks at others having fun before they proceed to "join in." I asked various people why, and the typical Hollywood self-consumption syndrome seems to be a trait of the secretary-model types rather than of the actor types. There are some out on the dance floor who I'm sure do not realize they even have a partner.

Presently, the original good humor man, Frank Sinatra, steps in, and a hushed reaction by the crowd acknowledges his presence. Flanked by his bodyguard "Sarge," Frank is brandishing his left hand in a sling. I stepped over to find out that he just had a cancerous growth removed from the hand and is doing just fine, thank you. Frankie will discuss his recent endorsement of Ronald Reagan with any and all. I wondered if he wasn't instead simply opposing Jess Unruh, one of the clan who kept President Kennedy from visiting Sinatra at Palm Springs in 1960. "You got it, pal!" Sinatra looked like he remembered graphically the who and where of the incident(Continued on Page 32)

ing to meet new girls while Sinatra is brandishing his cast "goodbye" to all; he and Sarge have a good comedy act going, as they stop at each table to take pokes at each other.

I am told to notice all the out-of-work actors: Dennis Cole, who's no longer on "Bracken's World," and Don Marshall, whose "Land of the Giants" got cancelled by ABC and who's better known to my "Julia" cronies as Diahann Carroll's ex-boyfriend. Rejoice, for the next time I saw Don, he had news of just forming his own production company, and he was getting lots of work.

Good pal Dan Doran, an ABC publicist, shrugged at the early-morning hour, speculating how rough it would be to get going in the morning. "I can tell them I was looking after Joey Bishop and Don Marshall," he chided, adding that he at first didn't recognize Bishop when he first started coming to the Store. "And I worked on his show!"

The Candy Store, like Hollywood itself, is a state of mind more than a place. If you have got a motive for having a good time, then it's phonysville; and phonics contrive motives. Yeah, there are seads of people to be seen and to be seen by. The concept of the Store is pure fun with a little status involved; suddenly Jim Brown, Frank Sinatra, Dean Martin, et al, are not considered for their professional stature but instead are your friend and mine.

I can think of very few people asking what I did workwise. They figured I must be something to get in. Otherwise, they knew you because you were there to have a good time. The Store is a place to really dig!

Memories of One-Station TV Markets, TV Digest Magazine, August, 1971

Inside the Tube

By HANK MOORE

The following is a commentary on an era gone by. Thank goodness! It specifically applies to the past 15 years in Central Texas; so other readers out of that area may have to stretch their retired memories to remember when there weren't enough television stations to go around. When there are one or 2 outlets, some crazy shuffling of programs goes on, and Central Texas must be the only major metropolis in the United States that has been the last refuge of that maddening phenomenon of the Vast Wasteland: the DELAYED BROADCAST!

Where else but in Austin, Texas, or, heaven help us, Waco, could viewers see the Wednesday Night Movie on Saturdays, the

he was cancelled locally due to lack of viewer interest?

Ed Sullivan always ran 2 weeks and 3 hours later than on CBS, and in his place we saw a live Steve Allen Show, which is understandable. KTBC could rightfully boast that they carried all of the top 20 shows.

Yet there was some scheduling that made the live show obsolete. "Your Hit Parade" in 1954-55 was run on a one-week delay at the same time it was on the network. The same with "The 20th Century." The Western "Have Gun Will Travel" ran Saturdays on CBS at 8:30 p.m., with the film "Official Detective" running locally at 8:30, and "Have Gun" running at

politics were palatable locally, 4 years for "The Virginian," 3 for "Hawaii Five-O," 2 for "Rifleman," 4 for "My 3 Sons," 3 for "The Real McCoys," 5 for "Father Knows Best" (it had gone into daytime reruns), and 7 for "The Donna Reed Show" (also on daytime reruns before she debuted). And how about that great summer replacement show we've been enjoying this particular year: "Medical Center." I hope it clicked with viewers, seeing as how it's been in the Top 20 nationally for 2 years!

Many network series later had their coming-out parties locally as, you guessed it, syndicated reruns: "M Squad," "Honey West," "The Detectives," "Wanted Dead Or

Lament To the Delayed Broadcast....

Sunday Night Movie on Thursdays, the Tuesday Night Movie on Sundays, and the Monday Night Movie on Saturdays. The only time in history that it made sense was when ABC ran "Spartacus" on Sunday and Monday; naturally, we saw it as a double feature on Saturday! In a way, it's sad that such times are gone; I was eagerly anticipating seeing ABC's new "Movie of the Weekend" on Wednesday mornings.

As viewers know, the Austin market had one station for 13 years. For another 6 we've had 2. This week, : KVUE—TV, Channel 24, makes it an even 3. In the past 19 years, TV antenna sales have multiplied 30-fold. The cable's thousands of subscribers attest to public quandry over delayed broadcasts.

I think the folks over at KTBC should be commended for juggling so many programs all those years. They'll probably enjoy laughing over some old times because programming was wierd for so long.

There was a time that "The Price Is Right" was being run here on a 6-week delay, which means we were celebrating Christmas via commercials in February. The older they could buy the kinescopes, the cheaper they were; yet it was bad in that "Price" had contests every month, all void by some few days before they were ever unveiled here.

The daytime show "Championship Bridge" ran Monday nights at 11:30. Lawrence Welk did his thing at such hours a Tuesday nights at 11:15 and Sunday afternoons at 4:00; Welk appeals to a crowd which was, for health reasons, napping at both ends of the day; is it any wonder that

10:00; it would have been half as many films to run "Official" at 10:00. And there were a couple of legendary weeks that airing all the football games meant one live on Saturday afternoons and another delayed on Sunday nights!

The network ran "Lawman" while Channel 7 was running the film "Whirlybirds" and delayed "Lawman" to some other time. Worthy of note is that the network shows were debirthed of the most prime viewing periods by syndicated shows, which, locally sponsored, were more lucrative to the station and which served the needs of retail advertisers. Yet the shows have since hardly been immortalized. Will anyone remember such titles as "26 Men," "The Case Of the Dangerous Robin," "Decoy," "Manhunt," "Coronado 9," "Johnny Midnight," "Tombstone Territory," "Lock Up," "Law Breakers," and "MacKenzie's Raiders"? "Sea Hunt" made local furniture dealer Louis Shanks a bigger star than it did its leading man, Lloyd Bridges.

Sometimes the juggling meant running shows a couple of weeks behind yet within a half hour of their network run (ala Walt Disney, Loretta Young, and "Dennis the Menace"). I sat home a couple of months ago and was able to watch a double feature of "Room 222" episodes by flipping the channel selector!

When you're running only half of the network product available; you have to let some programs "prove themselves" before they can be scheduled. We waited 2 years to see if that bomb "Bonanza" would make the grade, a year before the Smothers Brothers'

Alive," and "The Law And Mr. Jones." NBC's "Bat Masterson" (starring Gene Barry) ran on one station with local commercials inserted.

The shows were run at all kinds of times: "Ozzie And Harriet" on Sunday afternoons and "Face the Nation" on Sunday nights. When the networks put shows together, it is done several days ahead of time, mixing the filmed show and commercials on videotape or kinescope and then shipping them out to TV stations for delayed broadcast. There were even past cases where shows hit the air (via advanced film) earlier in the day than they appeared on the networks. Examples: "National Velvet" here at 3:30, on NBC at 7:00; "Gomer Pyle" on a San Antonio station at 7:30, on CBS at 8:30; "Profiles In Courage" here at 4:30, on NBC at 5:30.

There have been scads of shows which played on both local stations before it was all said and done. "The Tonight Show," "Marcus Welby," "The Monkees," "The FBI," and Carol Burnett have been sporadically on Ch. 7 and Ch. 42.

The incident that tickles me most is the week that CBS (fall of 1965) debuted its dual movie nights. The premiere offering was "The Guns Of Navarone" and ran as Part One Thursday over Channel 42. Sheepishly, they had to announce that viewers who insisted on seeing Part 2 could do so the next evening . . . over Channel 7!

No harm intended to the station we picked on for the most part, it was the darndest era in the history of broadcasting. I cannot believe it is over!

The Lazy Student's Little Helper, Texas Monthly, 1972

The Lazy Student's Little Helper

By Hank Moore

Student X worked all weekend on his Shakespeare theme and nothing else, reading three plays and several books of criticism. He spent about eight hours on his rough draft and finished off his final version in two hours. He ruined his weekend, but he earned an A.

Student Y drank beer, played tennis, watched a movie, listened to stereo, and slept late. Monday morning he wrote a check for $25. He bought an A.

There is still a majority of students like Student X in college, but a growing number are joining Student Y. Today in Austin there is a booming trade in ghost-writing themes. The anonymous ghosts find the field lucrative. The student-clients of means get a big boost to their grade point average. And academic standards suffer.

Three theme-writing services have been established in Austin. They rely not only on local writers to pen specialized topics, but also on catalogued essays on general topics. In newspaper ads the companies are billed as "research centers."

Collegiate Research System is located in a downtown Austin office building. The operators are out of Chicago, though they were out of Austin this summer setting up new offices in the South. Their three catalogues of themes, each three feet thick, list some 10,000 topics which may be obtained in carbon copies for $2.95 per page. It takes about a week to order a theme through the catalogue and receive it through the mail.

Customers are given a carbon or Xeroxed copy of the essay and are supposed to retype it and change the wording. Thus retyped, the purchased theme is impossible to tell from the real thing, which is a big factor in the growing appeal of the fake theme to students.

"More often the student has toyed with the topic and deadline time is upon him," said one local theme-writing businessman. "He then brings in the theme as a rush order and we don't have time to get copies by mail. Then we have to turn it over to a writer."

He lists the only qualification to ghost-write for his service as possessing a college degree in any field, reasoning that four undergraduate years has taught a person the fine art of the snow job.

When original research and writing is done, the fee is $4.50 per page, of which the writer doing the work gets $2.25 per page. An extra 50 cents a page for special rush orders (under three days' lead time) goes directly to the writer, whose name the customer never knows.

Fact Finders, a second theme-writing service, operates out of an apartment in the University area, where the landlady doesn't even know what business is conducted within.

"Texas is one of the better markets in the nation," said another theme-writing manager. There are about

500,000 college students in the state and his service gets orders from San Antonio, San Marcos, and smaller area schools.

What kind of students come to these services to have their papers ghost-written? "Mostly coeds," said the manager. "They're sorority people with money and, I suppose, want to spend their time playing around. Then there are real dummies that come in."

In other words, the usual customer is not a diligent student who has an emergency need for just one paper. Clients come back again and again. "They're people who aren't meant for college," he said.

The theme-writing services do not guarantee grades. On the themes I

wrote for theme-writing services, my batting record was B+. I answered Government 610 essay questions on the relationship between Congress and the President. There were a few American History 315 exams last spring on the Depression and New Deal years. Philosophy courses are big on asking for papers on Plato's and Sir Thomas More's Utopias. I was able to use the same notes for several papers.

I'll admit that the experience, in addition to putting bread on the tables of starving writers, lets one research topics that otherwise he would not force himself to. I did a character sketch of women's lib activist Gloria Steinem, a political essay comparing President Nixon's "Checkers" and

Stuck on windshields, handed to passersby on Guadalupe Street, these are the business cards of three Austin theme-writing firms, including a newly founded one, Southwest Research Group.

Hank Knows Moore About Radio, The Houston Post
editorial page column by Tom Kennedy, May 2, 1987

Hank knows Moore about radio

Tom Kennedy

Hank Moore wears many hats. While he's wearing one, he often talks about another. So it wasn't unusual the other night when Hank the charity promoter began talking like Hank the radio/television historian.

As a person who has piloted his share of airwaves, Hank tells the story of radio station KTRH, which broadcast from the Rice Hotel for many years. Most people think the call letters stood for Texas' Rice Hotel, but the fine-tuned historian claims it was something else: Keep Tuned Right Here. Also, in earlier days, it supposedly stood for Come to the Rice Hotel.

In the 1950s, television station KTRK sponsored a contest to name its mascot, a woman wearing a black leotard and a cap with cat ears. The unforgettable Bunny Orsak delighted Houston's youth for 16 years on Channel 13.

How did "Kitirik" get her name?

"Some little boy put i's between each of the call letters of KTRK," Hank remembers, "and spelled Kitirik." KiTiRiK. Very clever.

Let's switch back to radio. You listeners out there may know that KRBE got its "name" because its studio was originally located on Kirby Drive. And you might have heard that KILT was named for "the ole Scotsman," radio mogul Gordon McLendon.

But didja know KMJQ (Majic 102) has its roots in Alvin? According to Hank, the station originally was KAJC, operated by Alvin Junior College. In the early 1960s, Shorty Powers, the

voice of early space missions, purchased it in partnership with fellow NASA officials.

After the purchase, the station was moved from Alvin to Clear Lake and called KMSC, the MSC standing for Manned Spacecraft Center. Eventually, it was sold again and almost became KMGC. However, another "magic" station threatened to sue, prompting station owners to take liberties with the "spelling." All of us listeners know magic is spelled with an M, a J and a Q instead of an M, a G and a C.

Hank, an adman in real life, says many stations adapt their call letters to an acronym or catchy phrase. Many consultants, he explains, recommend the use of letters that produce a pleasing pronunciation. That's why many stations are minding their Z's and Q's.

Thus, one might deduce that KKBQ is owned by a barbecue (bar BQ) firm, but the letters actually were put together to help establish the Q-Zoo. When you tune in John Lander et al, you likely call it the Q-Zoo, not KKBQ.

Stations seem to change formats and owners fairly frequently. KFMK began as an underground rock station and was shut down by the Federal Communications Commission for using profane language. It was resurrected in a religious format for a few years before reaching its current, yuppie-oriented status.

K and W, which represent the first letter of radio and TV call letters, come from the electrical term *kilowatt*. Years ago, the federal government decreed all stations west of the Mississippi River would have call letters beginning with K, while those east of the line of demarcation would begin with W.

There are a few exceptions grandfathered by the decree. Among them is WACO in — you guessed it — Waco. "That is the only station in the country where the actual call letters spell the name of the town," Hank claims.

KQUE is the most powerful FM station in Houston, the historian says, because of an FCC clerical error. Official FCC papers gave the station 280 kilowatts of power instead of 180.

Hank says the call letters of a country music station were changed to KIKK when the owner heard many people say, "Only a bunch of kickers listen to your station."

And when Channel 26 wasn't doing too well in the ratings, someone reportedly said, "It's a real *dog*." The next thing you know, they renamed it KDOG until it was changed to KRIV.

Thanks for tuning in.

Business Ethics, American City Business Journals, 2010

Houston Business Journal
FOCUS: ETHICS & VALUES

Week of June 13–19, 2003 houston.bizjournals.com **27**

PHOTO COURTESY OF MANAGEMENT RESOURCE INSTITUTE
Business consultant, speaker and author Hank Moore applies his trademarked Business Tree model to ethics and standards.

Companies take ethical issues off the back burner

BY THORA QADOUMI
HOUSTON BUSINESS JOURNAL

Company managers, often occupied with trying to "slay the last dragon," are finding it pays to take some easily neglected concepts off the back burner.

"Ethics," "diversity," and "team-building" should be main ingredients in the strategic planning recipe, rather than ideas taken out of context, left simmering and served as an afterthought, says business adviser

and speaker Hank Moore.

Moore, president of Management Resource Institute (www.selec.net/businesstree), is author of numerous books, including "The Business Tree," the 10-tape audio cassette series, "$50 Million Business Makeover" and, his most recently published volume, "The High Cost of Doing Nothing." A consultant who leaders of many companies turn to for help in achieving "big picture" plans, he has trademarked the term "corporate strategist" as

defining his role.

Moore's next book — with the intriguing title, "The Future Has Moved ... And Left No Forwarding Address" — is on corporate responsibility. It includes his "Seven Levels of Standards, Ethics", an application of his trademarked "Business Tree" approach to growing, strengthening and evolving businesses.

Moore defines "ethics" as "the science of

SEE ETHICS, PAGE 28

Houston Business Journal

Week of June 13–19, 2003

ETHICS & VALUES

ETHICS

FROM PAGE 27

morals, rightness and obligations in human affairs."

All levels of standards and ethics are part of the tree, starting with Level 1, "base-level ethics," represented as being high in the branches. This is knowing right from wrong and "trying to pursue a good life and aspiring to something better."

Level 2, lower in the branches, are prevailing philosophies and behaviors ("society's lowest denominators"); Level 3, "lessons learned from the school of hard knocks," and Level 4,

efforts to learn more and go further ("launching a quest").

Level 5 is "standards" — establishing and respecting boundaries. The trunk of the tree, which supports the whole plant, is Level 6, "values and vision," where it is recognized that "success comes from charting a course, encompassing value systems and methodically reaching goals."

Level 7, the roots of the tree, becomes the "code of ethics," which includes "fundamental canons, rules of practice, professional obligations, accountability-measurability, professional development, integrity, objectivity and independence."

"Company managers think that by putting more money behind technology or marketing, everything will be fine. They call in consultants," Moore notes.

What they really need, he says, is a plan that provides a true vision of the company that allows long-term growth. And part of the plan should be a carefully formulated, distributed and continuously reviewed ethics statement and program.

"Companies that fail to address ethical issues of the day are endangered species," he says. "You don't want to be too preachy. You just have to inculcate ethics in everything you do. Eighty-five percent of the time, if you plan for a crisis, you can avert it. You determine what could be the biggest ethical dilemmas and you take proactive steps to avert them."

Hank Moore
Management Resource Institute

'Companies that fail to address ethical issues of the day are endangered species.'

stocks.

"The program seeks to create conditions that support the right actions," Moore says. "It communicates the values and vision of the organization."

"A formal and well-documented corporate ethics program, developed as part of the planning process, will prevent ethical misconduct, monetary losses and losses to reputation," he says. "If communicated well, it may breed customer trust."

Moore recommends that companies establish organizational roles to manage ethics and send copies of their ethics statement to customers, suppliers, regulators and other stakeholders, demonstrating that the company is attempting to become a model.

"It becomes a good marketing mailing," he says, "and formal attention to ethics in the workplace is the right thing to do."

Every organization will differ in how it implements corporate responsibility and ethics programs. The main point, however, is that business ethics encompasses much more than accounting fraud and the publicly stated values of

Managing ethics in the workplace

· Recognize that managing ethics is a process.

· The bottom line of an ethics program is accomplishing preferred behaviors in the workplace.

· The best way to handle ethical dilemmas is to avoid their occurrence in the first place.

· Make ethics decisions in groups, and make decisions public, as appropriate.

· Integrate ethics management with other management practices.

· Use cross-functional teams when developing and implementing the ethics management program.

· Value forgiveness.

· Note that trying to operate ethically and making a few mistakes is better than not trying at all.

Hank Moore

Developing a code of ethics

· Review values needed for adherence to relevant laws and regulations.

· Review values that produce the top three or four traits of a highly ethical and successful product or service in the firm's area.

· Identify values needed to address current issues faced by the firm.

· Identify values needed, based on findings during strategic planning.

· Consider top ethical values prized by stakeholders.

· Collect from the above, the ethical values that are high priorities in the organization; for example, trustworthiness (honesty, integrity, promise-keeping, loyalty), respect (autonomy, privacy, dignity, courtesy, tolerance, acceptance), responsibility (accountability, pursuit of excellence), caring (compassion, consideration, giving, sharing, kindness, loving), justice and fairness (impartiality, consistency, equity, equality, due process) and civic virtue and citizenship (law-abiding, community service, protection of the environment).

· Compose the code of ethics, attempting to associate with each value two example behaviors which reflect each value.

· Include wording that indicates all employees are expected to conform to the values stated in the code of ethics.

· Get input from as many members of the organization as possible.

· Announce and distribute the new code of ethics.

· Update the code at least once a year.

Hank Moore

tqaddumi@bizjournals.com · 713-960-5901

Houston Legends column by Ken Hoffman,
The Houston Chronicle, May 31, 2015

HOUSTON ☆ CHRONICLE

and chron.com | **Sunday, May 31, 2015**

ZEST

We've got 2,000 Houston legends for you

KEN HOFFMAN
Commentary

Back when, I mean way back when, there were lots of newspapers in Houston. They had names like the Houston Gazette, the Daily Times and the Daily Post.

"In 1869, one newspaper editor called the other a 'liar, coward' and 'scoundrel.' The two met in the street for a duel the next day. They exchanged several gun shots, missing each other, but killing a bystander."

It's my favorite newspaper story — ever.

It's just one of hundreds of little tales about Houston and Houstonians in Hank Moore's new book, "Houston Legends: History and Heritage of Dynamic Global Capitol." On practically every page, you'll find something that you didn't know about our city.

The book is set for national release in July.

Moore, a business strategist and former public-relations wizard, spent five years digging for details about famous people who were either born, grew up or made their reputation in Houston.

The book will have you saying, "I didn't know Mary Kay Ash, you know, Mary Kay Cosmetics, was from Houston" or "I went to Lanier Middle School ... I didn't know Walter Cronkite went there, too."

Moore has quicky bios on more than 2,000 "Houston Legends," and they get right to the point

— what they're famous for. Billy Preston, the only outside musician ever to get his name on a Beatles record, was born in Houston.

The label on the "Get Back" single says "THE BEATLES" ... and in small print, "with Billy Preston."

I asked Moore, what is it about Houston that produces so many successful artists, businesspeople and scientists?

"Houston never says no. Houston doesn't tell people, no, you can't accomplish your dreams. Houston says, if you want to become somebody, you've come to the right place," Moore said.

Moore has written eight other books, most of them about business strategy, including "The Business Tree," "Chicken Soup for the Entrepreneur's Soul," "The High Cost of Doing Nothing," and I love this title, "The Future Has Moved ... and Left No Forwarding Address."

In 2005, Moore wrote "The Classic Television Reference," an analysis of the industry including interviews with stars such as Tim Conway, Buddy Ebsen, Jack Lord, Eva Gabor, Sonny and Cher, Captain Kangaroo and Dick Clark.

"That book got me on the 'Oprah Winfrey Show.' She did a show about great television shows and I was sitting on a couch with a bunch of old has-beens," Moore said.

Come on, you *have* to tell me who was on the couch.

"I was on there with Florence Henderson from 'The Brady Bunch,' Ed Asner from 'The Mary Tyler Moore Show' and Leslie Nielsen from 'Po-

lice Squad.' We had fun with Oprah," he said.

Moore divides his "Legends" by chapters on Energy, Entrepreneurs and Innovators, Banking and Finance, Retailers, Media, Arts and Entertainers, Music, Sports and Medicine.

OK, sometimes he's generous with what becomes a legend. There are some legends in the book, frankly, I've never heard of them. And, after reading about them, I still have no idea who they are. And the chapter on media contains some names ... let's just say I knew them, I worked with them, and sir, they are no legends. Remember the story about the dueling editors who missed each other but killed an innocent bystander? I used to work for editors whose aim was just as bad.

The book is more than just a Who's Who or Who Was. The chapter on music talks about old clubs and concert venues that aren't around anymore, such as Dome Shadows, Van's Ballroom, Teen Hall and the Sam Houston Coliseum.

The coliseum played a big part in Moore's own legend. He grew up in Austin, and went to work for radio station KTBC in Austin in 1958. The sta-

tion was owned by Lady Bird Johnson, whose husband was U.S. Sen. Lyndon B. Johnson. Moore's goal was to become the "Dick Clark of Texas."

Bill Moyers, the assistant news director at KTBC, took Moore aside and said, "Look kid, suck it up, you're not going to be Dick Clark. We're here to be groomed for if and when Lyndon becomes president."

Johnson was elected vice president in 1960 and became president in 1963 when President Kennedy was assassinated. Moyers became Johnson's press secretary and Moore, still a teenager, was a "special adviser" to the White House, while continuing to spin records back in Austin.

One time, a University of Texas professor asked Moore how come he rarely came to class. Moore told him, "I'm an adviser to the White House and I'm a disc jockey, too." He added, "Those two jobs are pretty similar."

Here's where Moore deserves a chapter all to himself in "Houston Legends."

This year is the 50th anniversary of the Beatles' one and only visit to Houston, two shows at the Sam Houston Coliseum on Aug. 19, 1965. Moore was one of the disc jockeys invited to make announcements from the stage.

In 1975, Moore introduced Elvis Presley at Hofheinz Pavilion.

"I'm one of very few people who can say they were on the same stage with both the Beatles and Elvis Presley," Moore said.

That's pretty legendary.

ken.hoffman@chron.com
twitter.com/KenChron

ABOUT THE AUTHOR

Hank Moore is an internationally known business advisor, speaker and author. He is a Big Picture strategist, with original, cutting-edge ideas for creating, implementing and sustaining corporate growth throughout every sector of the organization.

He is a Futurist and Corporate Strategist™, with four trademarked concepts of business, heralded for ways to remediate corporate damage, enhance productivity and facilitate better business.

Hank Moore is the highest level of business overview expert and is in that rarified circle of experts such as Peter Drucker, Tom Peters, Steven Covey, Peter Senge and W. Edwards Deming.

Hank Moore has presented Think Tanks for five U.S. Presidents. He has spoken at six Economic Summits. As a Corporate Strategist™, he speaks and advises companies about growth strategies, visioning, planning, executive-leadership development, futurism and the Big Picture issues affecting the business climate. He conducts independent performance reviews and Executive Think Tanks nationally, with the result being the companies' destinies being charted.

The Business Tree™ is his trademarked approach to growing, strengthening and evolving business, while mastering change. Business visionary Peter Drucker termed Hank Moore's Business Tree™ as the most original business model of the past 50 years.

Mr. Moore has provided senior level advising services for more than 5,000 client organizations (including 100 of the Fortune 500), companies in transition (startup, re-engineering, mergers, going public), public sector entities, professional associations and non-profit organizations. He has worked with all major industries over a 40-year career. He advises at the Executive Committee and board levels, providing Big Picture ideas.

He has overseen 400 strategic plans and corporate visioning processes. He has conducted 500+ performance reviews of organizations. He is a mentor to senior management. This scope of wisdom is utilized by CEOs and board members.

Types of speaking engagements which Hank Moore presents include:

- Conference opening Futurism keynote.
- Corporate planning retreats.
- Ethics and Corporate Responsibility speeches.
- University—college Commencement addresses.
- Business Think Tanks.
- International business conferences.
- Non-profit and public sector planning retreats.

In his speeches and in consulting, Hank Moore addresses aspects of business that only one who has overseen them for a living can address:

- Trends, challenges and opportunities for the future of business.
- Big Picture viewpoint.
- Creative idea generation.
- Ethics and corporate responsibility.
- Changing and refining corporate cultures.
- Strategic Planning.
- Marketplace repositioning.
- Community stewardship.
- Visioning.
- Crisis management and preparedness.

- Growth Strategies programs.
- Board of Directors development.
- Stakeholder accountability.
- Executive Think Tanks.
- Performance reviews.
- Non-profit consultation.
- Business trends that will affect the organization.
- Encouraging pockets of support and progress thus far.
- Inspiring attendees as to the importance of their public trust roles.
- Making pertinent recommendations on strategy development.

Hank Moore has authored a series of internationally published books:

- The Business Tree™ (with multiple international editions)
- Pop Icons and Business Legends
- The Big Picture of Business
- Non-Profit Legends
- The High Cost of Doing Nothing. Why good businesses go bad.
- Houston Legends
- The Classic Television Reference
- Power Stars to Light the Flame…The Business Visionaries and You.
- The Future Has Moved…and Left No Forwarding Address.
- The $50,000 Business Makeover.
- Plus monograph series for the Library of Congress Business Section, Harvard School of Business, Strategy Driven and many publications and websites.

Follow Hank Moore on:
Facebook: http://www.facebook.com/hank.moore.10
Linkedin: http://www.linkedin.com/profile/view?id=43004647&trk=tab_pro
Twitter: https://twitter.com/hankmoore4218
YouTube: https://www.youtube.com/watch?v=vELOvp-Kljg
Pin Interest:http://www.pinterest.com/hankmoore10/
Google+:https://plus.google.com/u/0/112201360763207336890/posts

Skill Pages:http://www.skillpages.com/hank.moore

Atlantic Speakers Bureau: http://atlanticspeakersbureau.com/hank-moore/

Business Speakers Network: http://directory.espeakers.com/buss/viewspeaker16988

Silver Fox Advisors: http://silverfox.org/content.php?page=Hank_Moore

Facebook business page: https://www.facebook.com/hankmoore.author/?fref=ts

Additional materials may be found on Hank Moore's website:

www.hankmoore.com

Printed in the USA
CPSIA information can be obtained
at www.ICGtesting.com
JSHW082228140824
68134JS00017B/786